D1106814

DISCARDED

Staging Masculinity

Staging Masculinity

*Male Identity in
Contemporary American Drama*

CARLA J. McDONOUGH

McFarland & Company, Inc., Publishers
Jefferson, North Carolina, and London

ACKNOWLEDGMENTS: I have many people to thank for the completion of this work. In particular, I'd like to thank Stan Garner for his close readings and extended discussions of the project, and for his support of its angle on gender issues, which at the time I started it in 1991 were far from popular. Further helpful feedback was provided by both Mary Papke and Chuck Maland. On later stages of the project, I'd like to thank my colleagues Ruth Hoberman and Lauren Smith for editorial suggestions about sections from the Shepard and the Mamet chapters.

Along the way, I received much support and encouragement from close friends and colleagues willing to listen to my ideas and my frustrations. Mary Moss, Robert Warrior, Jeri Swatosh, and Cecilia Stinnett come chiefly to mind in that regard, as do my parents, especially my father, James McDonough, who has always served as a model of good scholarship and writing that I have benefited from observing. And above all, the peace of mind necessary for any extended project was made possible for me by the support and encouragement of my husband, Eric Hobson. His editorial work on this manuscript, as well as his willingness to put up with my work habits, made this project much easier and better than it would have been otherwise.

Finally, I gratefully acknowledge permission to reprint sections of this project that have already been published. Sections of chapter 3 appeared originally as "The Politics of Stage Space: Women and Male Identity in Sam Shepard's Family Plays," *Journal of Dramatic Theory and Criticism* 9, 2 (Spring 1995): 65–83, and are reprinted here by permission from the *Journal of Dramatic Theory and Criticism*. Sections of chapter 4 appeared as "Every Fear Hides a Wish: Unstable Masculinity in Mamet's Drama" *Theatre Journal* 44, 2 (May 1992): 195–205, and are reprinted here by permission of the Johns Hopkins University Press.

British Library Cataloguing-in-Publication data are available

Library of Congress Cataloguing-in-Publication Data

McDonough, Carla J., 1963–
    Staging masculinity : male identity in contemporary American
drama / Carla J. McDonough.
        p.   cm.
    Includes bibliographical references and index.
    ISBN 0-7864-0268-7 (library binding : 50# alkaline paper) ∞
    1. American drama — Men authors — History and criticism.
2. Men in literature.   3. American drama — 20th century —
History and criticism.   4. Masculinity (Psychology) in literature.
5. Shepard, Sam, 1943–   — Characters — Men.   6. Wilson,
August — Characters — Men.   7. Mamet,   David — Characters —
Men.   8. Rabe, David — Characters — Men.   9. Group identity
in literature.   I. Title.
PS338.M46M33   1997   96-44555
812'.5409052041— dc21   CIP

©1997 Carla J. McDonough. All rights reserved

No part of this book, specifically including the table of contents and index, may be reproduced or transmitted in any form or by any means, electronic or mechanical, including photocopying or recording, or by any information storage and retrieval system, without permission in writing from the publisher.

Manufactured in the United States of America

McFarland & Company, Inc., Publishers
  Box 611, Jefferson, North Carolina 28640

Table of Contents

SHATFORD LIBRARY

FEB   2011

1570 E. Colorado Blvd.
Pasadena, CA 91106

SHATFORD LIBRARY

FEB   2011

1570 E. Colorado Blvd.
Pasadena, CA 91106

· Introduction

Manhood ... Some of us may think we have it when really it is
someone else.—Caryl Churchill, *Owners*

A new study exploring masculinity in American drama might seem, at first
glance, unnecessary in the midst of a dramatic tradition already heavily weighted
toward the actions and experiences of male characters. All too often, however,
the male protagonist or male playwright has been critically treated as if he were
non-gendered. Men in plays such as Arthur Miller's *Death of a Salesman* or Sam
Shepard's *True West* are often presented as universal referents; their stories are
viewed by author and critics as encompassing dynamics relevant to humanity
rather than specifically to men. Although it is quite possible to recognize the universal experience in almost any particular story, consistently refusing to consider
the particulars of gender dynamics for male characters leads us into critical blind
spots. Such an approach tends to write over the status of individual men in a
desire to empower their voices as "universal," thereby both avoiding the lived
experiences of the individual man whose life may not fit this universal pattern
and fallaciously assuming to speak for different gender, ethnic, or economic
groups. This problem of conflation is articulated by Jane Flax in her recent analysis of gender relations:

> In a wide variety of cultures and discourses, men tend to be seen as free from or as not
> determined by gender relations. Thus, for example, academics do not explicitly study the
> psychology of men or men's history.... Only recently have scholars begun to consider the
> possibility that there may be at least three histories in every culture — his, hers, and ours.
> *His* and *ours* are generally assumed to be equivalents, although in contemporary work
> there might be some recognition of the existence of that deviant — woman (e.g., woman's
> history) ["Postmodernism" 45].

This study explores the issue of masculinity as it appears in the plays of some
of our generally accepted leading male playwrights in order to consider how the
question of male identity is staged by these men, and how this staging reflects and
affects men's social interactions, interactions which themselves are powerful
reflections of our social systems. The overt masculinity of plays by Sam Shepard,
David Mamet, and David Rabe should be readily apparent to readers or viewers

of their work. Their fondness for male-cast plays alone highlights this bias toward male issues,[1] yet consistently, they are most often critically presented as universal American voices, not qualified by gender (or race, or ethnicity) in the way that so many other contemporary playwrights find themselves qualified. In contrast, consider some of our leading *women* playwrights, or *Hispanic* playwrights, or *gay* playwrights who, by such descriptions, are located within a specific subset of playwriting for which the heterosexual white male playwrights Shepard, Mamet, and Rabe are offered as prototype. The fourth playwright to be treated in depth here has assured himself a significant place on the American stage by winning two Pulitzer prizes during the 1980s, among other honors and numerous productions and publications, quickly endowing him with the kind of critical weight that has been afforded the playwrights listed above. August Wilson's theater, while not as overtly male oriented as those of Shepard, Mamet, and Rabe, has nevertheless followed masculinized thematic interests that many feminist critics have observed are common among African American male writers who have tended to confuse the African American experience with the African American male experience.[2]

These four contemporary playwrights have been selected for examination because increasingly they are listed in studies of American drama as "the" important playwrights of the latter half of the twentieth century and (except for Wilson) have rarely been given qualifying adjectives that would tag their theaters as offering a partial rather than a universal view of American experience. Even within his qualification as an African American writer, Wilson's work has been interpreted as widely representative of the entire African American experience with little to no attention paid to gender. Although the plays of each of these four playwrights often explore quite brilliantly the conflicts and issues confronted by many men in America, the issue of gender for men is all too often ignored. Instead, the stories told by these playwrights tend to be presented and accepted as universally American — confusing, as Flax has described, "his" culture with "our" culture — and overlooking a highly provocative thematic consonance among these writers.

The impetus for examining the gender issues that shape the theatrical presentations of these writers responds both to feminist theory and to the rise of men's studies, which help to highlight the confusion of the male story with "the" story of a culture, as well as to express the confusion that exists regarding what it means to be a "real" man in American culture. Discussions of masculinity within what has come to be known as "men's studies" have recorded a sense of crisis concerning masculinity in the past two decades and have begun to address the issues of men's psychology and men's history that Flax calls for. However, the recent issue or crisis of masculinity has not appeared from nowhere as merely some sort of response to or backlash against feminism. Male playwrights have always been gendered writers whose work is colored by their experience as men. As demonstration of this, chapter 2 offers some background regarding the presentations of masculinity in modern American drama, focusing specifically on select plays by Eugene O'Neill, Arthur Miller, Tennessee Williams, and Amiri Baraka as the "founding fathers" for the work of the contemporary playwrights to be treated at length in subsequent chapters. But before approaching these four earlier playwrights, chapter 1 positions this discussion within recent studies of masculinity that appear in men's studies and in feminist studies, particularly postmodern gender theories. Both theoretical fields demonstrate the problematics of gender, positing gender as an unstable concept that constantly tries to hide its own instability. Although rarely in any real dialogue, these fields provide points of intersection for thinking about masculinity that shed light on its positioning in regard to power and to subjectivity. As Victor Seidler writes in *Rediscovering Masculinity*, it is precisely the empowered position of speaking *for* (or as representative of) others that also makes men "strangely invisible to themselves ... estranged from the personal aspects of their experience" as men (4). In a manner of approach similar to those of Flax and Seidler, this study sets out to read the works of Mamet, Shepard, Rabe, and Wilson as relevant to the gendered experience of American men in order to explore the issues involved in enacting an "acceptable" masculinity. This book further explores the tradition out of which these playwrights arise and some alternative directions being pursued by more recent playwrights. In doing so, I hope this study illuminates how our leading male playwrights today return often to issues of troubled manhood, although they usually mask these issues behind other topics such as family, business, war, success, and personal freedom. Their protagonists tend to be haunted by perceived threats to their manhood as much as (if not more than) by any other problem they face, although they consistently refuse to acknowledge the source of these problems as being gender. However, as attractive as the often illusive image of masculinity proves to be for these men, a close examination of the image being pursued indicates the precarious nature of — even perhaps the impossibility of — attaining this image as it too often fractures and fails the characters who pursue it. By examining this thematic concern with masculinity, I hope to further considerations as to how gender might be restaged in a manner that is more flexible and more tractable, for both men and women.

Notes

1. The prevalence of male-cast plays in American drama is itself an indication of concern with masculinity within that drama. Robert Vorlicky's recent study of male-cast plays, *Act Like a Man*, explores what interactions among men in these male-only worlds demonstrates about problems of communication for men.

2. See, for example, Michele Wallace's influential *Black Macho and the Myth of the Superwoman.*

Chapter 1

Masculinity and Performance

Because there is neither an "essence" that gender expresses or externalizes nor an objective ideal to which gender aspires, and because gender is not a fact, the various acts of gender create the idea of gender, and without those acts, there would be no gender at all. Gender is, thus, a construction that regularly conceals its genesis.— Judith Butler, *Gender Trouble*

If gender, as opposed to biological sex, is a construct, as feminism has argued for decades, it is a construct for both men and women. As Jane Flax comments in *Thinking Fragments*:

Men and women are both prisoners of gender, although in highly differentiated but inter-related ways. That men appear to be and in many cases are the wardens, or at least the trustees, within a society should not blind us to the extent to which they too are governed by the rules of gender [139].

If, as Simone de Beauvoir indicates, one is not born a woman but becomes one, so too it would seem that one is not born a man but becomes one. Just as women are shaped and limited by a compulsory femininity (body shape, dress, gesture, movement, hair, skin, makeup, emotional behavior, dependence),[1] so are men constantly challenged to enact a compulsory masculinity (body shape, dress, gesture, movement, suppressed emotions, strength, independence).[2] The emphasis on strength, both emotional and physical, on power, and on dominance is not necessarily any more natural to a boy than is the emphasis on weakness, dependence, and ineffectualness natural to a girl. However, the performance of masculinity is subject to greater rewards than is the performance of femininity: if masculinity is performed successfully, its performer attains power and privilege that can offer him a greater sense of self-determination, something not generally offered the forced participants of femininity. Seemingly, then, it is precisely this sense of power and self-determination that blinds enactors of masculinity to the limitations of what they can "determine" to be. If a specific ideal of masculinity is accepted as the norm against which all other gendered behavior by men and women is measured, how can we see what may be problematic or even abnormal about this norm? How do we pull off the cloak of invisibility that masks the dominant ideology so that we can see possible problems with that ideology? This question is at the root of the present study that seeks to consider the questions, fracturings, and failings that surround the "normative" gender — masculinity — as portrayed by our leading male playwrights who, as men in this culture, have a stake both in shoring up those fracturings and in escaping them.

Within the sexual politics of America, males can attain the highest positions of power and prestige, and can become directors of their own dramas rather than always actors only. This politics allows men control, however, only if they follow certain scripts, only if they perform an acceptable masculinity and are born into certain races or attain certain classes. Generally, the construct of traditional masculinity within their economic class or race limits what range of performances individual men are allowed if they hope to maintain their power. Self-determination is thus allowed only within the constraints of a narrow range of socially acceptable selves. Yet, the plays treated in this study tend to demonstrate, as do many of the discussions in men's studies, that this enactment of a socially acceptable self occurs at great cost to men forced to participate in the performance of masculinity, often limiting their ability to exhibit, value, or even to see other possibilities for themselves. This cost ultimately calls into question the benefits of the patriarchal system in which acceptable masculinity is to be enacted.

Due to the "rules" that limit and maintain "normative" gender, the male's empowerment is actually extremely precarious within his own life. The necessity of policing the boundaries that delineate behavior that is privileged as male has often led, among other things, to the fear and hatred of women that feminism documents. Susan Faludi's influential study *Backlash: The Undeclared War against American Women* indicates that the connection between a backlash against women's rights and cultural confusion regarding the male role in American society deserves further study. She questions: "What exactly is it about women's equality that even its slightest shadow threatens to erase male identity? What is it about the way we frame manhood that, even today, it still depends so on 'feminine' dependence for its survival?" (65). In examining the impetus behind the backlash to feminism that Faludi covers with exhaustive research, she also records that this backlash is always accompanied by a "crisis of masculinity," a fear that somehow women in demanding to be treated fairly are challenging men at the heart of their identity — their manhood. She notes that if masculinity is such a fragile thing, perhaps "social investigators" should pay more attention to "the man question." Perhaps American culture's "woman problem" is the effect of the causal gender problem, which is the fragility and intractability of our concept of manliness (59–70).

In seeking to lash out against the social constraints inherent in the male gender role, the easiest target for men within the current social hierarchy is women, whose sexuality has, after all, been set up by this politics supposedly to absorb and to tend to the psychic wounds that masculinity creates for men. Flax notes that "men and masculine discourse have an ambivalent relation to woman and the dark continent of her sexuality — they both fear it and need it" (*Thinking*

Fragments 172). This view of female sexuality as a "dark continent" that frightens and seduces men appears frequently in literature, unacknowledged by many writers but often foregrounded in feminist texts. It is clearly evoked, for instance, in Caryl Churchill's drama *Cloud Nine*, in which the "dark" continent of Africa is connected with the female body: masculinity must "conquer" both in order to prove itself.[3] Similar to *Cloud Nine*, Churchill's *Vinegar Tom* examines male fear of female sexuality and of the female body as the driving force behind witch-hunts, one of history's most severe backlashes against women. I bring up these examples to help foreground the paradox of this binary relationship of gender for men and women — that men are encouraged to fear as overpowering and threatening the women that the social system makes powerless. Male fears that women, who are actually physically and socially disempowered, will ravage their manhood demonstrate that "masculine discourse" is, in fact, the locus of its own precarious relationship to masculinity, manhood, and virility. It creates a need to "conquer" the female body, or at least the feminine, in order to establish its own existence. And because it must "conquer" women, this discourse establishes the female as the adversary to be feared, even as her complicity in her subjugation is sought. Masculine dependency upon the complicity of women, on women's participation in its fantasy, insures that masculinity is much more dependent, more fractured and precarious, than it wishes to appear.

While traditional masculinity relies on conflict with the female body and with femininity for self-determination, recent gay studies and men's studies have explored how self-determination is denied to many men who either do not, cannot, or prefer not to perform traditional masculinity.[4] Likewise, studies of race and class also demonstrate the limitations imposed upon many men in their quest for self-determination.[5] Gay theorists assert that in addition to the manipulation of women, the male gender role is maintained through homophobia. Men are encouraged to be heterosexual and to fear and hate homosexuals due to the ostracized position of homosexuality within the heterosexual system. Boys and men are encouraged to behave like "men" rather than like "fags," thus establishing that homosexual men are not "real men," just as "real men" are supposedly not homosexual. This dynamic teaches men to fear certain behavior — anything typically labeled "effeminate," such as tenderness or affection for other men. This fear, of course, leads to further — often extremely restrictive — limitations regarding "masculinity," leaving masculinity as an increasingly shrinking and endangered position; it must be constantly policed and defended. This image of policing appears in David Savran's recent study of Arthur Miller and Tennessee Williams. In his discussion of Miller's theater, Savran comments upon the boundaries that Miller's men try to control regarding women and effeminate men: "The fantasy of a community defined by strictly homosocial bonds and yet aggressively heterosexual in its professed orientation puts enormous stress on the already fractured male subject, the one who must exert a control as rigorous over his own desires as over the desires of others" (40).[6]

While gay theory posits the need to control or contain certain desires within the self and the culture as part of the politics of maintaining "proper" masculinity, black activists have pointed out how racial issues also have to be policed and contained within this model. "Real men" who have and can wield the power and privilege of masculinity in American society must also, by the traditional definiticn, be white, and this power of white masculinity relies on subjugation of racial minorities. What it means to be black and a man in this society is extremely affected by these traditional concepts of "color-coded" masculinity, which becomes apparent in the theaters of Amiri Baraka and August Wilson. So, it would seem that the space for masculinity is increasingly narrowed, and challenged, by the performances that it excludes. The borders of exclusion become increasingly important as ways to define masculinity in contrast to what it is not: it is not female, it is not gay, and it is not black (or any other distinctly "ethnic" group).

This vision of masculinity as defined negatively is supported by contemporary psychological theory. Christine Di Stefano's *Configurations of Masculinity: A Feminist Perspective on Modern Political Theory* offers an excellent summary of psychological theory that establishes this negative approach to masculinity. As Di Stefano describes it:

> The rudimentary building blocks of the boy's struggle to understand what it is that makes him a boy, a masculine subject and agent in a gender-differentiated and gender-organized world, consist of negative counterfactuals garnered through comparison with the mother: as a boy, I am that which is not-mother, not-female, not-feminine. Within privatized family settings, where the father is not likely to be continuously available as a positive source of substantive information on masculinity, proceeding by way of negative comparison is a sensible strategy.... Early dependence on a maternal figure in the household may require an even more vigorous and aggressive response on the part of the boy who is struggling to achieve a masculine identity. His society may lend him a helping hand by providing elaborate and rigorous rituals with which to mark his entrance into manhood [46].

Whether through gender, sexual preference, or race, masculinity is thus constructed within a narrow range of possibilities. This masculinity, however, like the masquerade of femininity extensively discussed by feminist theorists, is clearly always already a role, a construct, a performance that has been scripted and is directed by the boy's society. While feminist theory offers us a paradigm for viewing masculinity — like other gender behavior — as a construct rather than as a given, this theory of gender is offered its most pertinent discussion for this study via poststructural and postmodern theories. Postmodern feminists such as Jane Flax and Judith Butler, who are influenced by the poststructural theories of Jacques Lacan and Michel Foucault, clearly view gender and sex as unstable and contested concepts rather than as inherent "givens." Judith Butler opens her study of gender issues, *Gender Trouble*, by analyzing the problem that feminism has encountered in marking the category of "woman" as a stable subject. She sums up the theoretical problem:

> The very subject of women is no longer understood in stable or abiding terms. There is a great deal of material that not only questions the viability of "the subject" as the ultimate candidate for representation or, indeed, liberation, but there is very little agreement after all on what it is that constitutes, or ought to constitute, the category of women [1].

As we have come to question the accepted "norm" of femininity, that norm has become ever more unfixed, unclear. If "woman" can no longer be taken as a stable subject, then it seems logical that neither can its traditional opposite, "man." The body and gender, far from being an autonomous, self-contained subject, becomes the site of "gender trouble," and identity is nothing more than what we choose to perform. Thus, Butler arrives at her chief question: if gender is a performance we choose to enact, why can't we perform gender differently?

Butler's question implies a need for change regarding modern performances of gender. In order for new performances of gender to be created or imagined, it seems that we must first more clearly examine the issue of this perceived need for change. What is wrong with the traditional concept of gender that feminists and writers in the men's movement are both calling for changes? A good part of the following chapters, which explore portraits of masculinity in contemporary plays written by men, will be devoted to examining if and where traditional concepts of gender, specifically of masculinity, fail its participants. Interestingly enough, masculinity itself in many of the plays to be discussed seems to have become the current "problem that has no name." Just as Betty Friedan examined the undefined dissatisfaction felt by middle- and upper-class suburban housewives of the late 1950s who supposedly lead protected and therefore privileged lives, the resulting discussions of the plays to come reflect the deep-seated dissatisfaction shared by many of the male characters despite their advantageous power position regarding gender roles. Yet this dissatisfaction is precisely what cannot be overtly voiced by these characters who have been trained to privilege the masculine position. How can privilege be disadvantageous? Our society is already filled with ideas regarding the burdens of leadership, the sacrifices that a man must make in order to achieve this traditional masculinity, but these sacrifices are traditionally viewed as acceptable given the advantages of the powerful position allotted to masculinity in American society. Interestingly enough, the advantages of the powerful position of masculinity become increasingly hard to pin down as a close examination of male characters in the following plays indicates. Rather than seeing themselves as privileged, these male characters are more likely to see themselves as limited, confused, and victimized by gender expectations, as deserving power, but powerless. Rather than critique their male systems of identification that offer them power only in return for acceptance of a limited version of "real" masculinity, they instead transfer their own problems with the expectations surrounding "normative" masculinity onto others, usually women and "effeminate" men.

If male characters find themselves dissatisfied and confused in a culture that privileges masculinity, the chief question becomes "why?" The rules of masculinity would seem to be clear-cut and the outcome rewarding, especially given the obviously disadvantageous position offered femininity. In response to much of this confusion, men's studies offer discussions and debates concerning masculinity that intersect in useful ways with the concept of gender as a troubled performance. Men's studies, which developed somewhat concurrently with feminist thinking in the late 1960s, reflect the questioning of gender taken up by feminism and have since grown into a quite different movement of their own throughout the 1970s and 1980s, focusing on issues of masculinity, male rights, and male liberation (particularly in regard to divorce laws and child custody laws).[7] Although not at all simply a male version of feminist politics, this movement at times employs theoretical approaches similar to feminist readings of femininity in order to explore masculinity and the male gender role as contested ground.

"Men's studies" or "the men's movement" is an extremely diverse and even self-contradictory field that has yet to produce a highly sophisticated theoretical voice, although it has several charismatic leaders. The most visible, no doubt, is Robert Bly. He stands, however, for the more personally oriented sections of the movement, those quite apart from the politically active groups involved in father's rights, which have been in part represented by Richard Doyle. However, despite such problems as an often limited focus on white, middle-class, heterosexual males, the entire project in all its derivations serves to highlight masculinity as a troubled, arbitrary performance that can be, and needs to be, refigured. Although often fraught with a dangerous essentialism (dangerous in that this essentialism tends to reinscribe the very concepts that first created the gender problem being discussed), many of the approaches in the men's movement attempt to find new ways of thinking about manhood, manliness, and masculinity that do not reinscribe the homophobia and misogyny that feminist, gay theorists, and certain members of the men's movement find problematic. Those who favor essentialism, however (many of whom are the most vocal spokesmen for various sections of the movement), often end up reinscribing antagonistic positions between men and women and between heterosexuality and homosexuality in their desire to rescue (as they see it) masculinity from the slurs laid upon it by feminism.

Robert Bly's interest in finding the archetypal, and essential, "deep male," in order to reinforce the positive aspects of being male in an age when to be male is theoretically in bad taste, is informed by a covert fear of femininity and of homosexuality. This fear is best indicated by his too fervent assertions that men can feel emotions and be physically affectionate with each other without being "feminine" or "effeminate," implying that to exhibit any feminine or effeminate qualities is inappropriate for a man.[8] He teaches his followers that they need to get away from the influence of the mother and to find their "father's house" in order to appease the "father hunger" brought about by the absence of literal or figurative fathers in this feminist age (at times implying that the absent father is somehow the fault of women rather than of the absent men). In many ways, Bly's theories simply restate in new terms an old, hierarchal division that privileges "masculinity" over "femininity" and that basically seeks to avoid any trace of "femininity" in order to be "masculine." At the same time it implies that women (the feminine) are still to blame for many male problems because they "emasculate" men. In addition, his tendency to present the current crisis of masculinity as unique to a "postfeminist" age ignores the insecurity regarding masculinity that has long been a part of the American culture, as will be discussed more thoroughly later in this chapter.

Other men involved in the movement, chiefly though not exclusively gay men, are attempting to throw out the concept of a true masculinity in favor of accepting multiple masculinities, which would make irrelevant such anxieties as "am I a real man," "am I truly masculine," by challenging what is "real" and "true" about any gender. For instance, in an article collected in Engendering Men, Ed

Cohen argues for a change in the way we think about "identity" in general. Following Teresa de Lauretis, he prefers to see identity (sexual or otherwise) not as a set position but as a "point of departure" and a "process" (170). This line of reasoning rejects the implied archetype represented by the "deep male" as being that almost indefinable something every man is duty bound to find and enact. Critics who reject "essential" masculinity argue that a desire for an essential masculinity — or a specific masculinity — leads to the oppressive, aggressive overassertiveness of many men that, fed by insecurities, leads to actions such as verbal and physical abuse of women, children, and other men.

Although the work of men such as Cohen and Bly examines the current debate over masculinity, two histories of masculinity that appeared in the late 1970s and early 1980s demonstrate that the question of masculinity is not exclusively a contemporary problem but that it has long been seen as unstable and precarious. Joe Dubbert's *A Man's Place* traces American concepts of masculinity from the 1840s to the 1950s and reads this history as one crisis after another. Dubbert's study could be seen as addressing "the man question" that Susan Faludi touches upon in her book. He treats in detail the crises of masculinity that have often accompanied the various waves of American feminism, but does not indicate that these crises are caused only by feminism, implying instead that they seem to be a part of America's general fears and insecurities regarding masculinity. The fear in pre–Civil War days that young boys were being emasculated because they were being raised by women did not, interestingly enough, encourage more active fatherhood but, instead, encouraged activities outside the home that were supposed to "make" men. The Civil War, the Spanish-American War, and World War I are three examples Dubbert gives of how political policy reflected this perceived need for a "testing ground" for men, war supposedly being the optimum test. In accord with this argument, Tania Modleski's *Feminism Without Women* also examines how the experience of war is often held up as the ultimate "authoritative" experience "that is felt to endow men with superior truth and insight" (66). Outside of military activities, Dubbert argues that the establishment of the Boy Scouts and the rise of professional sports (particularly the rise in favor of the "tougher" sport of football over baseball) during the first part of this century were also inspired by this desire to save boys from a perceived emasculation by women.

In a similar type of study, Mark Gerzon's *A Choice of Heroes* looks at a more contemporary America, particularly at how television and movies influenced the way young men were encouraged to view themselves in the 1950s and 1960s and how that influence affected U.S. involvement in the Vietnam war. Dubbert's and Gerzon's studies demonstrate that perceptions of masculinity have been in flux in this country at least since the early 1800s and often have inspired worry concerning emasculation of American men who, constantly perceiving themselves as threatened by the powerful influence of women, fear they are not living up to an idea of manliness seen as stronger in a previous age or generation. Even Robert Bly's current concern with the "soft male" emasculated by feminism reflects this vision and is but a more recent manifestation of what Dubbert describes as a series of male responses to the assumed threat by women (whether those women are feminists or not), and could perhaps be read as part of the backlash against women that Susan Faludi has explored. Viewed through the lenses offered by these critics, manliness becomes something like a receding horizon of expectation located in some past, obscure origin, an origin that is perceived as constantly receding from each generation of American men, but one that can also never be located (easily) in documented reality.

According to the above views, masculinity becomes an increasingly unstable position oscillating between traditional conditioning (harking back to those misty origins) and contemporary demands and desires, never settling fully into either. As the increasing publications of works for men that appear in popular psychology also attest, many men today are searching for a discourse of masculinity in a feminist age, seeking to define its essence (itself something difficult to agree upon) or to broaden its definitions. The 1970s and 1980s saw the publication of such books as *The Masculine Dilemma, The Male Ordeal, The Hazards of Being Male, Changing Men, The Myth of Masculinity, Absent Fathers/Lost Sons, Men Freeing Men, New Men/New Minds, Iron John*, and *Fire in the Belly*. These writings seek to cope with enervated and unstable definitions of gender, sexuality, and sex, while also beginning to acknowledge the entrapments and limitations inherent in these definitions and searching for ways to cope with the instability. The tone of some of these books is angry and bitter, blaming women for male woes; other studies take on a self-recriminatory tone that often becomes self-defeatist as well. However, the rise of men's studies in all its varied forms indicates a male concern with the value or use of our society's concept of masculinity and thus begins to pick up the challenges regarding masculinity's definitions and boundaries that have been raised by feminism concerning the traditional gender roles.

Without involving myself deeply in the often contradictory arguments within the men's movement (a brief history of which has been written by Tom Williamson in *Men Freeing Men*), I find it useful to draw upon some of the gender concerns behind the various projects of writers in men's studies as a way to examine the gender issues in the theaters of the country's leading male playwrights. The variety of questions, the confusion about position, place, and behavior recounted in these studies provide a background of unease, of insecurity, against which the dramatic male's plight is thrown into high relief. Male characters, like their real-life counterparts, seem to be haunted by the questions raised by both feminism and men's studies: What does it mean to be a "man"? What are the dynamics that create the current cultural concept of masculinity? How are those concepts enforced? Do such concepts limit the personal growth and fulfillment of men? Can there be multiple perspectives on masculinity instead? In changing our definitions of masculinity, what should we retain of the traditional performance or construct of maleness? And finally, why does it seem to be so difficult to perform gender differently?

As an example of work inspired by these concerns with male gender, psychologist Ray Raphael's study of male rites of passage in America, *The Men from the Boys*, though hardly a conclusive study, offers some pertinent views regarding our understanding of gender as a culturally coded performance or construct. Raphael interviewed one hundred American men, ranging in ages from 15 to 50 and drawn from the working and middle classes, about their ideas of manhood and the rites of passage they have enacted in their struggle to "become" men. Although this limited sample cannot be viewed as reliably representative of all men in America, it is interesting to note how these interviews repeatedly testify to the trouble that these American men have had in attaining a sense of identity as men and to the pressure they feel to do so. Raphael interprets this trouble as stemming from a deep-seated cultural need for some public acknowledgment that a boy has become a man, acknowledgment such as that supposedly offered by initiation rites in the past. Raphael argues that unlike womanhood (and here he seems to deny de Beauvoir's assertions), manhood is viewed as something not simply grown into but achieved or earned. According to this interpretation, one is not born a man; one *proves* himself to be one. And it is precisely this need to "prove" one's manhood that Raphael treats when he writes the following:

> At a time in history when male insecurity is rampant, formal rites of passage seem to offer dramatic definitions of manhood that are otherwise lacking…. How does a boy in any culture undergo the transformation from the weakness and vulnerability of childhood to the strength and self-confidence required of manhood? *The primary role of an initiation is to dramatize this change and thereby to facilitate it. A rite of passage places a difficult problem of personal growth into a social context; it gives a public dimension to private problems; it calls upon the combined force of a culture and all its traditions to help the individual get through this time of crisis* [12, Raphael's emphasis].

Increasingly, so Raphael speculates, American culture offers no established, universal rite of passage for its men, and this lack accounts for the fact that the majority of the men Raphael interviewed continued to question their identity as men even after asserting that identity through self-styled rites of passage. The male gender role of this model, then, is presented as a performance that requires acknowledgment and acceptance by an audience. It must be dramatized.

Perhaps, some might argue, feminism deprives men of important reinforcement of masculinity by encouraging women not to play the role of audience for this drama (of supporter, encourager, and reflector of men); however, Raphael argues that although the female body may be used in male rites of passage, female recognition of masculinity is not of ultimate importance. What is most desired and most needed is recognition from other men, because the belief is that while women can create boys, only men can create other men. Such a reading complies with the psychoanalytic model of masculine identity that Christine Di Stefano summarizes in which a boy establishes his male identity in opposition to the feminine as represented by his mother, and in which "his society may lend him a helping hand by providing elaborate and rigorous rituals with which to mark his entrance into manhood" (46). So, too, Luce Irigaray's study of gender dynamics in patriarchal societies demonstrates that women's bodies are used only as signs to signify the communion and relationships between men, to solidify their "hom(m)o"-social bonds.[9] In Raphael's model, which is typical of Freudian psychology, women represent emasculation (lack), immaturity, and perpetual dependency — all of the things that a "man" must overcome or escape. Raphael's interpretation of his patients' confusion regarding masculinity not only follows widely shared psychoanalytic models of masculine identity, but also places his patients' stories neatly within canonical American literature in which, as Nina Baym has pointed out, manhood beset must perform some task to prove itself.[10] If such a need for acting out masculinity is present in the psyche of the American male, then it should hardly be surprising that so many of the stories written by men take as their subject male coming-of-age or initiation into manhood.

This need to "act out" one's masculinity in front of an audience connects quite clearly to the postmodern feminist idea of gender as masquerade and as performance rather than as essence, a concept of gender that is at the root of the present study. Gender as *performance* would seem to be especially relevant to the genre of drama, wherein performance is understood as the end result of most dramatic texts. Theatrical representation is generally recognized as being metaphorically relevant to the human experience of self-presentation.[11] In Shakespeare's "All the world's a stage," the military lingo that refers to "theaters" of operations in which soldiers enact battles, and even in the term "gender *role*," human behavior is often linguistically tied to the site and act of theater and of performance. These connections have not been lost upon social scientists and theorists who study humans and their cultures. Anthropologist Victor Turner's *The Anthropology of Performance* explores connections between culture and performance, demonstrating that rituals and ceremonies intrinsic to culture are much like acts of theater. Anthropological approaches to the study of humans and their self-presentations have made their way back into theatrical discourse, particularly through the work of such theatrical theoreticians as Richard Schechner, Peter Brook, and Eugenio Barba. My use of the term "performance" throughout this study borrows from these dramaturgical analyses. If theater and culture can be read intertextually, as these theoreticians posit, then a study of gender presentation in American theater is relevant to an understanding of how gender is figured in the culture.

James Clifford's ethnographic study of the twentieth century, *The Predicament of Culture*, encourages readers to consider how mutable are performances of cultural selves. His study indicates that culture is hardly a stable enactment but one constantly restaged and improvised upon. It is precisely the ability of humans to incorporate new elements into their culture — to rescript the players, as it were — that makes a culture more likely to survive. Such a reading of cultural fluidity as important to survival offers a model of adaptability that might profit our thinking regarding gender. Both Faludi and Di Stefano indicate that problems within the masculine gender may arise largely due to the rigidity of that formation. Di Stefano notes that

> because the defining bounds of masculinity are so strictly set, they are all the more susceptible to invasion. This insight provides an alternative perspective on classically conceived masculine ego "strength," which until recently was compared favorably in the psychological literature on sex differences to women's notorious ego boundary "problems" and cognitive "field dependence." Indeed, a related aspect of such strength may be a brittle rigidity, the diminished ability to accommodate a shifting and unpredictable environment inhabited by independent fellow creatures and an enigmatic nature [47].

It would seem that rigidity of thinking about "true" or "real" masculinity may be precisely the root of the problems experienced by men in forming their identity. Perhaps chasing after this rigidly defined "real" or "true" masculinity is a doomed project in that, if found, that masculinity may not be appropriate for coping with the fluidity of human experience. Clifford, in borrowing from William Carlos Williams' poem "To Elsie," argues that no such things as "pure products" of culture exist because culture is, rather like the gender that Butler posits, always comprised of a series of positions that constantly shift in relation to each other and in response to new experiences. Only when a people have ceased to exist does their culture become fixed. Change, in Clifford's theory, is the ally rather than the enemy of culture — adaptability is the very thing that keeps culture alive. With such models that encourage adaptability and diversity available to us, why do we so often insist on intractable behavior in our concepts of identity — why cling to behavior that might actually be detrimental?

This desire to cling to a certain model of masculinity, even as it fails, and at times destroys, its participants is the pattern that drew me into a deeper study of the gender issues in so many plays by America's leading male playwrights, issues in much of American drama's traditional canon. America, as a country that supposedly is constantly recreating itself, remains nonetheless tied to a rigid concept of masculinity and manhood. As critics of that canon such as Nina Baym and Annette Kolodny have pointed out, this concept is an intricate part of our canonical literature. The man beset, taking up a "glorious" struggle or even a doomed fight, carries great romantic weight in our culture: our stories often pit the (male) hero as an underdog fighting (sometimes reluctantly) against a powerful and ruthless antagonist. The hero "proves" himself (and, by implication, proves his manhood) by winning, or if not always winning, at least by meeting the challenge. We can trace this pattern in our historical stories (such as the American Revolution and Civil War), or literature (*The Last of the Mohicans, Absolom! Absolom!, The Crucible, The Lords of Discipline*), or movies (*Casablanca, Shane, Rocky*).

Theatrically staged masculinity follows this pattern as well, and so offers readers/viewers an excellent position from which to consider cultural reflections of gender construction for men. Perhaps because they are writing at a time in which traditional concepts about masculinity are under debate — and under attack from some quarters — that masculinity seems to become more problematized in the work of contemporary authors such as Sam Shepard, David Mamet, David Rabe, and August Wilson. Their work offers us visions of ways that masculinity is rigidly constructed and how it is problematized within American society.

Notes

1. For a concise discussion of the way that femininity is prescribed by a patriarchal discourse, which requires women to become their own disciplinarians as they enact the ideal of feminine beauty in their approaches to food, body, dress, movement, and cosmetics, see Sandra Lee Bartky, *Femininity and Domination: Studies in the Phenomenology of Oppression*, 63–82.

2. For discussions of enforced "acceptable" male behavior, see several articles within men's studies such as those appearing in the collections *Men Freeing Men* (ed. Francis Baumli) and *Changing Men* (ed. Michael Kimmel). These discussions usually avoid celebrating the privilege that comes as reward for enacting the male role "properly" but, instead, attest to the limitations and psychic damage that results from the discipline necessary to enforce this behavior.

3. Churchill's model of the colonizing of gender has also been treated by feminist theorists such as Gayatri Spivak and Trinh Minh-ha in their influential cultural studies.

4. For examples of approaches by gay men, see selective readings in the anthology edited by Franklin Abbot, *New Men, New Minds*. This collection includes memories of growing up gay in a homophobic world of enforced heterosexuality, and offers insight into some groups' attempts, such as those of the Radical Fairies, to offer positive outlets for expression of the gay life. Other collections that offer perspectives from both gay and straight men who are disillusioned with traditional masculinity appear in Francis Baumli's edited collection *Men Freeing Men: Exploding the Myth of the Traditional Male* (1985), Michael Kaufman's edited book *Beyond Patriarchy* (1987), and Michael S. Kimmel (ed.) *Changing Men: New Directions in Research on Men and Masculinity* (1987).

5. For discussions of racial and economic issues, see Manning Marable's *How Capitalism Underdeveloped Black America* (1983), and Jewelle T. Gibbs's *Young, Black and Male in America: An Endangered Species* (1988). For a Marxist approach to masculinity, see Andrew Tolson's *The Limits of Masculinity* (1977).

6. Savran's *Communists, Cowboys, and Queers* relates Miller's theater to the Cold War politics of masculinity, an image of masculinity that he defines in his introduction as part of the "cowboy" politics of the Cold War. He has discovered an excellent term for the kind of gender policing I am referring to here in the work of Elaine Tyler May whose examination of the parallels between U.S. politics during the Cold War and the politics of the family indicates that the U.S. created a "domestic version of containment" concerning gender roles that was modeled upon that of the "containment" policy for our foreign affairs (Savran 6–9).

7. For an overview of studies of masculinity, see Kenneth Clatterbaugh's *Contemporary Perspectives on Masculinity*, and for representative voices within men's studies, see Harry Brod (ed.) *The Making of Masculinity*, Frank Baumli (ed.) *Men Freeing Men*, Franklin Abbot (ed.) *New Men, New Minds* (which includes a brief history of the men's movement by Tom Williamson), and Robert Bly's *Iron John*.

Popular versions of "men's studies" are more and more becoming connected with the theories of Robert Bly, whose Jungian-based concepts of gender have strongly influenced many psychologists and therapists (e.g., Lee, Osherson, Shapiro, Baumli, Abbot). Followers of Bly basically argue that male development creates a psychic "wound" related to the "wounded father" (an emasculated version of manhood represented often by the physical or emotional absence of the father). This "wound" keeps a man incomplete until he can go on a journey away from his mother and women, or from his psychological past, into the "wilds" where he can discover his own masculinity, touch the "deep male" within himself. As such, a fear of femininity (as represented by either women or the effeminate male) underlies this search and so tends to reinscribe antagonism between masculinity and femininity, positing the male psyche as the territory over which the gender battle is fought.

Bly's theories also promote an essentialism that can lead to dangerous positions in that it excludes certain behavior by men in favor of the traditional male role. Other essentialists within this field include theorists such as George Gilder, whose theories are radically different from Bly but who basically argues that the traditional gender roles are "natural" or inherent and that in abandoning those roles Americans are committing "sexual suicide." Men need women, so Gilder argues, to tame them, and women need men to protect them so that we must return to the old ways, those practiced before feminism disrupted and corrupted our supposedly stable and happy societies. For Gilder's theories, see his *Naked Nomads: Unmarried Men in America*.

Other branches within the men's movement position themselves much closer to the political agendas of some strands of feminism that recognize that a change in current systems in America or England requires men to lose privilege and power but that also argues that the loss will or can be compensated for by men discovering other aspects of the male psyche, such as the importance of parenting (caregiving) and other types of personal relationships (see Carrigan, Connell and Lee, in *The Making of Masculinities*).

Political activists within the movement are working for child custody laws and divorce laws that offer men more contact with their children and less absolute responsibility for financial support of ex-wives and/or children whom they may seldom get to see. Some of the writing in this movement is focused on what is perceived to be the greater evil done men via gender roles by turning men into working "machines" or "success objects" that are used for their earning potential and then tossed away (for example, see the work of Richard Doyle). Other activists seek to open up support for gay men, who are often ostracized from roles as fathers or are given less legal status in cases of sexism in the workforce.

8. Bly has been developing his approach throughout his writings of the past decade. His book *Iron John* is a compilation of these approaches centered on an archetypal reading of the fairy tale "Iron John." He sets up a dichotomy between the "soft men" of the feminist age who have abandoned true masculine qualities in order to accommodate feminist-preferred versions of maleness (i.e., men who cry) and the "deep male" or "wild man" who reflects the strength and untamed influences of the warrior archetype. His fear of femininity fits the psychoanalytic model of modern masculinity that Di Stefano summarizes:

We should also keep in mind that in modern western societies, there are strong sanctions against effeminate behavior on the part of boys. This is consistent … with the suggestion that modern masculinity resembles a reaction formation rather than an originary model of selfhood.... . There are significant links between masculinity as an achieved and precarious identity on the one hand, and a negatively conceived femininity represented by the objectified mother.... . The horror of identification with the feminine, the strictness with which masculinity is defined and established in opposition to femininity, suggests an intimate pairing of rigidity and vulnerability in modern constructions of masculinity. Because the defining bounds of masculinity are so strictly set, they are all the more susceptible to invasion. This insight provides an alternative perspective on classically conceived masculine ego "strength." … Indeed, a related aspect of such strength may be a brittle rigidity, the diminished ability to accommodate a shifting and unpredictable environment inhabited by independent fellow creatures and an enigmatic nature [46–47].

9. See Luce Irigaray's *This Sex Which Is Not One* (1985).

10. See her influential "Melodramas of Beset Manhood: How Theories of American Fiction Exclude Women Authors," reprinted in *The New Feminist Criticism: Essays on Women, Literature, and Theory*, ed. Elaine Showalter (1985).

11. See, for example, Erving Goffman's *The Presentation of Self in Everyday Life* and *Frame Analysis: An Essay on the Organization of Experience*.

Chapter 2
Canonical Forefathers

Because the 1970s and 1980s witnessed a revolution in critical thought about gender as well as the rise of men's studies, today's readers/viewers of drama have perhaps been made more aware of the subtle and often not-so-subtle ways in which gender assumptions shape human interaction. Yet we are still used to seeing the particularities of female gender while overlooking the particularities of male gender. Though hardly surprising that male writers' experiences are shaped and colored by their gender, critical interpretation has traditionally glossed over the male gender issues present in plays by men in favor of more universal themes, confusing, as Jane Flax puts it, "his" history with "ours." The result is that a central issue within much of American drama written by men has been virtually ignored, or at least certainly not given the in-depth analysis that has been afforded the (seemingly exclusively) gendered subject of women in American drama. What happens to our vision of the canon of male drama, though, if we acknowledge that men, too, are gendered subjects who are constructed by social concepts of masculinity? What do we discover about gender roles for men if we listen not to how these male writers speak in "our" voice, but to how they speak in men's voices?

In a highly influential essay first published in 1981, Nina Baym critiqued the male bias behind the definition of "the" American story — in regard to the critical reception of the novel — as a subtle and pervasive way to exclude women authors and women's stories from the canon. Her examination of the primacy that stories of "beset manhood" have had in American criticism and literature carries over easily into American drama, confirming a thematic tendency that ought to be readily apparent to any careful reader of plays by the widely acclaimed American playwrights attributed with establishing a distinctly American drama: Eugene O'Neill, Arthur Miller, and Tennessee Williams. The reluctance by both writers and critics to admit to gender bias — to recognize the particularity of male experiences recorded by these writers — can be seen to reflect the insecurity regarding masculinity that perhaps led to the (usually unacknowledged) emphasis on the theme in the first place.

The issue of American writers' concern with masculinity has been addressed by David Leverenz in a 1989 study entitled *Manhood and the American Renaissance.*

Leverenz demonstrates quite convincingly that nineteenth-century male writers such as Thoreau, Emerson, Melville, Hawthorne, and Whitman were troubled by issues of masculinity, by a fear of emasculation, because their career of writing was not generally perceived as being a "manly" pursuit. The need for these writers to find a masculine identity within the establishment of American literature, so Leverenz argues, in many ways reflects the need to establish a strong, powerful identity for the country. If such has been the case with the men attributed with founding American literature, it seems hardly surprising that the "founders" of American drama also reflect both the fear of emasculation and the need to assert and validate a powerful manliness within their pursuit of an American voice for the stage. The prominence of the question of masculinity within these writers' works is simultaneously accompanied by attempts to deemphasize the theme, turning critical attention to other issues within these plays that certainly deserve attention (such as the immigrant experience, the business ethic, the American Dream, and race relations). However, this desire to cover up or to ignore the often central problem of gender identity that besets the heroes of countless American plays has not diminished the impact that gender identity has had for the characters portrayed. After all, it is very difficult to conquer — much less to fight — an enemy that one does not see or acknowledge. Examining male gender issues within works by some of America's leading dramatists reveals the confusion and discontent regarding masculinity that men's studies acknowledges.

The logical starting point regarding the "founding," or at least the securing, of a distinctly American drama is with Eugene O'Neill, acknowledged father of our drama. He was soon followed by the powerful theatrical voices of Arthur Miller and Tennessee Williams. While O'Neill, Miller, and Williams presented their strongest drama between 1920 and 1960, the fourth predecessor to be discussed here came to prominence in the 1960s, contemporary with the early work of Sam Shepard: Amiri Baraka. Although a contemporary of Shepard can hardly be said to be a predecessor, Baraka does precede the other playwrights to be discussed in subsequent chapters. But more importantly, he stands as a powerful and representative voice of avant-garde theater as well as of African American theater, both of which have influenced the contemporary playwrights of this study. Although some literary studies already exist that examine direct influence or close correlations between O'Neill and Shepard, and between Miller and Mamet, my interest here lies not so much in direct influence as in establishing a pervasive concern regarding gender in the drama written by these men. I aim to explore issues that in their repetition — if not in their open acknowledgment — by so many male playwrights in America indicate a common concern with male identity that is, however, generally not treated critically as a central issue for these playwrights. By pointing out the gender dynamics for men that are usually not openly acknowledged by playwrights or critics, this chapter sets out to expose how deeply issues of gender, and specifically masculinity, are embedded into the fabric of so much of American theater history.

While many plays by O'Neill, Williams, Miller, and Baraka would be fruitful to study in light of their stagings of masculinity, I have chosen for brevity's sake to focus on only one representative play by each, while also briefly attempting to place it in some context of their other work. My selections were made chiefly in light of thematic concerns of the plays that follow and with the obvious awareness that my coverage of these playwrights is limited. My purpose in this chapter, however, is not for exhaustive coverage but to establish in these highly influential playwrights how issues of masculinity are consistently embedded into the very structure of their theater, though this issue has often been overlooked by critics until recently. In fact, despite the contributions by numerous feminist theater critics in the past two decades who have opened up new avenues for thinking about gender in the theater, it has only been in the past few years that a few theatrical studies have begun to address issues of masculinity. Robert Vorlicky's *Act Like a Man* takes on this issue in his consideration of communication among characters in the overwhelming number of male-cast plays that appear in American drama. His study analyzes a male-cast play by each of the above playwrights. David Savran's *Communists, Cowboys, and Queers* examines the works of Arthur Miller and Tennessee Williams in light of the political atmosphere of the Cold War and its construction of gender (specifically what he terms "Cold War masculinity"), sexual orientation, and power. Taken in consort with these two studies, I hope that the present discussion helps to further reveal the extent of critical analysis there is yet to do in regard to the politics of masculinity and its construction of our social and cultural self-concepts, both within the theater and without. The plays I have selected to discuss here, *The Hairy Ape* (1922), *A Streetcar Named Desire* (1947), *Death of a Salesman* (1949), and *Dutchman* (1964),[1] are generally hailed as significant additions to the dramatic canon, and each also presents male characters struggling to assert or to find their identity as men. Viewed together, these four representative plays serve to demonstrate the importance that gender issues regarding masculinity have traditionally had within American drama.

Eugene O'Neill: Father of American Drama

Selecting one representative play for O'Neill is difficult given the number of plays he wrote and the range of styles he employed. However, even when his earlier experimental style of drama later evolved into domestic realism, the issue of identity (particularly for his immigrant characters), and chiefly of male identity, remained a theme he returned to often in his work. As an early example of this theme, *The Hairy Ape* treats both class and gender relations outside of the family relationships that pervade so many of O'Neill's other plays. The later plays are often more obsessed with sexuality than are the former, the presentation of which is informed by Freudian psychology and influenced by Greek drama. The family and, more specifically, the Oedipal conflict of the son, is central to plays such as *Desire under the Elms* (a son trying to defy his father and to escape his mother's memory), *Mourning Becomes Electra* (a son unable to right the family wrongs), *Long Day's Journey into Night* (two sons unable to escape the devastation of their parents' mistakes), and *Strange Interlude* (the dead Gordon's manliness contrasted to that of Masden, the feminized academic). Sons have key roles in these plays and are always trapped within family dynamics that define, limit, and shape their struggles for masculine identity. The heavy hand of family history is figured as inescapable, implying that, for O'Neill, a man's identity is not possible beyond this history but is always determined by it. We will see this approach developed further in Shepard's family plays (in the father-son conflict that James Robinson and Henry Schvey argue owes much to O'Neill), as well as in the family plays of Wilson.

But before immersing himself in the familial issues that became a mainstay of his theater, O'Neill offered an almost archetypal quest for self-knowledge undertaken by Yank, a character whose name indicates his status as the "average Joe" American male. *The Hairy Ape* examines class structures that dehumanize the lower echelons of society; however, the main character also embodies a key aspect of traditional masculinity — physical power or "brute" strength. Yank's concerns regarding his place in society have as much to do with his manhood as with his class. Although Yank is able to construct a sense of manhood for himself in order to feel somehow superior to the rich men who ride the steamship he works on, he loses his concept of himself when confronted by a rich woman, Mildred. Initially proud of his strength, he comes to see himself as alienated from humanity, at last seeking refuge among the apes in the zoo where even there he does not fit and so is finally killed by the "hug" of an ape. Although Yank's struggle for identity revolves around his image of his own manhood, most critics of the play have tended to universalize the issues of alienation, "belonging," and identity that Yank confronts rather than interpreting these issues as gender specific.[2] From a class angle, Yank can certainly be read as representative of the lower classes, but the gender dynamics call for a slightly different reading.

While *The Hairy Ape* documents the abuse of the lower classes within America's capitalistic, materialistic society, Yank also represents an image of masculinity reduced to its lowest common denominator — brute strength. Yank's "power" is his body, whose superior strength places him at the top of the hierarchy of firestokers, and it is Yank's strength that gives him his initial sense of himself as a man. O'Neill notes in his stage directions that Yank should seem "broader, fiercer, more truculent, more powerful, more sure of himself than the rest" of the stokers (105). He is the one who lectures the other men on how they should behave and how they should think of themselves, emphasizing their relation to the machinery that has the power to move the ship. Through their connection with the fire, they attain their power:

> What's dem slobs in de foist cabin got to do wit us? We're better men dan dey are, ain't we? Sure! One of us guys could clean up de whole mob wit one mit. Put one of 'em down here for one watch in de stokehole, what's happen? Dey'd carry him off on a stretcher.[...] Dis is a man's job, get me? [109].

Yank's connection with the ship not only emphasizes his physical power as a man but his sexual power as well. In encouraging the other men to keep stoking the fire, he uses terms ripe with sexual innuendo: "Let her have it! All togedder now! Sling it into her! Let her ride! Shoot de piece now! Call de toin on her! Drive her into it! Feel her move!" (118). The ship is clearly figured as a female entity over which these men exert control, reflecting the need among men, discussed in the previous chapter, for a feminized presence to "conquer" in order to shape their identity as men. In consort with this reading, Linda Ben-Zvi notes in her discussion of the masculine myth of the frontier in this play that the "feminized" ship is similar to the feminized frontier, as posited by Annette Kolodny, which the male hero must master in order to prove his manhood (221).

Into this assertion of brute, masculine power comes Mildred, a bored, anemic aristocrat, "dressed all in white," who is determined to tour the stokehole, mainly to see "how the other half lives" in an attempt "to be sincere, to touch life somewhere" (114). Virginia Floyd describes Mildred as "emerg[ing] out of darkness like the unconscious shadowed side of Yank" (241). Mildred's brief look at this "other half," which causes her nearly to faint, certainly touches Yank's life. He cannot look at himself the same way after that moment. Mildred stands as an emblem of the real source of power in the play — the wealth of the upper classes in a capitalist society — which, in owning the brute power of the stokers, also "owns" any identity that Yank thinks he has. This emblematic female presence breaks his faith in his body's superiority, a faith that has been the locus of Yank's identity as a man. Paddy tells Yank that Mildred looked at him "as if she'd seen a great hairy ape escape from the Zoo" (123). Another stoker claims, "You scared her out of a year's growth," leading Yank to respond, "I scared her? Why de hell should I scare her? Who de hell is she? Ain't she the same as me?" (124).

Yank is prompted by this last question to leave the ship in order to assure himself that he is not less than this woman, and that despite being poor he still deserves to be treated as a human being rather than as an animal. However, on the street among the wealthy classes, he can get no one even to acknowledge his presence. He has no identity among the rich, but he also learns he has none among the working class unions, either.[3] In both situations, Yank's bodily strength is not enough to confirm his identity. Among the rich, his physical actions have no effect. Among the unions of the working class, his intellectual weakness makes him dangerous and unwanted. After trying and failing to be recognized as at least a part of some social group, Yank finally retreats to the zoo, where, still searching for a group with which to identify, he meets his death in the superior brute strength of an ape. Whether or not he has actually found his place at last is left ambiguous, however, and this ambiguity further highlights the troubled and indeterminant performance of Yank's masculinity.

Of note in Yank's dilemma regarding his gender identity is the issue of power. Masculinity is, in our patriarchal culture, traditionally associated with power, but that power is not exclusively physical. Social position is ultimately where the power resides, and the American society that Yank inhabits structures its power hierarchy according to both gender and economics. Mildred, whose presence first shakes Yank's faith in himself, is only a representative of the real power in the play, her father who owns the steamship. Although she is a woman, Yank recognizes that she represents a power with which his physical strength cannot compete. That power is not her sex, but her economic class. Furthermore, that class is created for her not by her own actions but by her father, so that Yank's sense of self (purpose, place) is challenged, ultimately, by the power of the man she represents.

Even before Mildred entered, Yank had already indicated a sense of competition with the rich men who ride the ship by asserting that he and his fellow stokers were the real men, unlike "dem slobs" on the upper decks. Yet in actually being confronted by a representative of that other world, Yank realizes that in contrast to its power, he lacks something, but he is unsure what. He goes on his quest to fill his lack, to attain the respect and recognition that are necessary for real power, and, by his definition, real manhood. Ultimately, though, Yank does not fit the definition of "appropriate" masculinity necessary to gain the kind of power that the rich, educated white man who owns the ship has attained.

Yank's story would seem to indicate the dangers of an identity structured solely on the physical characteristic of brute strength in a society that values economic power and influence, although it affords that power and influence only to certain of its men. Viewed in this way, Yank's story indicates the illusion of power that the traditional concept of masculinity holds out to all men, yet that it denies to most men who cannot "compete," because they are seen as unfit for the role of "real" manhood. Yank fails, ultimately, because he cannot perform his role successfully. He is destroyed in the act of trying to perform the masculinity he believes should save him, but the rules of which he does not understand.

Tennessee Williams: Masquerades of Masculinity

Like O'Neill's later plays, family is also key in the plays of Tennessee Williams. And as in *The Hairy Ape*, Williams often shows how society's hierarchal code validates one person's experiences rather than another's, making that decision based upon who in the culture is afforded the most power. In fact, Anca Vlasopolos's reading of *Streetcar Named Desire* focuses on how authority within the play moves from Blanche to Stanley precisely because society legitimizes his masculine "history" of events over her feminine one. Unlike O'Neill, Miller, or Baraka, however, Williams is often praised for the sensitivity and complexity with which he draws his female characters. He is often discussed in light of his heroines, such as Blanche Dubois, Alma Winemuller, and Maggie the Cat. For instance, John Timpane, in his discussion of the ambiguity of Williams's tragic heroines, remarks upon Williams's own tendency to emphasize his identification with these women (171).[4] Many of his critics further argue that his heroines are embodiments of Williams's homosexuality by reading the nymphomania of these characters as an expression of Williams's own desire for young men as well as his shame regarding this desire.[5] Yet in contrast to these tortured heroines, Williams tends to set up a powerfully heterosexual masculine world — a world no doubt heightened by his own homosexual feelings of entrapment, ineffectuality, and shame brought on by the culture in which he was raised, which condemned and belittled the homosexual man. Williams's portrait of the heterosexual man is what interests me most in the context of this study because this character is often portrayed as a brute not far removed from O'Neill's Yank, and he is often trapped within this portrayal — yet unlike Yank, he usually triumphs in the end. As Georges-Michel Sarotte argues, Williams's plays often contain the "handsome and sensual brute" best epitomized by Stanley Kowalski: "Stanley Kowalski is the Other; he is what Williams is not but would have liked to be" (110). Sarotte assumes, in this remark, that homosexual desire is actually heterosexual envy, but it is equally possible that Kowalski represents not what Williams would like to be but simply what he would like. The male body in this play is, after all, overtly presented as an object of desire.

A Streetcar Named Desire offers perhaps the best example of the complex of male positions that Williams creates. The "sensual brute" Stanley, Blanche's young husband Allan, and the naive Mitch together epitomize the conflicting masculine identities available in Williams's stage world. All three of the men in *Streetcar* are insecure about their identities. Allan, the young homosexual, has committed suicide even before the play begins. Mitch is stumblingly apologetic about his manners and behavior in the presence of the classy Blanche until he learns that he has been "duped" into a cat and mouse game as old as the institution of marriage. And even Stanley's assertiveness is clearly dependent on his relationship with Stella and his ability to crush opposition. This play, then, examines how a man asserts, and performs, male (hetero)sexuality even at the expense of other people and survives, basically, because he remains unaware of his sexuality as performance.

While most of Williams's homosexual men are not allowed on stage but are represented — spoken for — by other characters, usually women, the heterosexual men are all too dominant. The aggressive sexuality of Stanley Kowalski, however, does not necessarily indicate he possesses any more security concerning his identity and social position than do the other male characters. If male homosexuality must be protected or defended by being masked in shame and sheltered off-stage, by being figured by tragic characters who are "too good for this world" (as Blanche says of her young husband), male heterosexuality evidently must be aggressively assertive of stage space, defending (oftentimes violently) its preeminent position in order to maintain that position. This defensive posture suggests an imperiled masculinity, one that needs to be defended but that is, nonetheless, subject to its audience, which must accept this posture in order for the posture to survive. In this regard, Stanley's masculinity is simply another "masquerade" not far removed from that of the Southern belle enacted by Blanche.

Although Stanley calls Blanche's bluff concerning her performance as a chaste lady, he remains unaware that his own posturing is every bit as calculated.[6] Like Blanche, Stanley has his own costumes, particularly the sweaty t-shirt and the gaudy silk pajamas. Like her, too, he performs his sexuality in gesture and movement. Blanche cringes from lights and plays up her physical delicacy. Stanley smashes lights (and tables and bottles) and plays up his physical strength. Blanche pretends innocence and ignorance, while Stanley pretends experience and intelligence. Of chief importance to Stanley's self-presentation is his actual sexual "performance," which he uses to win and to subdue Stella, and which he finally enacts upon Blanche in Stella's absence. Stanley's antagonism towards Blanche stems in part from the threat that Blanche's presence might disrupt the "routine" that Stanley has been able to create with Stella, leaving Stanley with no partner in his performance and no one for whom to perform.

Stanley's relationship with Stella is not simply romantic or sexual but also somewhat Oedipal, with Stella representing both his mother and his sex toy. "My baby doll's left me.[...] I want my baby," he screams when Stella leaves him (65). And when she returns, he grasps at her like a child clings to a mother after waking from a bad dream. In return, Stella remains fiercely protective of Stanley even when challenged by Blanche, defending his image whenever he is not there to defend himself. When Blanche chastises Stella for Stanley's brutishness, Stella's response is to leap, literally, to Stanley's side for a "fierce" embrace, seemingly sheltering him from her sister's criticisms. Stella as mother-to-be has already been playing "mother" to Stanley on a certain level, cleaning up after his messes and comforting him when he begins to doubt himself. Through her support and admiration of him, she also provides Stanley with a reflection of himself as the type of man he would like to be.

In contrast to Stanley, Mitch contains some qualities of refinement, which Blanche compares to the behavior of her young husband, Allan. Mitch is from the gruff, poker-playing, beer-drinking world of Stanley, but he is aware of the more sensitive parts of life. He is capable of sentimental rather than merely sexual attachment, as is indicated by his relationship with his mother as well as by his memory of the young girl who gave him his cigarette case. He is modest about — even a bit ashamed of — his body, wishing to cover up his perspiration, to hide the bigness of his shoulders. Unlike Stanley, he does not assert his own sexuality, although he is every bit as proud as Stanley is of the strength of his own body and is eager to show it off to Blanche by literally picking her up. When faced with the "truth" about Blanche's promiscuity, however, Mitch chooses to enact not the tender, sensitive lover but the sexually aggressive male guided by the principle that women are only either angels or whores. He feels threatened by Blanche's deception concerning her chastity, sure that she has simply been making a fool of him, and thus feels duty-bound to reassert his sexual power in regard to her. This "duty" has clearly been encouraged in him by Stanley who is the impetus behind Mitch's confrontation with Blanche, and who later prevents Mitch from helping Blanche when she is being taken away to a sanitarium at the end of the play. In Mitch resides the only possibility in the play for a masculinity that does not fall into the stereotypes of either weak homosexuality (Allan) or brutal heterosexuality (Stanley), yet Mitch cannot break through the sexual code upheld and policed by Stanley. In the closing scene, Stanley literally pushes Mitch down and forces him to accept Stanley's authority, his ideology, his control.

In *Streetcar*, we enter a world haunted by the moods of New Orleans with its carnival atmosphere of masks and masquerades. Although Blanche is aware of the performance of sexuality she enacts in order to captivate Mitch, Stanley remains blind to his own participation in sexual masquerades. The final irony of the play is that Blanche's awareness of the game does not save her from being brutalized by its other participants, who remain (despite Mitch's brief insight into Stanley's "brag" and "bull") unaware of their participation. Male heterosexuality is given the privileged position of remaining unaware of its own constructedness, blind to its own games, its own instabilities, and to the support system that keeps it in place.[7]

Arthur Miller: Portrait of the Common Man

Although not addressing the "performance" of masculinity as centrally as does *Streetcar*, *Death of a Salesman* provides American drama with one of its most well-known portraits of troubled masculinity. Among the plays of modern American drama, perhaps no other captures the instability and dilemma of traditional American masculinity better than does Arthur Miller's *Death of a Salesman*. However, it has only been recently that this fact has been treated by such critics as Linda Ben-Zvi, Kay Stanton, Eugene August, and David Savran.[8] Earlier criticism tended to discuss the play in terms of its fulfilling or failing the definition of tragedy, in terms of its dramatic form or style (particularly realism), or in terms of its political or social critique.[9] While questions of identity have also interested some critics of the play, the tendency has been to read these issues as universal to Americans rather than as specific to American male identity.[10] However, August writes more recently that *Death of a Salesman* is "a profoundly *male* tragedy, one in which its protagonist is destroyed by a debilitating concept of masculinity" ("Men's" 5). David Savran's exploration of how Miller's concept of masculinity pervades most of his theater, particularly *After the Fall* and *The Misfits*, comments that Miller's work "vividly illuminated the pressures and anxieties circulating around the normative constructions of masculinity and femininity" during the 1940s and '50s (9). And in *The Making of Masculinities*, Harry Brod states that *Death of a Salesman* is "still the most eloquently profound single statement of mainstream American male dilemmas" (47).

These dilemmas are embodied in Willy Loman, a man who stands at a crisis point, torn between rugged individualism, with its version of the self-made man (as epitomized by both his father and his older brother Ben, as well as by the old salesman Dave Singleman), and his commitment to the domestic sphere of the family. Willy is trapped between competing versions of manhood, and his unwillingness to see the two versions as incompatible leads to his failure and death. He wants to be both the adventurer like Ben and the hero of the hearth and home, refusing to see that the two are mutually exclusive and impossible for him to attain.[11]

Willy's insecurity about his identity is summed up in his first flashback scene with his brother Ben. He asks Ben about their father, whom he barely remembers, explaining that because he does not remember his father, he has always felt "kind of temporary" (51). This statement speaks of Willy's profound need for a father figure on whom to model his own identity. His subsequent psychological reliance on Ben and on the old salesman further indicates his need for substitute father figures. We learn that Willy's father was always on the border of the American frontier — taking his family with him in a wagon, "through Ohio, and Indiana, Michigan, Illinois, and all the Western states" (49) and ending up in Alaska, evidently without his family, where Willy as a young man thinks about going in search of him. Willy's only memory of these trips is himself in a wagon and the sound of flute music, which Ben tells him came from his father's flute playing. For Willy, then, the father figure is something like the pied piper, never known but always heard, mysteriously, calling Willy to places far away.

Although his father, always pushing against the edges of the frontier, stands as a shadowy embodiment of the Manifest Destiny that beckons Willy, Ben is the main representative of the frontier lifestyle for Willy.[12] Ben's adventures in Alaska and Africa represent colonial exploitation and frontier individualism at its most idealized. As Ben reminds Willy several times, "when I was seventeen I walked into the jungle, and when I was twenty-one I walked out. And by God I was rich" (48). Explanation of what he did in that jungle, of how he became rich, is never forthcoming. We are left with a vague impression of Ben as representative of not merely survival but *success* of the fittest, a sense that Ben somehow wrested from the jungle the riches he now possesses, riches that he can hold in his hand, tangible objects such as diamonds. He is the independent man who has "pulled himself up by his own boot straps," offering American literature as well as Willy Loman yet another version of the Ben Franklin myth of the self-made man — hence his name.[13]

However, the model of masculine identity that Willy actually chooses is epitomized by the old salesman Dave Singleman (the single-man), whom Willy met early in his career as a drummer. This salesman had contacts, friends, acquaintances. He could make deals by phone from his hotel room because, unlike the adventurous Ben, Dave was connected to a community where he could attain monetary comfort by virtue of his reputation, by being well liked. And so Willy became a salesman too, notably a *traveling* salesman. Tied into the capitalist industry, he is also the adventurer or emissary to areas outside the main office. In becoming a traveling salesman, Willy seems to be attempting to combine the freedom of the open road (his father's identity) with the conquering of new spaces and "opening up whole new territories" (Ben's identity), as well as with the idea of being "well liked" and having "connections" (Dave Singleman's identity). Obviously, however, he commits more to the life of the businessman than to any other choice, and this choice is made clear in a flashback of Willy's "one chance" with Ben — to go to Alaska, which Willy refused because he was already established in his life with Linda. In this scene, Ben warns Willy:

> Get out of these cities, they're full of talk and time payments and courts of law. Screw on your fists and you can fight for a fortune up there [Alaska] [85].

To which Linda responds: "He's [Willy's] got a beautiful job here.[...] Why must everybody conquer the world?" (85). This exchange sets up the contrast of the "feminized" city and the "masculine" frontier, a tension explored by Kay Stanton in her discussion of "Women and the American Dream" in *Salesman*. Willy's fear of seeming emasculated in his choice of careers encourages him to overassert a role for himself as an important man at the office, claiming to have brought in huge commissions and high sales. At the same time, he feels compelled to prove to Ben that he has not given up the old ways of the frontier:

> It's Brooklyn. I know, but we hunt too. [...] there's snakes and rabbits and — that's why we moved out here. Why Biff can fell any one of these trees in no time! [50].

Willy passes this rugged, frontier image on to his sons, who also struggle to become important men in offices where, at the same time, they feel confined and emasculated. They, too, want to assert a physical identity within the world of business. As Happy says:

Sometimes I want to just rip my clothes off in the middle of the store and outbox that goddam merchandise manager. I mean I can outbox, outrun, outlift anybody in that store, and I have to take orders from those common, petty sons-of-bitches till I can't stand it any more [24].

This desire for some physical act, for some tangible proof of their masculine identity, is summed up in the idea that a man must be "building" something — a house, a family, a future. Willy assures his brother, "I am building something with this firm, Ben, and if a man is building something he must be on the right track, mustn't he?" To which Ben responds, "What are you building? Lay your hand on it. Where is it?" (86). Tangible indications of success are what Ben values and what Willy tries to come up with at the end of his life, but he does not even possess the intangibles of being "well liked" anymore, if he ever did. This desire to build something is reflected in Willy's carpentry skills, which Biff eulogizes at his funeral: "There's more of [Willy] in that front stoop than in all the sales he ever made" (138). The only other tangible evidence of Willy's struggles consists of the house, which has finally been paid for now that there is only Linda to live in it, and his two sons who are basically a reflection of Willy's own failures.

Willy's relationship with his sons is chiefly intended to increase his own reputation and sense of self-worth. He is proud of his sons' physical prowess and boasts of this to his neighbor Charley, clearly seeing his sons' physical success as a reflection of his own. This is not to say that he does not exhibit genuine interest in and love for his sons, but these feelings seem to grow as much as anything out of Willy's need for more support for his own ego and identity. His sons are the only tangible evidence of his life's work. They are his creation, and by being "Adonises," they can reflect well on him. However, Willy's confusion concerning identity and masculinity has led his sons into confusion as well. Neither Biff nor Happy has been able to "make" anything of himself. Happy is setting up to live his father's life all over again, mistakes included, in his promise to "show you and everybody else that Willy Loman did not die in vain. He had a good dream" (138–139). Only Biff seems to have come to any realization regarding the entrapments of his father's masculinity when he begins to strip away the lies and to face his own limitations, to realize what he wants rather than what he thinks he ought to want: "Why am I trying to become what I don't want to be? What am I doing in an office, making a contemptuous, begging fool of myself, when all I want is out there, waiting for me the minute I say I know who I am." What Biff finally admits to is his being not unique, not "individual," in his identity but "a dime a dozen" (132).

Anthologized in countless literary texts, translated and produced around the world, *Death of a Salesman* has stood for the past 40 years as a major statement on that ubiquitous American theme, the American Dream. Willy Loman's struggle and failure to become a self-made man, a financial success as a salesman, resonates with ideas and beliefs concerning manhood and masculinity. The story of an aging man, losing his grip not only on his job and family but also on reality, thinking back endlessly on the choices he has made that have led to his present failure, Willy's drama is that of a man who failed to understand how to be not a *successful* man but a successful *man* — how to integrate conflicting definitions of identity and masculinity. He is caught between two models of manhood — the independent explorer in the wilderness as represented by his father and Ben, and the community man tied into both the capitalist enterprise and the family wherein he must be husband, father, and provider. Torn between these two ideals and unable to see or to commit to either fully, he is unsuccessful at both. In its conflicting worlds of the frontier and business, as well as its conflicting concepts of the American Dream, *Death of a Salesman* contains many of the gender issues that will concern the dramatists to come.

Amiri Baraka: Angry Young Men

While O'Neill, Miller, and Williams were produced chiefly on the main stages of Broadway, the avant-garde, off-Broadway plays of Amiri Baraka (LeRoi Jones), which were often written within and for the Black Revolutionary theater, became a powerful voice for issues of race within American culture, an issue that is at the heart of American identity. His confrontational style of theater is at the forefront of the 1960s off-off-Broadway movement that cultivated Shepard and opened the way for the other dramatists to be discussed here. Baraka's theater, however, is distinctly masculine in its orientation, as Michele Wallace's *Black Macho and the Myth of the Superwoman* has so vividly and controversially demonstrated. Wallace argues that, like many other leaders of the Black Power movement, Baraka's fight for black power and black liberation in his plays and essays is focused chiefly on black manhood. Referring to Baraka's essay "American Sexual Reference: Black Male," which opens with the statement "Most American white men are trained to be fags" ("Home" 216), Wallace shows that "according to Jones the struggle of black against white was the purity of primitivism against the corruption of technology, the noble savage against the pervert bureaucrats, the super macho against the fags" (63). Baraka's equation of white men with "fags" is clearly intended to be the worst insult he can think to throw at another man, a concept based on homophobia, which Wallace also critiques (65–67). This homophobia has traditionally been a key to maintaining and protecting the dominance of a certain type of heterosexual masculinity, as is apparent, for instance, in *Streetcar Named Desire*.

Though many critics may have been taken aback by Wallace's critique that demonstrates how the African American fight for power was collapsed by its male leaders into the black man's fight for his manhood, Baraka himself has indicated that *Dutchman* is first and foremost about black masculinity. In "LeRoi Jones Talking" he wrote:

> *Dutchman* is about the difficulty of becoming a man in America. It is very difficult, to be sure, if you are black, but I think it is now much harder to become one if you are white. In fact, you will find very few white American males with the slightest knowledge of what manhood involves. They are too busy running the world or running from it [188].

This highly provocative statement regarding white males running from the world is one that I will return to in later chapters, but the first half of this statement begs for attention now.

True to Baraka's statement above, perhaps no other play within the American theatrical canon illustrates more vividly the dilemma that results from being black and male in America, a country that insists that its men enact an assertive and powerful masculinity at the same time that it crushes and even kills black men who attempt to do so. The issue of enacting gendered behavior, of gender as performance, is as crucial to this play as it is to *Streetcar*. The audience of *Dutchman* is encouraged to view Clay's actions — his masculinity — as a *performance* he has chosen to enact. Lula calls Clay a well-known "type," and Clay later admits to being so out of choice. When pushed by Lula's insults to take a stand for himself, Clay tells her:

> If I'm a middle-class fake white man ... let me be. And let me be in the way I want. I'll rip your lousy breasts off! Let me be who I feel like being. Uncle Tom. Thomas. Whoever. It's none of your business. You don't know anything except what's there for you to see. An act. Lies. Device. Not the pure heart, the pumping black heart [34].

This self-knowledge seems to be the ultimate cause of Clay's murder. Clay is acting the part of a "middle-class fake white man," and warns Lula that he does so "to keep myself from cutting all your throats" (34). He reveals to Lula that although he pretends to be an "Uncle Tom" he is actually hiding or repressing his anger and hatred, and it is this anger that Lula wants revealed so that she will have a reason, or an excuse, to kill him. As long as he plays the Uncle Tom "type" (as does the conductor whom Lula ignores at the end of the play) without acknowledging his performance, he is no threat to the system, but Clay both enacts a demure exterior as a defensive measure *and* remains aware of "the pure heart, the pumping black heart" within him. Subsequently, he is considered to be dangerous to the white patriarchal system, ironically represented (in a more vivid way than we saw in *The Hairy Ape*) by a white *woman*. Clay's "danger," as his final speech indicates, is that he might at any moment choose to perform his role differently.

Clay's self-knowledge is somewhat akin to that of Blanche, who performs a role created for her by the white patriarchy of her Southern culture, at the same time knowing it is a role. Although it is not always comfortable for her, though it is often even hypocritical, that performance is also necessary for survival, something that Blanche understands. Like Clay, it is her self-knowledge that destroys her because she cannot reconcile the performance with the reality, although Stanley manages to do so for himself by simply not acknowledging his performance as anything but reality. In a certain way, Blanche and Clay both expose the danger and dilemmas of self-knowledge if the self does not fit into neatly, predefined social categories. In Stanley's world, there is no place for Blanche because she does not fit into only one of the "appropriate" roles he envisions for women: wife, mother, or whore. In Lula's world, there is no place for Clay because he resists neat dichotomies: he is neither a white man nor an Uncle Tom.

Clay's emphasis on his performance reveals, however, the extent to which performance is necessary to his survival. In proving that his performance is a way to mask his rage, Clay's references are to professional entertainers from the black community, notably Bessie Smith and Charlie Parker, who he claims also mask their rage behind their performances. The professional "performance" of music or poetry, Clay argues, is simply channellings of the rage that all blacks, all the "blues people," actually feel towards whites. Clay, Baraka's version of the average black man, is presented as playing the same game as the professional performer, what Richard Majors and Janet Mancini Billson refer to in *Cool Pose: The Dilemmas of Black Manhood in America* as a "relentless performance ... in a theater that is seldom dark" (4). To "pass" through a white world that refuses to acknowledge a black man's right to existence and chooses to see him as a threat, he must disguise himself in a manner that will be perceived by his white viewers as non-threatening. This image of the mask appears often in plays by African Americans that treat the difficulty of finding and knowing one's identity in a culture that seeks to take away that identity.[14]

In addition to the theme of masculine identity that Baraka details, *Dutchman* provides an influential style of theater for presenting this issue. The violence and rage of his male characters, while overtly motivated by racial injustice, are covertly reflecting a confusion regarding gender identity that is apparent in the rage and violence among the men in the plays of Shepard, Mamet, Rabe, and, to a lesser extent, Wilson. Violence and aggression are associated with masculinity not only by these playwrights, but by sociological definitions of masculinity, which will be discussed more thoroughly in chapter 6. Baraka's theater is an angry theater, his men are bitter and defensive, threatened and imperilled, but fighting back. We will see similar characteristics among men in the plays to follow, indicating that certain gender issues are at the heart of the anger and violence that are so often exhibited by male characters in contemporary plays by both black and white men in America.

The vagaries, the fracturings, the insecurities of male identity are all present within plays by O'Neill, Williams, Miller, and Baraka, who serve as sometimes direct, sometimes shadowy influences on the leading male playwrights of the next generation. Although all of the playwrights discussed in the following chapters indicate that they see their plays as encompassing a wide canvas of American experience (the family, business, war, the frontier), consistently within the plays of all four dramatists, that canvas shrinks as the American myths or subjects they treat reveal themselves to be gendered as male. The plays that follow reveal, at times unintentionally, the "invisible" or "unspeakable" idea that masculinity is often as disempowering for the men who seek to enact it as it is empowering. This disempowerment explains in part the defensiveness and even paranoia that plagues so many male characters. Masculinity, manliness and manhood, far from comprising a stable, monolithic construct, become fractured and insecure in these plays, yet masculinity is also the territory over which these playwrights and their characters fiercely fight for mastery.

Notes

1. All dates for plays in this study refer either to the first major (usually New York) production or to the first publication, whichever occurred first.

2. For representative discussions that treat Yank's search for identity as basically non-gendered, see Doris V. Falk, *Eugene O'Neill and the Tragic Tension*, which reads Yank's quest as a seeking after "self-knowledge" typical of the tragic hero; Virginia Floyd's *The Plays of Eugene O'Neill*, which equates the terms "man" with "humanity" in describing the play as examining "not only the nature of man's role in society but also the nature of being" (238); Travis Bogard's *Contour in Time: The Plays of Eugene O'Neill*, which describes the play as "a fable narrating man's war with a capitalistic society," yet which consistently confuses "man" with "human" (249); and Peter Egri's "'Belonging' Lost: Alienation and Dramatic Form in Eugene O'Neill's *The Hairy Ape*," which gives a detailed reading of the theme of alienation and Yank's search for "belonging."

3. For an extended reading of Yank's inability to belong among either the rich or the working class, see Peter Egri's article. (Note 2)

4. For some representative readings of perhaps his most famous heroine, Blanche Dubois, see Constance Drake's "Blanche Dubois: A Re-evaluation"; Susan Spector's "Alternative Visions of Blanche DuBois"; Leonard Berkman's "The Tragic Downfall of Blanche Dubois"; and Durant Da Ponte's "Tennessee Williams' Gallery of Feminine Characters."

5. See, for example, discussions in John Clum's *Acting Gay*, John Timpane's "'Weak and Divided People': Tennessee Williams and the Written Woman," and Georges-Michel Sarotte's *Like a Brother, Like a Lover*.

6. For further development of this point, see John Clum's discussion of Stanley in *Acting Gay* (215–216).

7. Vlasopolos's reading of *Streetcar* highlights how patriarchal assumptions within the play ultimately support Stanley's version of "history." Clum's reading also emphasizes how Blanche is aware of her "performance" while Stanley remains oblivious to his own.

8. See Ben-Zvi's "'Home Sweet Home': Deconstructing the Masculine Myth of the Frontier in Modern American Drama"; Stanton's "Woman and the American Dream of *Death of a Salesman*"; August's "*Death of a Salesman*: A Men's Studies Approach"; and David Savran's *Communists, Cowboys, and Queers: The Politics of Masculinity in the Works of Arthur Miller and Tennessee Williams*.

9. For examples of articles concerning *Salesman* as tragedy, see Robert A. Martin, "Arthur Miller and the Meaning of Tragedy" (1970); M. W. Steinberg, "Arthur Miller and the Idea of Modern Tragedy" (1960); George D. Schweinitz, "*Death of a Salesman*: A Note on Epic and Tragedy" (1960); and Miller's own "Tragedy and the Common Man" first printed in *New York Times*, 27 February 1949. For representative articles concerning the dramatic form or style of the play, see Enoch Brater, "Miller's Realism and *Death of a Salesman*" (1982); Raymond Williams, "The Realism of Arthur Miller" (1959). Regarding political or social implications, see Eric Mottram, "Arthur Miller: The Development of a Political Dramatist in America" (1969); Paul Blumberg, "Sociology and Social Literature: Work Alienation in the Plays of Arthur Miller" (1969).

10. For representative articles concerning identity or American images, see Gerald Weales, "Arthur Miller's Shifting Image of Man" (1969); P. P. Sharma, "Search for Self-Identity in *Death of a Salesman*" (1974).

11. Enoch Brater's article discusses this conflict in non-gendered terms as being the tension between the home and the outside world. He argues that the set described by Miller epitomizes this tension. The Loman house (the domestic sphere) is both symbolically and physically threatened by the surrounding "inhuman towers," which represent the city or the outside world (119–120).

12. See Ben-Zvi's "'Home Sweet Home'" for a similar reading of Willy's relationship to the "masculine myth" of the American frontier (222–224).

13. Eric Mottram discusses Willy's father, his brother Ben, and Willy himself as embodying various versions of the self-made man (30).

14. Ntozake Shange's *Spell #7*, and Adrienne Kennedy's *Funnyhouse of a Negro* are prime examples of the tyranny of the mask, although these plays focus mainly on female subjectivity.

Chapter 3

Sam Shepard:
The Eternal Patriarchal Return

There's something about American violence that to me is very
touching. In full force, it's very ugly, but there's also something
moving about it because it has to do with humiliation. There's
some hidden, deeply-rooted thing in the Anglo male American that
has to do with inferiority, that has to do with not being a man, and
always, continually, having to act out some idea of manhood that is
invariably violent.— Sam Shepard, in interview with Michiko
Kakutani

   Perhaps more than any other contemporary playwright, Shepard is fascinated
by the patriarchal inheritance of American frontier mythology. If *Death of a Salesman* records the demise of the masculine myth of the frontier, Sam Shepard's male
characters are still not willing to abandon that myth. Their unwillingness to let
go of the frontier myth of rugged individualism and of the western hero that they
have inherited from their fathers reflects how deeply such concepts are imbed-
ded not only in the American self-image, but especially in American ideas of
masculinity. As we witnessed in *Salesman*, Shepard's theater also often presents
the family as that which encroaches upon a man's individualism, upon his manhood. This emphasis upon the family's role in defining and limiting men is reminiscent of O'Neill's theatrical explorations of the family, particularly of the father-
son relationship, as indicated in the last chapter.[1]
   Shepard's male protagonists are creatures of the West — of open spaces, of
plains and deserts and their concomitant images of freedom, isolation, and independence. His science fiction westerns such as *The Unseen Hand, Operation
Sidewinder*, and *Forensic and the Navigators* focus on a version of the western-type
hero in conflict with technology. *The Holy Ghostly, Angel City, Cowboy Mouth*,
and *Geography of a Horse Dreamer* concern characters whose talents are threatened by industry and exploitative schemes that cut them off from the roots of freedom and individual style that they need to survive. This conflict echoes that
between the "masculine" frontier and the "feminine" city that has been established
by a number of critics of American culture and literature.

In his history of masculinity in America, Joe Dubbert argues that there is a strong connection between America's concept of the frontier and its concept of masculinity. Borrowing from Frederick Jackson Turner's influential frontier thesis and from Edward Hall's theory of proxemics, Dubbert posits that American ideas of masculinity became intricately connected with the freedom and wildness of open, untamed frontier. Subsequently, American manhood faced a crisis as frontier gave way to urban sprawl. The masculine space of the frontier was seen as being crowded out, establishing in the American male a sense of loss. Dubbert also posits that this sense of crowding, which men experienced in the "woman's world" of the home, is in part responsible for the need that American men felt, and still perhaps feel, to assert themselves in business and in sports, outside of the home. The frontier, according to this argument, is more than a strictly physical reality. It has come to mean for American men a psychological space in which they may assert a gendered identity as men.

The image of the frontier as the vanishing point of American manhood has been ably critiqued from a feminist perspective by Annette Kolodny in *The Lay of the Land*, which points out that the above construct of masculinity was created by men. Kolodny refers to the metaphor prevalent in much frontier literature written by men of the feminine land that must be tamed, plowed, or fenced in by male hands. Thus, in the very act of asserting that the taming of the frontier is a masculine endeavor that helps to "make" men, this construct also reinscribes women into the scenario as the object of the taming. At the same time, frontier imagery, as Dubbert notes, also implies that the "encroachment" of society is somehow feminine as well. Within this mythology, then, masculinity is given the fleeting space between the supposedly feminine wilderness of the open land and the feminine institutions of civilization. Due to these constructs, men might seem to be threatened both before and behind by feminine presence, yet these entrapping images are, ironically, of male origin.

To the theories of Joe Dubbert, Annette Kolodny, and Frederick Jackson Turner it is important to add those of Leslie Fiedler in relation to Shepard's theater. The frontier and the wilderness function for Shepard's men much as Fiedler, in a now classic study, posits they function for heroes of the American novel.

Fiedler's *Love and Death in the American Novel* argues that

> the typical male protagonist of our fiction has been a man on the run, harried into the forest and out to sea, down the river or into combat — anywhere to avoid "civilization," which is to say, the confrontation of a man and woman which leads to the fall to sex, marriage, and responsibility. One of the factors that determines theme and form in our great books is this strategy of evasion, this retreat to nature and childhood which makes our literature (and life!) so charmingly and infuriatingly "boyish" [xx–xxi].

According to Fiedler, the great American novel is the story of adolescent boys who flee the responsibilities of civilization in favor of male bonding in the wilderness. Huck Finn's determination at the close of his narration to "light out for the territories" before Aunt Sally has a chance to "sivilize" him becomes for Fiedler the quintessential statement of the desires of male protagonists in American novels. Shepard's male characters also flee the confines of the East and the city for the open spaces of the frontier — usually represented in Shepard's plays not by the lush wilderness of forests and rivers but by the barrenness of the desert. In fact, his obvious fascination with western cowboys, represented in play after play, springs from his idea of their adolescent rebellion against the civilized East. In a 1974 interview he comments about cowboys:

> Cowboys are really interesting to me — these guys, most of them really young, about 16 or 17, who decided they didn't want to have anything to do with the East Coast, with that way of life, and took on this immense country, and didn't have any real rules [Chubb 190].

The adolescent rebellion against "civilization," which Fiedler defined as a driving force of the American novel, becomes in Shepard's drama the story of the western hero's flight from the rules of the eastern cities to the openness and even oblivion of the western deserts.

This fascination with the western hero, the cowboy, is evident in Shepard's own persona. Often photographed in cowboy hat and boots, Shepard himself is something of an American cultural icon representing the maverick, independent, modern-day cowboy, as well as the perpetual adolescent. In his article about Shepard, which appeared in *New York* magazine, Pete Hamill describes Shepard as being "as American as Huckleberry Finn; he often looks back upon his lost innocence, sometimes symbolized by the emptiness of the western desert, sometimes by the people of masculine myths, and his characters often long to join Huck by lightin' out for the territories" (78). Robert Coe also refers to Shepard's tendency to "run away" as reminiscent of Huck Finn's (66). In her *Esquire* profile of Shepard, Jennifer Allen tells her readers: "Think of Holden Caulfield's loathing of phonies, hypocrites, all the jerky grown-ups who compromise instead of dream, then cross Holden Caulfield with the cowboy ethic, and you get the idea" of Shepard (142). In this same article, Allen refers again to Shepard's youthfulness, describing him as being "as much a boy-man as a middle-aged man of letters; his life has been less a steady march toward maturity than an acting out of adventures" (142).

These images of Shepard are not merely the creation of critics but are fostered and encouraged by Shepard himself both in his personal life and in what he chooses to write about. Until quite recently, Shepard seemed to be living the lives of the characters he writes — the American male's quest for independence and for perpetual adolescence in preference to the responsibilities and repetitions of settled, adult life. In fact, his career as a playwright grew out of his desire to play rather than to take on "real" work. He establishes well this difference in a comment to the editors of *Theatre Quarterly* in 1974:

> The reason I began writing plays was the hope of extending the sensation of *play* (as in "kid") on into adult life. If "play" becomes "labor," why play? ["Language" 214].

For many of Shepard's male characters, the logic is the same: if becoming an adult means giving up their fantasies, of no longer being what *Fool for Love* terms "fantasists," then why grow up? Why exchange a fantasy of freedom for the responsibilities of adulthood? In the opening to her book-length study of Shepard, Ellen Oumano refers to the "personal mythology [Shepard]'s constructed for himself — Son of the West, inheritor of a divided nature" that reflects the longing for the fantasy of freedom in conflict with competing images. She describes this divided nature:

> The division is not psychological but archetypal, characterized by the American male who wants savagery and innocence, who yearns to be on the road at the same time he wants to settle down, who wants utter freedom yet feels his responsibilities [2].

Shepard's plays of the 1970s and 1980s, in particular, abound with images of men who abandon (or wish to) their responsibilities toward jobs and families in favor of a self-absorbed life alone in a desertic region (usually the Mojave) or in the bottom of a liquor bottle. Shepard's focus in play after play is the literally or metaphorically displaced cowboy who has lost the open spaces of the western frontier and become entangled in familial and/or business relationships that compromise his ability to be independent and free—qualities associated with Shepard's western-cowboy image of American masculinity. The desires of these characters to flee their entanglements, however, often indicate not a return to adult manhood but to adolescent self-absorption that is all too often destructive. The freedom associated with "originality" of personality obsesses Shepard's men in the plays to be discussed in this chapter, and this obsession revolves around Shepard's theories of fractured identity and his concern chiefly with male identity.

The "masculine space" of the frontier has become a psychological space in Shepard's drama that is nonetheless laid out within a specific geographic landscape. The West and the desert operate in marked contrast to the East and the city for Shepard's characters. One represents freedom and escape—a place to "disappear" into, as Lee and Austin discuss in *True West* (41)—while the other represents financial success and the death of the soul. This portrait of the "frontier" of the West as a place for men to escape the responsibilities of civilization, as Fiedler among others presents it, is certainly familiar in American literature. However, even as he locates this escape into the frontier as almost an inherent part of the American dream for men, Shepard also depicts this frontier ambiguously as both freedom and destruction. The abstract qualities of independence and originality that Shepard associates in his plays with the frontier are also connected with escape and erasure for the men who "disappear" into the deserts of the West. In Shepard's world, a man is a man when he owns his own identity, yet he is able to establish that identity only in relationships within the very civilization that he wishes to escape. The myth of the frontier is, after all, a fantasy of city folk for that ever-receding Eden wherein life is better, cleaner, purer, more real. If "real" masculinity is located in that frontier, then it too is an ever-receding fantasy. Embracing this fantasy, Shepard's man hopes to create himself *apart* from society and its inner workings by disappearing into the frontier, at the same time that he must create an idea of the frontier, and of himself, *out of parts* of the society he is supposedly fleeing.

This search for male identity is present in every stage of Shepard's career. Both *Rock Garden* and *Chicago* are early works that focus on young men attempting to assert themselves apart from their parents or girlfriends/wives. *Cowboys #2* and *Cowboy Mouth* also explore male identity as it is influenced by popular cultural images and by women's desires as these are perceived by men. However, Shepard's focus on the dilemma of male identity (that it needs the sphere of the social world in order to create itself but also longs to be uninfluenced and "original") becomes markedly clearer starting in the 1970s with what Felicia Londre has referred to as his "coming to awareness of a young adult masculinity" (20). This "awareness" includes dealing with the influence of one's roots — of one's immediate creators: the family. Shepard's move toward realism in his work in what have been termed his "family plays" of the 1970s and 1980s coincides with his developing ideas of character, which Shepard attributes at least in part to conversations he had with Peter Brook while in London (Hamill 96–98). Developing his explorations of character and of male identity within the family led to a change in his style of drama. The 1970s marked his movement from the more fractured and imagistic theater of his 1960s plays to a form of realism that Shepard employs, beginning with *Curse of the Starving Class* (1977), to explore family relations, and, particularly, male identity within the family.

The critical reception of Shepard's plays starting in the late 1970s also focuses increasingly on the issue of masculinity because his family plays call more and more attention to male violence, to father-son relationships, and to male resentment toward women and the feminine. Bonnie Marranca has noted Shepard's preference for "writing about male experience" to the point that he seems to be "unaware of what has been happening between men and women in the last decade" ("Alphabetical" 30–31). In discussing his frontier landscape, Florence Falk describes Shepard's domain as that "of Male Homo Erectus, whose bulging muscles and veins streaked with violence bespeak daring and conceal any trace of vulnerability" (91). Picking up the metaphor of muscular masculinity, Felicia Londre reads Shepard's career as a "'working out' to build up strengths in the playwright's craft," which activity parallels his "unconsciously developing masculinity" (20). According to Londre's model, Shepard's personal development is mirrored in the phases of his playwriting: early "masculine fantasies" gave way to a "coming to awareness of a young adult masculinity" in his plays of 1976–1980 and, finally, developed into "a mature masculinity" in his work of the 1980s (20–21).

Because his focus on the problems of establishing and maintaining male identity seems to crystallize beginning with his plays of the late 1970s, this discussion will be limited to the family plays: *Curse of the Starving Class* (1977), *Buried Child* (1978), *True West* (1980), *Fool for Love* (1983), *A Lie of the Mind* (1985), and his most recent exploration of father–son identity, one that marks a turn away from his previous version of realism, *States of Shock* (1991). As a preface to these plays, I will also treat the 1971 rock drama *Tooth of Crime* because it explores Shepard's fascination with the performance of identity, the performance of self, which is crucial to his presentation of masculinity. This play offers the paradigm of dueling images of masculinity that serves as a foundation for each of the family plays.

In examining these plays, I hope to offer a counterpoint to the early feminist criticism that focused on Shepard's presentation of masculinity as it related to his treatment of female characters. Perhaps the best example of this critical stance is voiced by Lynda Hart in her powerful analysis of Shepard's masculinist heroes. Hart argues in two key articles, which appeared in 1988 and 1989, that rather than acting as the maverick iconoclast writing against the systems of power in America, Shepard actually reinforces the patriarchy that drives those systems. Far from being the revolutionary, Hart contends, Shepard affirms the patriarchal myth that privileges male subjectivity at the expense of the female by objectifying and abusing her, relying on the male myths of the frontier as one support for this stance ("Pornographic" and "Spectacle"). I will start with Lynda Hart's accusation that rather than subverting or deconstructing the masculinist bias — male violence and an emphasis on male subjectivity at the expense of female subjectivity — Shepard's plays often reinforce this bias as a given and present it iconically as particularly American. However, I further wish to suggest that such a critique of Shepard at times reinscribes some of this defense of the patriarchy by failing to see the ambiguities (particularly the ambiguity surrounding male power) expressed concerning male and female identity within the plays to be discussed here. If we focus not on how the male mythologies in Shepard's plays affect the women, but on how those mythologies affect the men, we discover a very different power dynamic than early feminist critiques supposed.

Although many of the recent critiques of Shepard's plays are accurate in pointing out that his men get the better end of the deal than do his women, the ways in which his male characters are actually fractured have not been treated fully. Some reassessment of the male-female positions in articles by Anne C. Hall, Susan Bennett, and Janet V. Haedicke, published in the 1993 study *Rereading Shepard*, begin to explore the idea that the gender positions are less clear cut in Shepard's recent work (particularly in *Fool for Love* and *A Lie of the Mind*) than many critics originally argued. Approaching these plays from various angles, Hall, Bennett, and Haedicke show how May and Beth actually critique the patriarchal system within their plays. As valuable as these articles are, they tend to focus more on the female characters' experiences/voices than upon those of the male in order to explore the breakdown of male mythologies. Also, they tend to indicate that these last two family plays break from Shepard's previous canon by calling into question the efficacy of the male mythologies. Although *Fool for Love* and *A Lie of the Mind*, and even *States of Shock*, are more overt in demonstrating the destruction inherent in the male mythologies for men, the oppression, confusion, and instability regarding the patriarchal code has been apparent in Shepard's male characters from the beginning of his career. The closer one examines Shepard's men, the more apparent it becomes that his male character's victories are often Pyrrhic. Even so, the overriding critical tendency has been to focus upon the glorification of Shepard's male characters as icons of the American Male Hero (the original, cowboy, maverick, dreamer, and so on) without noticing the entrapments and failings of these images for his men. Shepard's men are hardly positive images of completed and individualized selfhood or identity, however much Shepard himself may or may not have intended them to be so. Their mythologies of gender usually do not lead them into security or even into real power.

Shepard's men are usually unable to cope with the worlds that they have helped to create, although they desire to blame the failings of their own creations on women or on systems of culture (Huck's "sivilization"). This desire to escape or to deny their own entrapments often leads to violent, abusive behavior. When

Shepard's men fail in achieving the impossible unity of their identity, they seek an avoidance or escape that nevertheless fails to free them from the problems of gender created by the patriarchal system they accept. They flee to the desert, to alcohol, to the past or to their fantasies of the past, but their problems of identity do not go away.

Ultimately, Shepard's men arc unable to come to terms with the notion that their fantasies of power and wholeness may never be made a reality — that they may, in fact, be impossible[2] — and furthermore that these fantasies may be the root of their problems in the first place. They lack the strength of character to face their own failures and to move beyond them. When Eddie of *Fool for Love* boasts, "I never repeat myself," May responds, much more accurately, "You do nothing but repeat yourself. That's all you do. You just go in a big circle" (67). Yet even May's remark is not quite accurate, because Eddie does not repeat *himself* so much as he repeats his father by accepting his patriarchal inheritance. This playing out of the father's identity is recorded "repeatedly" in Shepard's family plays of the 1970s and 1980s and is reminiscent of the Freudian patterns that O'Neill explored in his family plays such as *Desire Under the Elms*, *Mourning Becomes Electra*, and *Long Day's Journey into Night*.

In echoing O'Neill's Freudian patterns, Shepard directs his focus on the plight of the son. Our sympathies within Shepard's family plays are usually directed toward the sons who are confused and oppressed by their fathers or befuddled by women, yet who cannot think outside of these traditional relationships. From his early *Rock Garden* through *The Holy Ghostly* on up to *Fool for Love* and *States of Shock*, Shepard uses the father-son relationship as a central pivot of the plot. Shepard's plays of the late 1970s and the 1980s tend to examine the complex matrix of male identity as it is played out within a system of patriarchal inheritance. Sons lose their own identities as they take on that of their fathers, an identity that is itself merely borrowed from previous fathers or ideas of fathers. Fatherhood becomes simply another one of the male mythologies that fails to give Shepard's men any stable identity, leading to confusion, violence, and destruction of self and others.

Within their patriarchal system of inheritance, Shepard's men usually wield power over women both emotionally and physically. However, even though that system empowers him in regard to women, the individual man becomes invisible — starts to disappear — as he gives himself up to the system, paradoxically sacrificing self in order to gain what turns out to be a dubious identity. Shepard's male characters' chief desire is for an original moment believed to lie somewhere within the past and usually represented by the American frontier or the Old West.[3] This moment is perceived as the site of an original or "true" identity of which present identity is merely a reflection passed on from one generation to the next, growing dimmer with each generation. There is always the hope that the son can shrug off this past and create himself anew or that he can abandon the stale version of the present and return to a place where he can recapture the vitality of the original. Just as Samuel Shepard Rogers changed his seventh-generation name to Sam Shepard, a move also made by Ice in *The Holy Ghostly*, the sons in his plays attempt to escape their inheritance but always return to pick up where their fathers left off. These sons believe in what James Clifford, borrowing a term from William Carlos Williams, calls "pure products"—meaning a pure, unadulterated, uninfluenced, original identity. Although they use storytelling in an attempt both to create and to recapture this supposed original moment, Shepard's men reveal the impossibility of returning to that moment as well as the loss of autonomy that they actually suffer in this system of identification. Even in retreating to the wilderness, they do not find their manhood but find instead a perpetual adolescence amid the bits and pieces of male mythologies.

Dueling Identities: *Tooth of Crime* and *True West*

Before exploring male identity within Shepard's plays, we need to examine more fully the images and mythologies that underlie this identity. In examining Shepard's idea of identity, most particularly male identity, the influence of popular culture on his heroes immediately becomes apparent. His plays abound with references or allusions to popular culture: Kent and Salem of *La Turista*, the Marlboro Man mentioned in *Fool for Love*, "that guy who wrote *Treasure of Sierra Madre*" from *Curse of the Starving Class*, Mae West and Paul Bunyan of *Mad Dog Blues*, Johnny Ace and Mick Jagger of *Cowboy Mouth*, Safeways and toasters of *True West*, the Velvet Underground and Elvis of *The Tooth of Crime*. Film genres such as the western and gangster film, music (particularly rock and roll and jazz), the drug culture, and the world of advertising all influence and shape the lives and identities of his heroes.

Stephen Watt notes that "Shepard's characters define maleness by way of appropriations from popular culture" (79). This appropriation, however, does not add up to an integrated whole for his characters. The early *Cowboys* and its revision *Cowboys #2* both explore this appropriation as the two "cowboy" characters play a number of continuously shifting roles that are marked only by a shift in voice or body language. Rather than playing *a* character, they play with the *idea* of character, shifting in and out of identities, no one of which equals what traditionally has been defined as a character—a unified, logical unit of personality. This concept of character is derived from a game that Shepard and Charles Mingus, Jr. used to play and that Ellen Oumano describes as follows:

> Mingus recounts how the two of them played at roles, switching characters, mimicking voices of those who struck them as phony, in characters ranging from old ladies to gangsters—telling the "truth" through their private code. He attributes their need to try on characters like suits of clothes to their mutual lack of a father's consistent and positive influence. They picked and chose from the models offered by our society, trying on "ideas" of men … because there were so many to choose from, all the while searching for an identity that fit [22–23].

As early as his first play, then, Shepard presented the idea of masculinity as a performance or a game that defies any fixity or rules. Interestingly, in this comment, Mingus attributes this need to try on ideas of men to the lack of a real role model in their own fathers. His comment encourages us to see that failed father-son relationships are at the root of Shepard's troubled concepts of manhood and masculinity.

This "trying on characters like suits of clothes," evident in the extreme among Shepard's early characters, remained a staple of Shepard's theater. His preface to *Angel City* (1976) informs the actors:

> Instead of the idea of a "whole character" with logical motives behind his behavior which the actor submerges himself into, he should consider instead a fractured whole with bits and pieces of character flying off the central theme [61–62].

This focus on "fractured" characters indicates Shepard's suspicion of a logical, whole, complete, unified identity. Within Shepard's plays, masculine identity is marked by performance, the play of signs over surfaces, the masks and personas that are offered in place of reality (itself a troubled term). These masks for his men are not random, however. They are drawn from American myths and icons of maleness: the cowboy, the gangster, the rock star, the artist — all perceived as masculine pursuits that (in Shepard's world) have not been or should not be entered into by women. Women, in fact, further complicate identity for Shepard's men. Although they need women to reflect their ideas of themselves, they also fear that women shut down the possibility for play by supposedly fixing a man in an image and holding him to it.

This idea of women's influence on male identity drives the plot of *Cowboy Mouth*, in which a woman kidnaps a man from his wife and child in order to turn him into her vision of a "rock-and-roll Jesus with a cowboy mouth" (157). This play grew out of Shepard's experiences when he abandoned his first wife and child and lived with rocker Patti Smith, who actually helped him write, and co-starred with him in, *Cowboy Mouth*. Interestingly, though, in turning this personal experience into a play, Shepard displaces any blame he might bear for leaving his real-life wife onto the woman of the play who has "kidnapped" his male character. As with *Cowboys*, this play grew out of Shepard's personal experiences, establishing a connection between his private life and theatrical creations that make his personal stagings of masculinity relevant to an understanding of those of his male characters. Identity and persona become entangled seemingly for Shepard as they do for his characters, both of whom become "the people they're pretending to be" (*Motel* 42). His 1972 rock-drama, *The Tooth of Crime*, powerfully foregrounds the question of essence in regard to identity that Shepard returns to again and again throughout the 1970s and 1980s, and an examination of this play will help to illuminate the fracturing of male identity that is crucial in any reading of his later family plays.

Shepard worked on *Tooth of Crime* while living in London, where it received its premiere. Having left America, he says that he finally realized his true Americanness: "I mean it wasn't until I came to England that I found out what it means to be an American" (Chubb 198). Thus, the play would seem, in its exploration of male identity, to relate to a particularly American maleness. *Tooth of Crime* establishes quite clearly many of the issues concerning identity and the performance of self that inform not only his early works such as *Cowboys* but also his later "realistic" or "family" plays. Chiefly, *Tooth* presents this question: Is there an essence that a man can fall back on, or is male identity merely a performance with no center?

In *Tooth of Crime*, as occurred to a certain extent in *Cowboys*, the performance of self or the story of self becomes synonymous with the self. The play's main characters, Hoss and Crow, operate under the principle that the stories they tell and the way they tell them create who they are. However, Hoss has become uneasy with mere performance and wonders if there is not an essence to which his performances might be anchored. *Tooth* is the ultimate duel of identities based on presentation alone — on style, gesture, attitude. This duel resonates with masculine images taken from western showdowns, organized crime, sports competitions, and, of course, rock and roll. Hoss, the aging star, works for an unidentified "industry," which is represented chiefly by the woman Becky, whom Hoss views as a controlling, limiting presence even though she at times takes on the role of fawning and exploited groupie. The anarchy of Hoss's youth has been molded to fit the official rules of the industry. He abides by a code, set up by the industry and monitored by referees, which has caught him in the paradox that he can be true to himself only by following the rules set up by someone else. As Becky tells him, "the only way to be an individual is in the game" (219). Hoss is aware, though, that he has become "stuck in [his] image" (224) and begins to long for a self that is not part of the game. He tells his manager, "Ya' know, you'd be O.K. Becky, if you had a self. So would I. Something to fall back on in a moment of doubt or terror or even surprise" (225). Hoss realizes, then, that his gestures and styles are not ultimately the same as having a self, and this discovery worries him, making him question both the game and his place in it. Clearly he has come to want not merely "ideas" of self but an essence, which he has been unable to find within the game.

Hoss is at this point being threatened by Crow, a "gypsy killer," who operates outside the game and ignores the code. Crow has never been controlled by the system and evidently has never stood still long enough to encounter the doubts that plague Hoss. He does not have Hoss's longing for an original self to fall back on but, instead, tells Hoss that "image shots are blown" (229), and he sings a new creed that accepts self as simply a performance with no center, base, or essence:

> But I believe in my mask — The man I made up is me
> And I believe in my dance — And my destiny [232].

Crow seems to accept that masks are the only reality, so he embraces the life of the "gypsy" who is forever wandering, never pinned down to any place or person.

The duel between Hoss and Crow is not simply over territory ("turf") or "styles" but over a specific type of identity that reflects Shepard's images of masculinity, images he connects to that of the "original," the maverick, the cowboy. Interestingly enough, given the emphasis placed on competition in this play, the point of the duel is not who wins but who keeps playing the game. "Play," as we have already seen, has certain definite connotations in regard to Shepard's work. He views "play" as a denial of the "labor" of adult life. "Play" is, therefore, associated with youth, and we have seen in Shepard's comments regarding rebellious cowboys that he associates youth with the cowboy image of rebellion. Subsequently, in *Tooth*, as the "aging" Hoss begins to doubt the game as a "game" and to settle into it as industry or "labor," he begins to lose control over his performances. He no longer knows how to play the game.

Hoss, by taking on the "job" of being the best, has also become a part of the industry that now controls him. He is no longer independent, free, self-proclaiming, self-creating as is Crow and has thus lost the edge that perpetual "playing" gives Crow. Crow, the outsider, the gypsy, actually retains more qualities of traditional masculinity (calling his own shots, free from doubt, independent) than Hoss does precisely because he has yet to be industrialized, marketed, managed, and fixed by others — has yet to have his play turned into labor for the benefit of others. Although Hoss briefly disconcerts Crow by performing the "old time boogie," a cowboy routine, Crow ends up defeating Hoss by literally taking on his style, by performing Hoss until Hoss can no longer play the game in response, until he ceases to perform.

After Hoss's defeat by this master chameleon, Hoss and Crow's different reactions to this outcome further underscore the differences between the two men. Hoss believes that Crow must know the secret concerning "a self to fall back upon" that he earlier longed for, and so he requests that Crow teach him this secret in return for Hoss's turf:

> Hoss: All right. The turf's yours. The whole shot. Now show me how to be a man.
> Crow: A man's too hard, Leathers. Too many doors in that room. A Gypsy's easy [243].

The core that Hoss longs for is that of a man, something he believes that Crow, a winner and the stronger party, must know about. But Crow does not privilege being a man over any other image or performance. In fact, he indicates that he prefers acting like a gypsy to acting like a man because being a man is too difficult. He prefers the gypsy life precisely because it is a running away from the rules, a perpetual flight from any one fixed image. The essence that Hoss seeks is abandoned by Crow in favor of the gypsy's play of multiple identities. Crow's flight coupled with Hoss's escape through suicide reflects with a vengeance Baraka's comment that white men know nothing of manhood because "they are too busy running the world, or running from it." Neither the supposed position of power that Hoss has nor the flight that Crow embodies ultimately answers the question that Hoss poses as to "how to be a man." Instead, they work amid a confused jumble of images and identities and only the one who keeps moving manages to stay alive.

As Stephen Watt has noted, these characters are creating themselves out of images from popular culture. They are creating themselves if not in their own images at least into images that they have chosen from their culture. Shepard would later offer the previously quoted comment about Los Angeles that is appropriate to the action of *Tooth*, especially in regard to Crow: "people here have become the people they're pretending to be" (*Motel* 42). This is true of Crow, who easily appropriates and assimilates Hoss's style, territory, and place. But this is not as true of Hoss. Hoss does not want images or reproductions of images; he wants to make his mark by creating:

> A true gesture that won't never cheat on itself 'cause it's the last of its kind. It can't be taught or copied or stolen or sold. It's mine. An original. It's my life and my death in one clean shot [249].

Hoss's only chance of proving and of truly owning his identity according to his mythology is through suicide, whereby all of the signs and significations he has created will stop, fixed forever in death, and therefore be owned only by him. His gesture will be "original" because it cannot be replayed or reproduced. A person's suicide is, literally, a one-time shot that cannot be repeated. Dying well, as Hoss does, in the "old style," used to indicate a final affirmation of a man's worth. Hoss's ability to claim his original identity by dying well has, therefore, iconic significance to an audience raised on Hollywood westerns, but this significance, this old-world nostalgia, is weakened by Crow, who gets the final words of the play.

Hoss's manner of death impresses Crow only briefly as "a genius mark," which is part of the old creed. After Hoss's suicide, Cheyenne tells Crow, "you got big shoes to fill Gypsy," but Crow responds, "That's fer lames. I'm throwin' the shoes away. I'm runnin' flat out to a new course" (259). Crow flees in much the same way as Huck lit out for the territories at the close of his narrative, following a path already marked for him by what Fiedler has described as the quintessential American story. In "lightin' out for the territories" like the "quintessential American," Crow rejects Hoss's style utterly, choosing flight over the fixed niche in which Hoss has died. Hoss's dying moment is thereby cloaked in ambiguity, as Crow asserts that it is not stasis or stability or being "true" that counts but that you keep moving, keep alive, keep playing the game. Crow abandons all ideas of essences in favor of the endless play of "ideas" of self. By refusing to lock himself into any image, he aspires not to be blown apart as Hoss was but to accept identity as a performance rather than as a fixed and attainable essence. He privileges adolescent "play" over adult "labor" and, significantly, ends up the survivor of the duel.

While *Tooth of Crime* restages the problem of male identity present throughout Shepard's early plays, it also establishes a model of conflict useful for examining the family plays of the 1970s and 1980s. Among the family plays, *True West* has the most obvious structural similarities to *Tooth of Crime*, but even in this play, we can see how the idea of masculine identity becomes entangled in the familial relationships that drive the family plays. Although *True West* borrows from *Tooth* the structure of the duel, the later play takes place on and over vastly different turf. By locating the duel within both fraternal and paternal relationships, *True West* addresses the question of origins and originality much more concretely than did the allusive *Tooth*. Rather than question, metaphorically, essence and performance, the two brothers of *True West* argue over their own experiences, their specific differing versions of careers, lifestyles, and their father. These issues are represented by "The West" as the play's major symbol of frontierism, rugged individualism, and masculine space. This West is evoked not only by the desert in which Lee has been living and the city of Los Angeles where Austin works but also by the script for a western movie, which Lee wants to write.

True West, in fact, takes its structure from the genre of Hollywood's western. Lee, the outlaw figure, shows up in town, disrupting the domestic order of Austin. Austin tries to reason with Lee in order to defuse his violence, then must revert to Lee's own tactics in order to combat him. The conflict escalates in violence to a final showdown that has every indication of becoming a duel to the death. While the action focuses on the confrontation between the two men, the actual domestic world — the world of women and children that had been nearly obliterated in *Tooth* — is established as a backdrop or sketch of the ideals over which the men fight. The urges for violence, dominance, and independence vie against and overlap with the urges for reason, civility, and community. The set itself undergoes a transformation from the suburban kitchen at the play's opening to a "desert junkpile at high noon," which Lee and Austin have turned this kitchen into by act 2, scene 9 (50).

In its dialectic, *True West* is simply following the conventions of the western, which many film critics have discussed as being focused on divided images of masculinity with the world of women or the feminine as backdrop. Laura Mulvey, in an article about the western *Duel in the Sun*, describes the genre of the western as detailing how

> the tension between two points of attraction, the symbolic (social integration) and nostalgic narcissism, generates a common splitting of the Western hero into two.... Here two functions emerge, one celebrating integration into society through marriage, the other celebrating resistance to social standards and responsibilities, above all those of marriage and the family, the sphere represented by women [73].

The tension between social integration, particularly in the family, and a narcissistic allegiance to the self apart from society is discussed in different terminology and in much greater length by Robert Ray in his *A Certain Tendency of the Hollywood Cinema*. Ray views the western plot device of pitting a lawman against an outlaw as classical Hollywood's "thematic paradigm," the "certain tendency" that is revised and repeated in films as diverse as *Casablanca* and *The Godfather*. Both the outlaw and the lawman as split versions of masculinity usually experience a splitting within themselves, an interior split that is represented by the bodies of the two characters. This splitting is evident in *True West*, as most critics of the play note.[4] James Riemer describes the play as an exploration of "two contradictory American ideals of masculinity which the two brothers initially represent" (41). He sees Austin's "ideal of masculine success" and Lee's "frontier ideal of masculinity" as working toward a confrontation that will lead to integration of these two ideals. His reading sets up these two ideals as the only choices of masculinity, thereby excluding any possible alternatives, as the play also seems to do. However, Riemer fails to explain how these two conflicting ideas can be resolved or "integrated," especially as Shepard's play ends at the moment of highest conflict, far from implying any clear resolution.

In Austin's desire to ride into the desert and in Lee's inability to function in the city, we are once again facing the dilemma created by the American idea of the frontier discussed in relation to *Death of a Salesman* and touched upon in the opening of this chapter. The hero ventures out alone into the frontier in order to prove his own manhood by creating the very structures of society that supposedly repress his masculinity. He helps build the town or make it safe for its residents, but he cannot live in it. After playing his part, he rides off into the sunset. What was admirable and necessary in the openness of the frontier becomes criminal or impossible in the world of the city. To live in the city is to lose one's sense of self. As Austin expresses it: "There's nothin' real down here, Lee! Least of all me!" (49). Yet to ride away from the city and live independently in the desert is as much a mark of failure as of independence, something Lee asserts when he tells Austin, "I'm livin' out there 'cause I can't make it here!" (49). If neither the town nor the desert offers a solution to the question of male identity, where is that identity to be found?

The conflict in this play demonstrates how neither brother is fully aware that they actually share the same dilemma. This situation is paralleled in the western story that Lee dictates to Austin. In Lee's ideal western, two men chase each other across the Texas Panhandle, first in trucks and then on horseback. The pursuit was initiated by sexual jealousy, the pursued man having slept with the wife of the man chasing him. But this issue quickly becomes irrelevant for these two men as the chase itself becomes their reason for acting. At the close of act 1, Lee describes the mind-set of these two men as they take off "into an endless black prairie":

> What they don't know is that each one of 'em is afraid, see. Each one separately thinks that he's the only one that's afraid. And they keep ridin' like that straight into the night. Not knowing. And the one who's chasin' doesn't know where the other one is taking him. And the one who's being chased doesn't know where he's going [27].

This image of confusion accurately describes both Lee and Austin by the end of this play. They share more than they realize in that both are motivated by the same fears and insecurities, but these qualities are manifested in each man in different ways. Their dueling versions of masculinity are shaped by the same fears and by their ideas of their father.

Each brother recounts a visit with their father who lives out in the desert and is drinking himself to death, and clearly each brother has shaped his current life in reaction to their father. As a man of the city, of the university, of the business world, Austin has sought to live a life in opposition to that of his father. Lee has almost become his father, even down to living in the desert and obviously drinking heavily most of the time. Lee's decision to try to write a screenplay is ultimately connected with his desire to give something to his father, to set up a "trust" for him. At first Austin sees Lee's interest in screenwriting as a way of possibly civilizing his uncivil brother. He encourages Lee by telling him that selling a movie script "could really turn your life around, you know. Change things" (24). Upon hearing that a screenplay sells for "a whole lot of money" (25), Lee is hopeful and interested, commenting that he could then help their father:

> Lee: We could get the old man outa' hock then.
> Austin: Maybe.
> Lee: Maybe? Whadya' mean, maybe?
> Austin: I mean it might take more than money.
> Lee: You were just tellin' me it'd change my whole life around. Why wouldn't it change his?
> Austin: He's different.
> Lee: Oh, he's of a different ilk huh?
> Austin: He's not gonna' change. Let's leave the old man out of it.
> Lee: That's right. He's not gonna' change but I will. I'll just turn myself right inside out. I could be just like you then, huh? Sittin' around dreamin' stuff up. Gettin' paid to dream [25].

This argument over their father reveals the position in which each brother sees himself — connected in some way to a response to their father's life. However, although each brother initially claims the superiority of his own way of life, deriding the other for not being "in touch" or for living in a dream world, each also wonders if the other brother might have "the right idea" in his lifestyle. Austin has the clout and independence offered through money, but he has to kowtow to the big executives, thereby sacrificing independence, in order to make that money. Lee has the freedom and independence of being outside the law and outside society, but he has to depend, like a coyote, on periodic scavenging and hustling trips into the city in order to support himself. Each is compromised in some way, and each entertains fantasies that the other brother has something better.

This fantasy of the other's better deal is never resolved. Although the call of the western frontier is for freedom and independence (particularly to the young mind), the East offers comfort and security and a different place to be "somebody" (which Lee recognizes in Austin's way of life) that the West denies. The mutual attraction of each position for the other is equal only to their mutual exclusion, a fact that would seem to make resolution impossible. As difficult as it is to survive in the desert, the characters in the play seem to believe that this desert is necessary for the making of American men. Why else would Austin decide the desert could be his salvation? At the same time, Lee makes clear that life in the desert does not always mean a man is successful; he can also, like the two brothers' father, simply be escaping. The right or "true" answer eludes these men, just as the "true" West becomes increasingly illusory the more the brothers try to pin it down. Each keeps returning to that idealized vision, and the question is left unanswered as to the nature of the "true" West. Is it the sterile, independent life of Lee in the desert, or is it the life of the green suburbs, a wife, kids, money, and a career as Austin lives it? Or is it blurred somewhere in between by that great image fuser, Hollywood movies?

Robert Ray argues that classical Hollywood's thematic paradigm tries to prove that contrasting positions can be maintained simultaneously, that choice is not necessary because a person can be both things at once by "obscuring the necessity for choosing between contrasting values" (66). This is precisely the move that James Riemer makes in reading the possibility for "integration" and "resolution" into the last scene of *True West* (46). But this last scene resists resolution, providing instead a vibrant image of unresolved and, by implication, unresolvable conflict. Showdowns such as those to which Lee and Austin have committed themselves do not end in compromise but in the death of at least one party. *True West* would seem to say that its two versions of masculinity can exist together only in that moment of absolute unresolved conflict that we witness in Lee's story and at the end of the play. The "many doors" into masculinity are collapsed into two contrasting options, and so the American male remains at war with himself because he cannot figure out which of the two he wants to be — Dirty Harry or Andy Griffith. If we agree with Ray's contention, perhaps the American male does not realize that he has to make a choice who to be — that he may have to fix on one identity rather than playing the field.

Although they attempt to become each other (Lee by writing and Austin by

stealing), neither brother can actually do so. Neither can they pool their talents
as Austin suggests, trading off abilities to satisfy each other's lack. Lee's code of
the loner will not permit collaboration. The closing moment of the play freezes
the two brothers as they square off for a final showdown—a powerful image of
both the need for and the mutual exclusiveness of these two particular versions
of male identity. In Shepard's other family plays, the possibility for multiple versions of male identity is denied even more fully, collapsing the "many doors" into
masculinity still further by documenting the perceived lack of choice that sons
have in finding and asserting their identities as men and by exploring the image
of the father more fully than it is treated in *True West*.

Fathers and Sons:
Curse of the Starving Class and *Buried Child*

While both *Tooth of Crime* and *True West* present masculinity as a combina-
tion and confrontation of identities, Shepard's next two plays to be discussed, the
two that began his cycle of family plays, examine how stagings of masculinity are
shaped within father and son relationships. The images and versions of masculinity offered in these two plays are collapsed into the image of the father that
the son cannot deny or escape. In this regard, his family plays become reminiscent of O'Neill's explorations of paternal legacies visited upon sons. In a 1992
interview given to Carol Rosen, Shepard confirms his belief in the inevitable
inheritance of certain characteristics from one's parentage by saying that "it's like
the structure of our bones, the blood that runs through our veins" ("Emotional"
8). Shepard himself recalls how his own father projected upon him a "macho
image" of masculinity:

> I know what this thing is about because I was a victim of it; it was part of my life, my old
> man tried to force on me a notion of what it was to be a "man" [Cott 172].

According to his philosophy, such a notion may not be denied if it is part of what
Shepard describes as "characteristics, if you want to call them that, that run
through families that are undeniable" (quoted in Rosen, "Emotional" 8).

Within *Curse* and *Buried Child*, the confrontation of masculinities grows out
of the son's origin. He is in conflict with the father whose desires and whose body
actually help create those of the son. Lines of demarcation between father and son
are blurred in these two plays, as sons try to work out their claims to identity
within the family as well as apart from it, but fail to escape their patriarchal inheritance. The tension between "savagery and innocence," between "utter freedom"
and "responsibilities," which Ellen Oumano referred to in describing Shepard,
rings true of the sons in these two plays, Wesley and Vince. Unlike Hoss and
Crow or Lee and Austin, these two sons cannot break away from their fathers long
enough to experiment with other images or "ideas" of masculinity.

Numerous earlier glimpses of father-son relationships serve as precursors to
the exploration Shepard undertakes in his family plays. As early as *The Rock Garden* (1964), Shepard had offered the image of a son's attempts to overwhelm the

father figure through blatant declaration of his own sexual virility. At the end of the play, the father falls over, perhaps dead. Although father-son relationships are central to *True West*, *Fool for Love*, *A Lie of the Mind*, and *States of Shock*, the two earliest family plays, *Curse* and *Buried Child*, most clearly explore what I have chosen to call the eternal patriarchal return with very little distraction or complication from other relationships or characters. Although both *Curse* and *Buried Child* offer troubled portraits of husbands and wives and of siblings as well, the key movement of each play revolves around the sons, Wesley and Vince, who attempt yet fail to escape the patterns of identification set down for them by their fathers and grandfathers.

Curse of the Starving Class offers several powerful and intriguing characters, including the daughter Emma, who has been touted as one of the strongest female characters that Shepard has ever created (Marranca, "Alphabetical" 31; Whiting 497). She is vibrant and vociferous, determined to get away from the family and to create her own life, first as an auto mechanic down in Baja and later as a criminal. She speaks her mind to her brother, telling him: "It's the perfect self-employment. Crime. No credentials. No diplomas. No overhead. No upkeep. Just straight profit. Right off the top" (197). Her exploration of possible lifestyles and her seeming ability to choose her path stand in contrast to Wesley, whose sole thoughts and allegiances are to maintaining the family farm. Certainly Emma is not to be ignored as a powerful voice in this play, but ultimately she is of little consequence to the struggle for identity that becomes central in the play — that of her brother, Wesley. We hear more about Emma than we see, her scenes being fewer than his. And she is, we are led to believe, although this is never confirmed, killed — offstage — by a car bomb intended for her father, cut down in her attempt to escape by the patriarchal inheritance laid out for her.

Ella, her mother, also shows a streak of defiance and independence in trying to organize a life apart from her husband, Weston, who evidently is rarely home anyway. In an attempt to take care of herself, she tries to sell the avocado ranch that her alcoholic husband is never home to run and that her son cannot run by himself. Deciding to cut her losses from a bad marriage, Ella works out a deal with a "lawyer friend" to sell the land for development. Ironically, considering the way that they have usually been viewed by critics as weak characters, it is often the mothers in Shepard's plays who are willing to break their ties and to start a new life, just as Ella, Halie, and Lorraine each tries to do in her own way.[5] In contrast, because of their limited versions of male identity, their husbands cannot seem to create new lives for themselves once their old ways have failed. Instead of trying to open new doors, the men want to return to the past, and when they cannot (as Hoss could not), they turn to the oblivion of the desert or of the bottle or both, each a form of escape or a way to disappear. However, Shepard clearly privileges the male stagnation and nostalgia for previous relationships over the women's concerns for improvement or change. Rather than portraying these mothers and wives as struggling heroically, Shepard portrays them as betrayers of their men, implying by the way he positions them that while a man's first priority is to himself, a woman's is to her family and to her man. When the men leave, they are portrayed as being simply confused or as seeking something that they need and rightfully deserve (freedom, independence), but women who leave or who desire to leave are usually portrayed as selfish betrayers of the family and, particularly, of their husbands.

Ultimately, however, in *Curse*, both Emma and Ella are presented as complications for Wesley, the son who is trying to keep together the family home — the house and ranch. Lynda Hart describes Wesley as the hero of the play, the one "who strives to untangle the constrictive cords that at once bind the family together and threaten to cut off the lifeblood of the individual" (*Metaphorical* 69). Wesley's ties and curses bind him to his patriarchal duties inherited from his father. This notion of inheritance from the father is brought up several times in the play. For instance, Ella questions why Wesley is not like her father, his grandfather:

> Why aren't you sensitive like your Grandfather was? I always thought you were just like him, but you're not, are you? [143–144].

Wesley is not like his maternal grandfather because his inheritance does not come from the mother's side of the family but from the father's. Emma explains this connection between father and son when describing her father's personality to her mother's "lawyer" Taylor:

> A short fuse they call it. Runs in the family. His father was just like him. And his father before him. Wesley is just like Pop, too. Like liquid dynamite. [...] It's chemical. It's the same thing that makes him drink. Something in the blood. Hereditary. Highly dangerous [152].

Although Emma is no doubt trying to scare off this "lawyer friend" of her mother, her statement about the legacy from father to son proves to be quite accurate in the course of the play. Weston encourages this interpretation in a later conversation with Wesley wherein Weston refers to the "poison" he has inside him:

> Weston: [...] My poison scares you.
> ....
> Wesley: No
> Weston: Good. You're growing up. I never saw my old man's poison until I was much older than you. Much older. And then you know how I recognized it?[...] Because I saw myself infected with it. That's how. I saw me carrying it around. His poison in my body. You think that's fair? [...] You think I asked for it? [167].

This "poison" is, then, explained as the unavoidable result of being a son and is evidently the male "curse," just as menstruation is set up within the play as the female "curse." By the last act, Weston manages to cleanse himself at least temporarily of some of this poison through a series of almost ritualistic actions, which he describes to Wesley. He strips himself of his old clothes, and, after walking around the house naked, he takes a hot bath, then a cold bath, and shaves and puts on new clothes. Wesley soon tries this method only to reappear in Weston's old discarded clothes. He describes the experience to Emma:

> I started putting all his clothes on. His baseball cap, his tennis shoes, his overcoat. And every time I put one thing on it seemed like a part of him was growing on me. I could feel him taking over me. [...] I could feel myself retreating. I could feel him coming in and me going out. Just like the change of the guards [196].

Emma's matter-of-fact response undercuts Wesley's sense of self-conflict. She tells him simply: "Well don't eat your heart out about it. You did the best you could" (196). But Wesley continues to see himself as compelled to reenact his father for reasons he cannot fathom. As he says, "I didn't do a thing. [...] I just grew up here" (196). Wesley's transformation is confirmed by his mother, who takes him to be Weston. As in *Tooth of Crime*, once a character learns to mimic another character well enough, he becomes that character — as Crow became Hoss. Identity is based on appropriating surrounding images. In Wesley's case, the strongest image is of his father, whom Wesley becomes by the end of the play.

The closing story told by both Ella and Wesley resonates with significance concerning this central conflict of the play. They retell Weston's earlier story of an eagle and a tomcat locked in mortal combat, an image that critics have read variously to describe the fate of the family or of men and women who cannot survive either together or apart.[6] More significantly, however, the story is a new verbal version of the physical image of two figures locked in mortal combat that occurred at the end of *True West* and in *Tooth of Crime*. The warring parties of this showdown, the cat and the eagle, began their fight over the testes of lambs, over what Weston refers to as "little remnants of manlihood" (183). The mortal combat occurs in this play, once more, over issues of manhood — over male identity. In this battle, unlike the two previously discussed conflicts, there is no possibility of a winner because together "they come crashing down to the earth. Both of them come crashing down. Like one whole thing" (200). Although *Tooth* left us with Crow's method of survival and *True West* left us with at least the possibility that one brother would live, *Curse* leaves us with a vivid image of mutual destruction. If Wesley has simply become his father, two warring entities that have become "one whole thing," then he is destined to follow his father's path into ruin.

The son of *Buried Child* finds himself inheriting much of the same "poison" from his father and grandfather that Wesley inherited from his. Shepard explores in this play many of the same themes that appear in *Curse*. However, the family in *Buried Child* places on stage the three generations of the male line that are merely remarked upon in *Curse*. Dodge and Halie, the grandparents, exhibit the typical Shepardian marriage: they are estranged and contemptuous of each other. Dodge drinks and Halie philanders. The play opens with Dodge onstage in conversation with the offstage Halie concerning a previous liaison of hers. Immediately, then, the dialogue highlights the question of Dodge's manhood. He is clearly no longer able to control his wife's actions, much less the actions of his sons, due to his physical frailty — aggravated if not created by drink — which has confined him to the couch. The family patriarch's failings as a "man" are reflected in the dissolution of his family and the failings of his sons.

Tilden, the oldest son, had great promise as a young man when he was, as Halie tells us, an "All-American" football player. But Tilden has instead "turned out to be so much trouble" (72), ending up in jail in New Mexico and now residing in his parents' house, a slow-witted child-man. Bradley, the second son, embodies his own ineptitude, having lost a leg, which he himself severed with a chain saw. Only the youngest, Ansel, is referred to as a "real" man by Halie, although whether or not he deserves such praise is unknowable. However, since he is now dead (shot in a hotel room, perhaps, so Halie believes, by the Mafia), his image as created by Halie is used to upbraid the current males in the family with their failings. The only son/grandson who seems to be whole is the prodigal Vince, whom the family at first fails to recognize. Like many of Shepard's sons (Ice, Austin, Jake), Vince has fled the past failings of his family, particularly of his father, to try to establish his own life. He returns to the family farm more or less on a sudden whim, much like the impulse recorded in *Motel Chronicles* that led Shepard to show up on his own grandparents' doorstep unexpectedly as a young man (43–46). This incident from Shepard's life seems to be the prototype for the story of Vince in *Buried Child*, for the similarities are unmistakable. Vince, like Shepard, shows up unexpectedly to visit his grandparents, but they fail to recognize him. Dodge, his grandfather, asserts, "You're no son of mine. I've had sons in my time and you're not one of 'em" (97). Tilden, his father, tells him, "I had a son once but we buried him" (92). Vince's birthright is thus denied by both his father and his grandfather, putting the issue of inheritance in this family in question.

The heritage of the male line, however, is confirmed or maintained by women. Dodge tells Shelly, Vince's girlfriend, "Halie's the one with the family album. She's the one you should talk to. She'll set you straight on the heritage if that's what you're interested in. She's traced it all the way back to the grave" (112). We know, however, that Halie has very little allegiance to Dodge even though she has been entrusted with keeping the records intact. Her control over the "heritage" bespeaks the position of woman within the family: her chastity and loyalty is relied upon to keep the male line pure and intact. Halie, however, has failed to do so, at least according to Dodge, who tells of a child that Halie bore and that he did not father. Thus, it is made apparent that Halie is the one ultimately in control of the family line, because the heritage of father and son must pass through the body of a woman — out of paternal control and into maternal control, a fact that raises male fears and results in numerous betrayals in this play. Perhaps because of male fear of this maternal control, the maternal figure is written offstage as often as possible. Halie is a disembodied voice for most of her scenes, and Dodge remains constant throughout the play in trying to discredit or ignore her, or to distract the audience from everything that she says. The heritage she honors regarding Ansel is furiously denied by Dodge. Rather than wanting to recall past betrayals that reflect negatively on his identity as the family patriarch, Dodge insists that Shelly ignore any but his own version of events and evaluate him in terms of the present, saying, "That isn't me! That never was me! This is me. Right here" (111). True to his name, he seems to be dodging any responsibility for past actions.

With the past so clearly in question, Vince's arrival in search of past memories is not welcomed by Dodge or acknowledged by Tilden. Rather than fight for his place in the family heritage, Vince's initial reaction to his denial by his family is to escape on the pretense of going to buy a bottle of whiskey for his grandfather. He leaves Shelly, who, after strange exchanges with both Tilden and Bradley, wakes up the next morning feeling in control of the house, as if it were hers. She has, she tells Dodge, "the feeling that nobody lives here but me. I mean everybody's gone. You're here, but it doesn't seem like you're supposed to be" (110).

This is an accurate description in light of the behavior of the three men in the house. Shelly is as much a part of the house as any of its occupants. Dodge barely concerns himself with anything other than getting his bottle of whiskey and keeping his blanket (infantile obsessions). Tilden wanders vaguely on and off stage, brings in armloads of corn and carrots evidently from nowhere, and answers questions in one or two words, seemingly not operating on the same level as anyone else in the play. And Bradley, who does not live in the house, attempts to terrorize its occupants: cutting Dodge's hair while he sleeps, symbolically raping Shelly by sticking his finger in her mouth. However, after removing his wooden leg and falling asleep on the couch, he ends up helplessly taunted by both Shelly and later Vince. Halie, too, wanders off to a "lunch," which lasts until the next morning. None of these family members seems connected to the house as a home.

Despite her initial claim, Shelly cannot truly take over the house because she does not have a biological connection with these people; she does not have the face inside her face that Tilden claims he sees in Vince. However, within a short time she does manage to uncover the past that Dodge has tried to deny, this family's "curse" concerning the child of Halie that Tilden loved (and that may have been his child) and that Dodge drowned and buried in the backyard. Nevertheless, her knowledge of this secret does not give her power within the family because she does not have the heritage or what the Colonel of *States of Shock* calls the "history." Because she is not part of it, she cannot control the family, but she can escape its confines. She *can* leave, even though Vince cannot. Given the family and its treatment of her, Shelly's assertion of control is clearly a temporary survival measure "just to make it through this" (94) rather than a desire to remain. Her assertion of control in her confrontation with Halie is quickly abandoned when a means of escape arises.

Unlike Shelly, Vince is not aware of the secret or curse, but he is nonetheless bound to the family. Although denied by his grandfather and by his father, he returns in act 3 and recounts the story of his aborted attempt to escape from the family: "I was gonna run last night. I was gonna run and keep right on running" (130). But during this long drive, he could see his face in the windshield, and face to face with himself, he studied the image "as though I was looking at another man" (130). What he sees is the heritage he cannot escape. This other man's face changes:

> His face became his father's face. Same bones. Same eyes. Same nose. Same breath. And his father's face changed to his Grandfather's face. And it went on like that. Changing. Clear back to faces I'd never seen before but still recognized. Still recognized the bones underneath. The eyes. The breath. The mouth. I followed my family clear into Iowa. Every last one [130].

This speech follows Dodge's "last will and testament" in which Dodge recognizes and wills his house to his "Grandson, Vincent" (129). Although Tilden, Dodge's eldest son, is alive, Dodge designates Vince as the male heir. Tilden has been the first to bring life into the household of the dying Dodge, but his childlike behavior evidently makes him unfit in Dodge's eyes to carry on the patriarchy. Instead, Dodge turns to the now powerful presence of Vince, who enacts a violent, military-style masculinity upon his second return to the house, throwing beer bottles as if they are bombs and singing the Marine Hymn. Now determined to stay in this house and refusing to leave with Shelly, who makes a quick and painless exit once Vince returns with the car, Vince eagerly takes over the position of the family patriarch, which is, however, a prone position that hardly evokes virility or power. In the last scene, Vince lies on the couch that his grandfather, now lying dead, had occupied throughout the first act. As Tilden enters from the backyard again, this time with the dead baby in his arms, the Oedipal secrets of Tilden, Halie, and Dodge are uncovered, but Vince is the child that remains buried in his family history. He has become convinced that he must stay in this house, announcing, "I've got to carry on the line" (130). Yet we are left unsure as to his ability to do so. Although Vince seems to have brought virility back into the family by enacting a soldier's forceful "taking" of the house, Vince also settles into Dodge's former place on the couch, the seat of impotence and, ultimately, death.

Vince's presence, however, opens Halie's eyes to the vision of fertility that Tilden has discovered among the corn and carrots in the backyard. As the two corpses, Dodge and the baby, fill the stage along with the befuddled Tilden and the drunken Vince, Halie exclaims from upstairs: "It's like a paradise out there, Dodge. You oughta' take a look. A miracle.... I've never seen a crop like this in my whole life. Maybe it's the sun" (131–132). Although the closing visual image of *Buried Child* is of death (the bodies of Dodge and the baby, and, even, the prone body of Vince), the linguistic images bespeak birth and fertility. As Tilden carries the dead baby up the stairs to Halie, the two images are being brought closer together as the lights fall. Again, as in *True West* and *Curse*, we are left with contrasting images of vitality and death that remain in conflict and are associated with questions of male identity: the father of the child, and thus the male heritage, is still in question at the close of the play.

The patriarchal inheritance for the sons in *Curse* and *Buried Child* seems to be inescapable, or — at least — the sons in these plays are unable to recognize any alternatives for themselves. They play out what Shepard has described as the futility of even attempting to deny one's heritage. In reply to Carol Rosen's summary of the theme of these plays as being "unless a character embraces that family character or accepts it, he's doomed," Shepard states:

> Yes, I think so. I think that there is no escape, that the wholehearted acceptance of it leads to another possibility. But the possibility of somehow miraculously making myself into a different person is a hoax, a futile game ["Emotional" 8–9].

As demonstration of this perceived futility, we witness that even as Wesley and Vince try to purge themselves of the poison, to flee the secrets, they are brought back into their father's and grandfather's roles by being made to recognize themselves through their fathers. The new possibility that Shepard hints at above eludes these two characters unless we accept the death imagery that appears at the end of both plays as that possibility. Death accompanies each recognition. The sons' identities are not born so much as borrowed as the sons disappear into these new — and deadly — roles. In contrast to the seeming inevitability of the male's patriarchal inheritance, Halie's part in the male heritage of *Buried Child* indicates the wild card that female sexuality throws into the game of male identity, a topic that is explored more fully in Shepard's next two family plays.

Women and Male Identity:
Fool for Love and *A Lie of the Mind*

In the plays of the 1980s, *Fool for Love* and *A Lie of the Mind*, Shepard introduces into his dynamic of father-son identity the issue of romantic attachments to women. Shepard is quoted by more than one critic as commenting in regard to *Fool* that he had come to realize that relationships between women and men are every bit as complex as those between men (Hart, "Spectacle" 218). As numerous critics have noticed, however, this dynamic is usually explored from the viewpoint of the male character. His plays tend to explore how male identity is affected by women rather than actually treating the question of female identity.[7] This viewpoint is perhaps the main reason for the negative feminist critique of Shepard's plays, a critique that demonstrates how women in his plays are objectified and fragmented (as well as abused mentally and physically). More recent discussions of gender dynamics in the later family plays begin to examine the possibility of a feminine presence that disrupts the traditional power of the patriarchy.[8] However, the question remains as to whether or not the men in Shepard's plays are really any more integrated, any less fragmented than are the women. Certainly Shepard privileges the male struggles for identity over that of the female, but does he offer a positive or integrated or self-determining vision of male identity? It is the ambiguity of Shepard's position toward male identity that I wish to explore further in *Fool for Love* and *A Lie of the Mind*, plays in which these struggles are enacted upon or through the bodies of women or the idea of the feminine.

Both *Fool for Love* and *A Lie of the Mind* explore how women are used and abused in the quest for male identity, but they also offer us a look at the precariousness of that male identity, particularly as it is affected by the absence of the father. Both of these plays are continuations of the family plays, which Shepard began with *Curse of the Starving Class*. However, unlike *Curse*, *Buried Child*, and *True West*, both *Fool for Love* and *A Lie of the Mind* make the relationship of romantic (or at least sexual) attachment between a man and a woman — between the son of the family and his wife or girlfriend — at least as central as the father-son relationship. More precisely, these two plays explore how a son's relationship with women is profoundly affected by his relationship with his father, from whom the son has derived a precarious and violent concept of identity.

In regard to male violence, Shepard remarked in an interview with Michiko Kakutani that

there's something about American violence that to me is very touching. In full force, it's very ugly, but there's also something moving about it because it has to do with humiliation. There's some hidden, deeply-rooted thing in the Anglo male American that has to do with inferiority, that has to do with not being a man, and always, continually, having to act out some idea of manhood that is invariably violent [26].

Linked with Shepard's earlier quoted comment about the "macho image" his father encouraged in him, the above statement makes clear that the patterns of masculinity for Shepard — and for his characters — are intricately linked with a violence that stems from a need to prove one's self a man — to "act out some idea of manhood" that has evidently been instilled in Shepard's sons by their fathers. As in *Cowboys #2* and *Tooth of Crime*, manhood is presented as an "act" rather than as a stable, attainable, fixed essence: it is the constantly receding horizon that beckons individual men with reassurance that somewhere else they can find and prove themselves to be men. Charles Mingus, Jr., appropriately for Shepard's theater, attributed this impulse for acting out ideas of men to the absence of a stable father figure in his or Shepard's lives, to "their mutual lack of a father's consistent and positive influence" (Oumano 23).

This instilled need for violence and the fear of inferiority that Shepard explores is further linked not exclusively to the father but to the feminine as the thing that must be erased, possessed, or controlled in order to reach male identity. As noted earlier, Shepard's landscape is often presented in gendered terms — described by Annette Kolodny — in which the "virgin" land of the frontier is metaphorically presented as a woman that must be possessed or tamed and that in turn will give the possessor his manhood. Frank Rich's review of *A Lie of the Mind* makes clear this connection between the male's idea of the West and of the feminine when he describes Jake's vision of a suddenly healthy and nude Beth at the close of act 1. Rich refers to this vision as the call of the road to the male wanderer evoked by a woman: "a woman whose nude back beckons with the mesmerizing lure of a distant, flickering neon sign along a desolate Western highway" (3). The man looks to the frontier, yet he is also drawn forward in his quest by his images of woman, which he perceives as an extension or embodiment of that frontier to be conquered. Eddie travels over 2,000 miles to find May, all the while thinking about parts of her body, and he leaves her to pursue yet another idea of the feminine in the countess. Fleeing into the western frontier, Shepard's men are also pursuing an idea of the feminine. Both Eddie of *Fool* and Jake of *Lie* alternately desert and return to the women in their lives, acting out their conflicted desire for independence and their absolute need for contact with a woman to consolidate their self-images. Thus, even when they reject the civilization of women, they turn to a fantasy version of the feminine — yet that fantasy version also eludes their control.

In his struggle to assert a masculine identity, the male character of Shepard's family plays must discredit the woman's story, imposing in its place his own version of her story in order to maintain a central position within his own fantasy — to remain "a fantasist," as the Old Man calls Eddie in *Fool* (27). This task becomes increasingly difficult in the world of *Fool for Love* and *A Lie of the Mind* as the female characters, unlike those of the earlier family plays, do not simply abandon the stage space to their men. In reading these plays, it is important to note the emphasis placed on fantasy, and on lies of the mind, that place the man always in the center of the story, always looking to and for what the Old Man refers to as "the male side a' this thing" (54). In this fantasy of centrality, the male character creates a split between physical and psychological reality. The Old Man of

Fool for Love sums up this irreconcilable splitting in his often quoted comments on realism:

> The Old Man: Take a look at that picture on the wall over there. (*He points at wall stage right. There is no picture but Eddie stares at the wall.*) Ya' see that? Take a good look at that. Ya' see it? ... Barbara Mandrell. That's who it is. Barbara Mandrell. You hear of her?
> Eddie: Sure.
> The Old Man: Well, would you believe me if I told ya' I was married to her?
> Eddie: (*pause*) No.
> The Old Man: Well, see, now that's the difference right there. That's realism. I am actually married to Barbara Mandrell in my mind [27].

According to the Old Man, the life of the mind and the lie of the mind are the same: an interior reality projected on the outside world. Yet, as the women in these family plays demonstrate, the outside world refuses to operate according to this interior reality, and so Shepard's men erupt into violence in their attempts to control and to shape the physical world around them, especially as it is represented by women. Women — like May who leaves the trailer in Wyoming that Eddie had set up for her before he took off— refuse to stay in place, refuse, finally, to be faithful to the self-centered fantasies of their men, and so their men direct at them various degrees of anger and violence. The physical world of women, which is the recipient of this violence, is often presented as the cause of this violence, is made to bear the blame for the male character's inability to confront reality and to take responsibility for his actions — whether that is betrayal that leads to suicide (that of the Old Man), competition that leads to patricide (Jake and his father), or jealousy that leads to would-be murder (Jake towards Beth). The male characters, like the playwright, want to view "their" women simply as plot motivation that allows the man to act out his inner pain and confusion. Given this behavior of the male characters, the question becomes for the audience of Shepard's plays, Whom are we to believe and where are we to place our sympathies? The logic upon which these men operate, upon which Shepard seems to intend his audience to place its faith in order to sympathize with these men, is clearly skewed. Regardless of whether Shepard would like us to or not, do we merely accept that the Old Man of *Fool for Love* is really married to Barbara Mandrell simply because he believes it to be true? Or that Beth really did become the adulteress she was acting in a play, the belief in which prompts Jake to beat her up? If Shepard intends for his texts to reinforce patriarchal biases, as certain critics have argued, these same texts often also elude his biases by showing the male "truths" to be lies and, thereby, exposing the instability of this masculine identity that is built on lies.

In defining a lie, Eddie tells Martin (the man about to take May out on a date), "Lying's when you believe it's true. If you already know it's a lie, then it's not lying" (58). Shepard's characters, like his plays, elide truth and lies, reality and fiction, in ways that make them difficult to sort out. If what is real is whatever you believe in your mind, then the real is also a lie because "lying's when you believe it's true." What they give with one hand, Shepard's plays take away with the other. According to one version of truth — the masculine lie of the mind — the violence of Shepard's men is valid, but according to another — the female version of the men's stories within these plays — this violence is completely inexplicable and unjustified. Shepard thus offers a double vision that glorifies and nostalgically longs for certain versions of male identity and that simultaneously undercuts these versions as consuming and dangerous fantasies, not simply for the women but for the men as well.

Fool for Love contrasts the "male side a' things" with the female side in its playing out of the battle of the sexes between May and Eddie. Their romantic conflict mirrors the male desire to control the story of woman. In placing The Old Man onstage but in a separate playing space from that inhabited by Eddie and May, Shepard foregrounds the question of whose vision we are seeing. Are Eddie and May memories (fantasies) called up by the Old Man, or is the Old Man a memory or fantasy called up by Eddie or May? The plot of the play revolves around the slowly revealed, intermingled story(ies) of Eddie, May, The Old Man, and the absent mothers of Eddie and May. All three of the onstage characters tell contradictory stories of their mutual past, and each story reveals the splittings and mergings of identity within the adulterous and incestuous ties that bind them to one another. The Old Man's story is the most guarded and the most whitewashed as he attempts to absolve himself of responsibility for his sexual betrayal of both Eddie's and May's mothers. He does so by explaining that his love for these two women "was the same love. Just got split in two, that's all," something that "can happen to the best of us" (63). When the two women end up in the same town, however, May and Eddie both describe how he simply surrenders his attempts to control events and disappears. In leaving, he abandons his credibility as a witness to the events that lead to the sexual relationship between Eddie and May and to the suicide of Eddie's mother.

The Old Man's disappearance, both in Eddie's and May's stories of him and in his actual position onstage as both seen and not seen, highlights the erasure, disappearance, and escape that obsess the characters in this play. They both want and fear each of these things. For instance, when he first shows up in her motel room, May tells Eddie "you're going to erase me" (19). This comment leads Lynda Hart to note its "immediate, literal reality" in light of "the erasure of women from history and the gynocide that is routinely practiced in American society" ("Pornographic" 74). May is fighting against that erasure, but she is also drawn to Eddie in a masochistic desire for the very thing that will destroy her. Despite her love/hate relationship, which makes it impossible for her to break with Eddie as long as he is physically present, she asserts herself by pointing out the lies told by Eddie and the Old Man and by refusing to remain "in place" once Eddie leaves.

Eddie, like the Old Man, simply disappears from time to time, abandoning May but always with the implied assumption that he is coming back to her. His off-again, on-again relationship with May enacts both the desire for and fear of the domestic sphere of women that Laura Mulvey discusses in light of the western hero. He wants to resist "social standards" and "social integration" at the same time that he needs them. Eddie must always return to May in order to secure her for his fantasy life whenever she tries to disappear. His absence is predicated on her remaining where he left her, and his presence is evoked by her disappearance.

He speaks of setting her up in a trailer in Wyoming — a safe, domestic harbor in his view, hell in hers — and simply cannot fathom May's refusal to remain there. He asks, "Why couldn't you just stay put. You knew I was comin' back to get you" (26). The impossibility of these two views of life is made quite clear. Eddie expects May to serve him as a symbol of home, domesticity, and romance that anchors him — a symbol to be missed, to be thought of fondly and nostalgically at a distance of 2,000 miles — but not to be a part of his everyday world. May refuses to remain in this "dumb little fantasy" (24). She escapes from Eddie's fantasy by moving away, just as Eddie escapes her too-real demands that he remain with her through his fantasy of her, which fractures her physical reality into "just a part" of her (21). Their connection is created by a delicate balance of absence and presence, and neither can remain with the other in one space for very long without, seemingly, canceling the other out.

The Old Man's position as both part of the stage world but not part of his children's world perfectly demonstrates this precarious position between absence and presence. His physical absence ensures his presence in their minds, but when he steps into their playing space in his urgent need to gain Eddie's attention, he loses his control over Eddie, who suddenly has eyes only for May. This father-son dynamic is yet another positioning of the law of the father that we have seen within Shepard's plays, usually personified, as it is here, by an abusive though absent father figure. This power of the father figure is strongest when the actual father is absent and the law he represents is internalized. In *Fool for Love*, the Old Man never leaves the audience's sight during the course of the play, just as he never leaves the minds of Eddie and May as long as he stays physically distant. His concept of what is real becomes the basis of reality for his son and daughter despite their violent attempts to reject him. And ultimately, it is his pattern of manipulation that Eddie mimics in controlling May and that May mimics in leaving the places where Eddie has found or put her.

Like Wesley and Vince, Eddie seems destined to live out the story of his father, and in this instance, the father's story is of his inability either to part from or to commit to the two women who have borne him children. The Old Man's influence on Eddie, however, is briefly disrupted when the Old Man moves onto the stage to stand "between Eddie and May" (73) in a desperate bid for Eddie's attention. It seems that the Old Man, like May, has fears of being erased by Eddie. After May has told the full story concerning the suicide of Eddie's mother, the Old Man demands that Eddie take up his defense. His physical presence, however, strengthens the hold that the mother's absence has on both Eddie and May. Instead of taking up "the male side a' this thing" as the Old Man demands, Eddie supports May's story by telling him, "It was your shotgun" (73) that Eddie's mother used to kill herself. The Old Man continues to rant that "nobody told me any a' that" (73), implying that if he did not know of it, it could not have happened, once more highlighting the split between physical and psychological reality. But May and Eddie's reaction to this argument indicates that the father's fantasies seem to have lost out here to the story of the mother. Seemingly, then, both the Old Man and the "male side a' this thing" are negated by this communion between Eddie and May.

However, the play does not end at this moment. Even though May gets Eddie to accept her story of their past in place of the Old Man's story, no progress or change results. The father's influence is not completely shaken off; instead, Eddie and May go on to reenact the actions of her mother and the Old Man. They embrace passionately, then Eddie leaves, as Hart expresses it, to "pursue the feminine as mysterious Other, the disembodied countess" ("Pornographic" 75). May too leaves, evidently to try to disappear yet again until called forth by Eddie to reenact the same scene. The father's story returns with a vengeance as it is split into the double version enacted by both Eddie and May. Eddie mimics his father's inability to commit to the women in his life, and May recapitulates the Old Man's movements as she is pursued from town to town by a jealous lover. Her physical absence will evoke her psychological hold over Eddie's mind, just as the physical absence of the Old Man controls Eddie as well. This connection between May and the Old Man positions Eddie as constantly pursuing an identity that evades him, both in the body of his father and in the body of his lover. Eddie enacts May's mother's continual search for the beloved, a beloved who refuses to stay in place, like the Old Man whose wanderings are remarked upon by both Eddie and May. The audience is left to assume that Eddie and May's encounter will be repeated again in some future motel room or trailer as the characters "do nothing but repeat" themselves (67). However, a further rub is that these two lovers are not really repeating themselves as much as they are repeating the lives of their parents — her mother and their father — recapitulating a pattern of interaction they have inherited rather than created and upon which they have structured their identities. Eddie's initially powerful version of masculinity becomes, by the end of the play, much more fractured and insecure as his complex entanglements with May, the Old Man, and the past are revealed.

If *Fool for Love* was Shepard's first conscious attempt to create a fully realized female character, *A Lie of the Mind* is, no doubt, the most disturbing of the family plays in its treatment of women. However, consistent with his masculine bias, the fracturings of the female body in this play are set up as reflections of the fractured psyche of his male characters. Beth's bruised body and injured brain are the direct result of her husband's interior fears and insecurities projected upon her. Jake epitomizes Shepard's comment about the Anglo-American male's deeply rooted feelings of inferiority. The play's initial focus is clearly on Jake's struggles rather than on those of his wife. As Lynda Hart points out, Beth's position in this play is as an object. She is "simply [Jake's] vision," as the stage directions tell us (41). Thus, Hart argues:

> Beth is not a *real* character in the play; she is a culturally constructed fantasy — a "lie of the mind." ... Shepard's masculine perception renders his female characters as powerfully repressed concepts that must be subdued or annihilated ["Pornographic" 79–80].

The focus of the play — the implied sympathy — is, then, not upon Beth the beaten object but upon Jake, the suffering and "humiliated" subject. We are encouraged to focus on Jake's suffering, which is "rendered so intensely that Beth's pathetic efforts to recover are backgrounded" (Hart, "Pornographic" 80).

As far as Jake and Beth's relationship is concerned early in the play, Jake certainly seems to be the acting subject, the play's protagonist. But as the play progresses, this organization becomes more questionable. The character of Beth has drawn critical attention in that her voice — fractured and nearly silenced by aphasia — is also used by Shepard to cut through the entrapping language of gender employed by other characters in the play.[9] Beth's attachment to Jake's brother Frankie offers a different version of subject-object gender relations than is readily apparent in her relationship with Jake. When Frankie crosses the stage to travel to Beth's family home in Montana in order to see what his brother has actually done, he becomes a captive in Beth's house, partly due to his gunshot wound but also due to his personality. Beth imposes on Frankie a fantasy version of him as her new and better husband. After all, Beth is not, we are told by her mother Meg, "pure female"; she has "male in her" (104) and thus in Shepard's world can take her turn at projecting her fantasies on others. Frankie, for his part, is not purely male but is "soft" and "gentle. Like a woman-man" (76) and so becomes the victim of Beth's fantasies. Male and female — like truth and lies — begin to coalesce in this play, leading Bennett to remark that the "oscillation between masculine and feminine identification" can be used to "dismantle the hegemony of male spectatorship" that has hitherto ruled in Shepard's plays (175).

Sheila Rabillard offers a further exploration of the male-female positions within this play based on the premiere performance produced at the Promenade Theater in New York, which Shepard directed. She describes a marked difference between presentation styles of the actors and actresses in regard to their parts:

> Under Shepard's directions, *A Lie of the Mind*'s women characters have a stage presence different from the men's. Much of the play's humor comes from the women's lines, because they are self-regarding in a way that the men are not; they act as their own audiences, and see themselves as they are seen.... The men, in contrast, played their roles with no trace of self-mockery [68].

Following this discussion of the difference in self-perception between these actors and actresses, Rabillard turns to other plays by Shepard wherein the man "strive[s] to hold an audience, affirming himself by performing and controlling," while the woman "perceives herself as others see her and defines herself in those terms" (68). It would seem that the men create the lies and the women must live according to them, according to a logic which they do not themselves create. Subsequently, Rabillard argues, the incident between Jake and Beth that prompts the action of *Lie* builds on this logic: "Beth plays a loose woman in a local theatrical performance.... Perceived as a tramp, she is one" (68). On this level of perception, Jake's motivation for beating Beth seems no longer to be fantasy but fact; he is no longer "paranoid" that his wife is betraying him sexually, but he has a form of proof that she is: his internal visions. The persona becomes the person; people *are* the roles they choose to play, or are forced to play.

The metaphor of the theater and of the performance of the self, which has run through all of these plays, is given a particularly vicious realization in Beth's acting career. We have returned to *Fool*'s idea of realism: what you believe in your mind is real. Yet at the same time, *A Lie of the Mind* calls this reality a "lie," just as Eddie stated that a lie is when you believe it is true. As in *Fool*, lies and truths are elided in the world of *Lie*, calling into question the reality of Jake's life of the mind at the same time that the fantasy-logic of the play seems to validate it. The strict independent male-subject/dependent female-object dichotomy is not maintained in regard to all of the characters in this play, making *Lie* Shepard's most complex examination of male identity within male-female relations. The power dynamics between men and women are given a particularly ambiguous twist in the characters of Beth's parents, Baylor and Meg.

Baylor and Meg's relationship is the most fully developed of any of Shepard's older couples. When they first appear in Beth's hospital room, Meg's vagueness and seeming ineffectuality is accompanied by Baylor's bluster and orneriness. Back in Montana, however, the power struggle within their marriage is less clearly weighted toward Baylor. He may attempt to rule his roost, but his dependence on his wife becomes as clear as is his resentment of her, a relationship reminiscent of that of Dodge and Halie. Meg is much more aware of the dynamics of their relationship than Baylor allows himself to be. Her often-quoted lines sum up male and female differences according to traditional definitions. She tells Baylor, "The female one needs [...] the male one[....] But the male one — doesn't really need the other. Not the same way." When Baylor presses her for further explanation, she responds as follows:

> The male one goes off by himself. Leaves. He needs something else. But he doesn't know what it is. He doesn't really know what he needs. So he ends up dead. By himself [105].

Baylor, for all his bluster and brag, is stunned by this declaration that a man's flight from women results in his death. Meg, however, calmly asserts the folly of the logic upon which Baylor has structured his self-image. She gets him to admit that he blames the females in his life for his sense of entrapment, prompting from him what Frank Rich, in his review of the play, calls a "Huck-sounding" proclamation: "I could be up in the wild country huntin' antelope[....] But no, I gotta play nursemaid to a bunch a' feebleminded women down here in civilization who can't take care of themselves" (106). Such is Baylor's version of himself and of Meg, but Meg's version is quite different and, given the stage business that follows, seemingly more accurate. She tells him, "Why don't you just go off and live the way you want to live. We'll take care of ourselves. We always have" (106). Her declaration of self-sufficiency is further underscored by Baylor's helplessness. The man cannot even pick up his own socks or take off his own shoes. Immediately following this exchange, he orders Meg to pick up his socks, saying "I can't bend over." Meg does so, slowly, after a pause. While Baylor desperately, angrily, orders and pleads for his socks, the stage directions indicate that Meg "crosses slowly over to his socks, picks them up off the floor, holds them in the air. Pause.... Meg moves slowly to Baylor with the socks and drops them in his lap" (107). Meg's movement is strikingly similar to Halie's when she drops the single yellow rose between the legs of the helpless Dodge, thereby placing an emblem of her own sexuality upon the site of his impotence. After Meg's exit, Baylor still cannot put the socks on his own feet, which only increases his anger and resentment toward his wife who has thus shown Baylor his dependence. Male independence is sharply undercut by Baylor's obvious helplessness in this scene, providing an image of helpless, weak masculinity to stand in marked contrast to the violent masculinity earlier enacted by Jake. Neither image, though, turns out to be successful or even functional for these men.

In addition to Baylor, this household also now contains Frankie, another image of incompetence. Frankie's injury and gentle nature have left him helpless against Beth's determination to marry him. Outside of the house, the two violent brothers, Jake and Mike, enact a battle of wills, which Mike's family refuses to acknowledge — thereby replacing the importance of this macho version of the showdown, which was central to both *Tooth of Crime* and *True West*, with the male-female "showdown" being enacted inside. Although the play begins as Jake's story, he grows less central by the end. He has found his lie of the mind by restoring his fantasy of Beth, and he realizes that it is only the fantasy that he desires. He tells her, "Everything in me lies. But you. You stay. You are true. I know you now. You are true. I love you more than this life. You stay" (128–129). He kisses her on the forehead and then exits "into darkness. He never looks back" (129). And why should he? He has the fantasy of Beth, which is all he ever really wanted of her — the image that stays with him even in the darkness. But, must we accept this revelation as his salvation? Jake, like his father, chooses to abandon the real (Beth's person) for a fantasy (the lie of his mind). He exits the stage, but does he exit in triumph, or even to survive? Given his behavior, which we know has been similar to that of his father, we can easily envision him dying, like his own father, some horrible and confused death — a death that Meg has predicted is inevitable for "the male one" who "doesn't really know what he needs" (105). Jake's exit recalls that of the western hero who, at the end of the movie, rides off into the sunset without looking back. But unlike the iconic western hero, Jake's exit is not given the end note of the play, which instead belongs to Meg and, visually, to Lorraine and which indicates further the growing inability of the men in this play to maintain their hold over their women or over their own identity. By the end, even Jake has lost his originally powerful position as central protagonist, and the stage space has been taken over by the women who either ease into harmony with their men (Meg) or purge their lives of male control (Lorraine and Sally).

Previous to the above scene, though supposedly happening simultaneously on the other side of the stage, Jake's mother Lorraine has finally given up not only on her husband and her favorite son but on all of her ties to America. She is planning to return to her maiden name and maiden family in her home country of Ireland, and to burn her present life behind her. She plans to destroy, along with the entire house, the memories and souvenirs with which both her husband and Jake had entrusted her. Having handed over to Lorraine the responsibility for maintaining their family line and history, these men must now bear the consequences of that action by being symbolically erased by Lorraine's decision to abandon them. Neither Lorraine nor her daughter Sally bothers to keep any fantasies of her past life because neither plans to return or to repeat herself as have both Jake and his father. Instead of regressing into childish dependence, these women are obviously going to "take care of [them]selves," as Meg indicated women "always have" (106). The fire that they leave behind provokes Meg's closing comment: "A fire in the snow. How could that be?" (131). The fire in the snow is the seeming impossibility, in Shepard's masculine landscape, of woman's sign.

As powerfully and viciously as it began, the male voice in this play loses precedence by the final act. Having ranted away their brief moments on the stage, the men follow their fantasies into darkness while the women destroy those fantasies in order to light their own way.

Afterward: *States of Shock*

Shepard's family plays seem to culminate in the epic-length *A Lie of the Mind*. After this play, he remained absent from the theater for six years, a tellingly protracted absence considering that he had produced nearly 20 plays in the first six years of his career. However, in May of 1991, New York's American Place Theater staged *States of Shock*. This production marked a move for Shepard away from his own style of realism developed in the family plays and back to a theater more reminiscent of his earlier work. As such, it can serve as something of a coda to the preceding discussion of male identity presented throughout those plays. After opening up the possibility of images of men from the extreme collapse of the male-male showdown in *True West* to the greater complexities created out of the clash between men and women in both *Fool* and *Lie*, *States* seems to be something of a retreat back into a clearly male-dominated world.

States of Shock revolves around a Colonel and a paraplegic named Stubbs who have come to a "family restaurant" to celebrate the birthday of the Colonel's dead son. The family home recedes in this play, represented only iconically by the commercialized version of the family dinner table as it is recreated by restaurants. In place of the family as a center of patriarchal inheritance, this play offers the military — an institution that remains, despite the admittance of some women into its ranks, the most exclusively male-oriented of any in our society. Mothers and daughters are erased in this play as the drama focuses on father and son.

The son of whom the Colonel speaks died in combat at the same time that Stubbs, his buddy, was hit by the shell that left him in a wheelchair. The story of the son's death is told and retold by both the Colonel and Stubbs because of the Colonel's belief that by telling the story often enough he can figure out what actually happened — why his son was taken away. Here Shepard parodies the family stories of the past, in which more traditional families indulged over family picture albums or home videos. This dead son, however, becomes an increasingly elusive figure for the audience as well as for the Colonel once we realize that Stubbs may in fact be that son — but is no longer acknowledged as such by the Colonel. If so, the father is trying to erase his physical son and erect in his place a memory, a fantasy. As in earlier plays, there is the desire for discovering the "true" story, to return to the original moment when everything changed in order to set things right again, at the same time as there is a fear of this truth. By uncovering the secrets and curses, the Colonel hopes to resurrect an idea of his son, yet he also is unwilling to accept any version of his son's death other than the "official" version, and he seems to be the arbiter of this official version. Thus, when Stubbs refuses to cooperate (or corroborate), the Colonel erupts into violence and begins beating him. Ostensibly, this beating takes place because Stubbs "[has] to learn

to pay for [his] actions. Become a man" (26). The Colonel explains that in denying his story, Stubbs denies not only the Colonel but "the principles. The codes.
The entire infrastructure" (27). After this whipping, the Colonel resumes his
methodical approach, saying, "we're going to go back in time. You and me. Back
to the field of battle" (28).

The Colonel's methods of maintaining his version of reality derive from those
of the military, an organization rife with implications concerning the shaping of
masculinity. In her review of the play, Carol Rosen describes the Colonel as "a
souvenir of all soldiers — from his Revolutionary War dress uniform to his Robert
E. Lee cavalry saber to his Vietnam combat boots and camouflage" ("Marooned"
24). He is the embodiment not of any one war but of the military mind, which
demands a certain unemotional approach represented by his comment: "It has
to be studied coldly, from the outside, without investing a lot of stupid emotion"
(14). The military leaders who order their soldier boys/sons to sacrifice themselves
in battle provide an excellent metaphor for the law of the father that oppresses
and "erases" its individual sons in its all-out obsession with "making" men in
order to uphold and police the code of patriarchy.

While the Colonel embodies all that is traditionally, uncompromisingly masculine — hard, cold, powerful, forceful, virile — Stubbs embodies lack. This lack
is represented by his physical limitations, or more specifically, his sexual limitations. Stubbs's name refers not only to his body in general but also to the site of
his manhood — the "dead meat" that is his penis. Not long after entering the
restaurant, he announces to the waitress, "My thing hangs like dead meat" (12).
If the Colonel is Stubbs' father, he cannot fully accept Stubbs because of the damage the young man has sustained to the organ most vital to his manhood. In fact,
the Colonel states at one point "no son of mine has a 'thing' like that" (34). Neither the Colonel nor Stubbs ever makes clear whether the son is a separate person who is dead or whether this son is Stubbs who, in losing his mobility and
potency, can no longer be claimed as a man and therefore a son. Whether or not
they are biologically related, the Colonel and Stubbs have a tie that binds them
like family: they share a curse or a secret. The Colonel explains to Stubbs: "We
have to stick together in this. We've got a history" (15), referring to the battles
they have fought over the story of Stubbs's experiences. The two men are further
united by a common enemy, left vague and shadowy but constantly alluded to in
their toasts: "Long live the enemy" and "Without the enemy we are nothing. The
enemy has brought us together" (15). This enemy is evidently what the two men
define themselves against, and for the Colonel, that would seem to be the effemi-
nates of non-military manhood.

The indeterminacy of these two characters whose names are more representative than particular opens up this story to the level of myth. Here is the perpetual abuse of sons by fathers, the perpetual rebellion of sons against their fathers,
and the perpetual need of each for the other, enacted against a backdrop of war,
that most "manly" of pursuits. The longing for secure identity is made unresolvable. Stubbs finally concludes that there is "no way of knowing the original
moment," and so the "best way is to kill all the sons" (44). In supporting the violent policing of sons who would question the accepted code of manliness, he

speaks for the patriarchy, but his end action is a rebellion against the law of the father. As the Colonel enacts a battle scene, asking Stubbs to stand with him, Stubbs draws the Colonel's saber and raises it to kill him. The deed is frozen, however, as the characters sing together "Goodnight, Irene" in growing darkness. Although the conflict in this play seems to be leading most definitely to a resolution in which the son by killing the father can assume his authority, the freeze and the song both diffuse this resolution. "Goodnight, Irene" evokes the entrapments of unrequited romantic love, which has already been touched upon in the Colonel's flirtation with the young waitress. The singer's "goodnight, Irene" is a farewell prefiguring his death. He sings of drowning himself and of taking morphine and dying if Irene does not return his love. This song superimposes a male-female conflict onto that of the father and son who are frozen in a death scene. It seems that whether he seeks his identity through the father or through relations with women, death becomes the only solution to conflict for the male, reminding us of the destruction at the core of the pursuit of male identity evident throughout Shepard's drama.

The conflicts in Shepard's family plays of the last two decades —*Curse of the Starving Class, Buried Child, True West, Fool for Love, A Lie of the Mind*, and *States of Shock*— revolve around father and son and reflect their unresolved Oedipal conflict. The son wants to overcome the father so as to establish his own identity and dominance, but ultimately he becomes exactly like his father, a reincarnation simply recapitulating his father's personality. In fact, identity and its illusions of autonomous self-creation (the self-made man) are the shared themes of all these plays. Along with battling the influence of the father's identity, Shepard's sons also battle their desires and fears concerning women. Ideas of the feminine are treated most fully, and with great complexity, in both *Fool for Love* and *A Lie of the Mind*. Whether exploring fathers and sons or ideas of the feminine in relation to masculinity, Shepard continuously refuses a wholeness for male identity. Instead, he shows how images or ideas of men actually fracture his characters. They can find only lies and fantasies and illusions of wholeness or of masculinity, and the masculinity they embrace is always (self-)destructive. Although Stubbs states that you must "lock onto an image or you'll be blown to KINGDOM COME," it is clear throughout the dramaturgy of Shepard's plays that the images of gender they embrace are the lies that destroy his men.

Notes

1. For further discussions of O'Neill's influence on Shepard, see James Robinson's "Buried Children: Fathers and Sons in O'Neill and Shepard" and Henry I. Schvey's "The Master and His Double: Eugene O'Neill and Sam Shepard."

2. Ann C. Hall's Lacanian reading of *Fool for Love* argues that wholeness is itself imaginary, always a misrecognition. Thus Eddie's attempts to use May as a mirror in which he can recognize a complete self can be read as one more of the fantasies that confuse and fail Shepard's men. This argument appears in "Speaking without Words: The Myth of Masculine Autonomy in Sam Shepard's *Fool for Love*."

3. Sherrill Grace's discussion of Shepard's use of expressionism also emphasizes his characters' fascination with origins. She refers to their "nostalgic longing for origins" as a fantasy that places

value on what it perceives to be a more real, more true existence, best portrayed in the metaphor for the "true west." See pages 184–185 of her article "Lighting Out for the Territory Within: Field Notes on Shepard's Expressionist Vision."

4. See, for example, William Kleb's "Worse than Being Homeless: *True West* and the Divided Self," Tucker Orbison's "Mythic Levels in Sam Shepard's *True West*," Peter L. Podol's "Dimensions of Violence in the Theater of Sam Shepard," and James D. Riemer's "Integrating the Psyche of the American Male: Conflicting Ideals of Manhood in Sam Shepard's *True West*."

5. These mother figures have usually been lumped with all the women characters in Shepard's plays and viewed as weak, powerless, and ineffectual. Few critics have distinguished between the positions in which Shepard places his women in his masculine-biased plays and the actual strength of character demonstrated by many of these women. For some examples, see Florence Falk's "Men without Women"; Marranca's "Alphabetical Shepard" (especially page 30); and Doris Auerbach's "Who Was Icarus's Mother?", which argues that the mother's inability to avert or change the masculine violence within the family shows a weakness on her part. For discussion of a stronger positioning of the mother figures, see my article "The Politics of Stage Space: Women and Male Identity in Sam Shepard's Family Plays."

6. In her *Metaphorical Stages*, Lynda Hart refers to this image as representing "the bond of the family, the wife and children dependent upon the father, whose flight from responsibility carries the family with him to destruction" (74). William Demastes in his *Beyond Realism* also reads this image as a portrait of the family in conflict (104), as does Ron Mottram in his *Inner Landscapes* (135–136).

7. For discussions of how the woman's viewpoint is written over, see articles by Lynda Hart already noted; also Ann Wilson's "Fool of Desire: The Spectator in the Plays of Sam Shepard," Sheila Rabillard's "Sam Shepard: Theatrical Power and American Dreams," Stephen Watt's "Simulation, Gender, and Postmodernism: Sam Shepard and *Paris, Texas*," and Rosemarie Bank's "Self as Other: Sam Shepard's *Fool for Love* and *A Lie of the Mind*."

8. See Janet V. Haedicke's "A Population [and Theater] at Risk," Ann C. Hall's "Speaking without Words," Susan Bennett's "When a Woman Looks," and my article "The Politics of Stage Space: Women and Male Identity in Sam Shepard's Family Plays."

9. For discussions of Beth's language and its effect upon the gender dynamics of the play, see Jane Ann Crum's "'I Smash the Tools of My Captivity'" and articles by Susan Bennett and Janet V. Haedicke, already cited.

Chapter 4

David Mamet:
The Search for Masculine Space

> When the secrets of the age were clear to him he took it like a man,
> which is to say as one who has no choice. — David Mamet, from
> "All Men Are Whores: An Inquiry"

While Shepard's men looked to the masculine myth of the frontier, to the open spaces of the West, for the touchstone of their identity, David Mamet's men try to find their masculine frontier in the realm of business. Mamet's male characters are every bit as stubborn as those of Shepard in being unwilling to abandon American myths of masculinity, even as those myths shatter around them. Joe Dubbert's description of the encroachment of the feminized city upon the masculine frontier is certainly appropriate in reading Mamet's men as they struggle to assert a masculine space amidst the urban sprawl. Mamet's contribution to the record of this struggle provides us with portraits of men trying to carve out a space for themselves in the jungle of the city. Subsequently, his work embodies the contradictions concerning the assertion of and threats related to a "masculine" space that were defined in the opening of the last chapter.

Although Mamet's plays do not explicitly treat the frontier of the American West as do Shepard's plays, they do exhibit the transference of frontier terms to the activity of business. Rupert Wilkinson in *American Tough* details this frontier obsession in American business, citing metaphors of hunting, wilderness survival tactics, and the like, evidently used to give the business of paper-pushing desk work an image of the virility, strength, and even freedom that it clearly lacks. The jargon and attitudes that Wilkinson sets forth are significantly prevalent among Mamet's businessmen. The frontier mythology that both Joe Dubbert and Annette Kolodny discuss as being central to male identity in America has thus been transferred in Mamet's plays to the idea of "free enterprise," which Teach defines in *American Buffalo* as "the freedom ... of the *Individual* ... to Embark on Any Fucking Course that he sees fit" (72–73).

The physical space may have been altered, but the rules of acquiring masculinity remain the same. That is, the idea of masculine space in Mamet's work is always made dependent on the destruction or exclusion of female subjectivity in order to glorify male independence or strength. Yet, that exclusion is also never truly possible. Even when his male characters — and even Mamet himself — seek to remove women and the feminine to the margins, to offstage space, they are unable to maintain a separatist male space precisely because they are obsessed with a fear of femininity. At least linguistically if not always physically, a feminine presence is continually evoked by Mamet's male characters as they attempt aggressively to deny, attack, or degrade what they perceive as feminine qualities in themselves and others. This chapter examines, first in Mamet's essays and then in several of his plays, the psychic "space" that Mamet's male characters seek to establish and defend. This space is a positioning that is actually impossible to achieve by its own definitions because of the rules of competition that offer the truly masculine space to only a handful of winners of the "games" his men enact. Yet Mamet's men constantly blame the failure of their own system of identification, or their own failure to succeed in this system, on women or on what they perceive as "feminine" qualities within themselves.

Since the beginning of his playwriting career, David Mamet has dealt extensively and almost exclusively with a vision of men's frustration in trying to understand and establish their place in society. His collection of essays, *Some Freaks*, provides fertile ground for establishing his obsession with masculinity as a continually threatened position. Whether describing the men who hang out at the hardware store in small-town Vermont, rhapsodizing about poker, recounting his adventures at the fifth annual convention of *Soldier of Fortune* magazine, speculating about what women want, or defending the pleasure of "spending time with the boys," Mamet often presents a defense of and a tribute to male activities in a time when such activities have become suspect. Most specifically in these essays, he seems to be defining and defending a masculine space, which he presents as threatened by changes in our society's concepts of gender and sex roles.

The opening and title essay of *Some Freaks* treats the issue of finding and validating a masculine space that is not strictly "macho." Addressed to the Signet Society at Harvard University, this essay discusses attitudes toward choosing a career in the fine arts. Mamet's goal in this speech is to prove that there is room and need in every society of men for the fine arts, regardless of their usefulness or practicality, or concepts of normalcy, arguing against an implicit assumption that "men" do not do artsy things. Yet, in his attempt to change that notion, his defense in some ways helps to substantiate the dominant concept that literature and the arts are not things that real men do. For example, Mamet claims that an interest in the literary represents a "deviant personality" (5). As he says: "Sometimes an individual is thrown up *who does not fit the norm*" (3). But he also goes to great lengths to explain that this deviancy is nevertheless acceptable. To give this deviancy acceptability, he refers to frontier mythology and the concept of male strength embodied not within the frontiersman but within Mamet's image of "the Indians of the Plains." He describes how this "magnificent society," never clearly defined and seemingly created in part from Mamet's own imagination, incorporated "deviant" behavior:

Among the warrior race, a young boy, subject to visions, incapable of assimilating, of taking up the major burdens of the culture, of being a Man of the Culture, if you will, was given the option of becoming a Man by another, by a more solitary route, as a seer, or a sage, or Medicine Man, and so was exempted from the daily task of his brethren, and afforded a certain living, and a position in the society. And that Individual and Society as a whole benefited [3–4].

This passage is rich with assumptions about and assimilation of masculine mythology. Referring first off to the "warrior," an image currently celebrated in the essentialist thinking of Robert Bly, Mamet, like Bly, draws upon the warrior image from the mythology of the American Indian as it has been recuperated for white man's use. To examine further the implications of this passage, it is necessary to understand what Mamet means, or may mean, by "Culture" in this context. He seems to be using the term in its more anthropological sense of the customs, beliefs, and social systems of a race or society rather than in its more contemporary sense, which would incorporate the idea of the fine arts within its definition. Culture seems to entail, in the context of the tribe he creates, hunting, gathering, and other manual labor necessary for survival — the ostensibly useful and practical endeavors of people — while fine arts represents the thinking, visionary, creative, less obviously useful or practical activities, which, he argues, a society can make room for and find beneficial for everybody. In his view of culture, only men's roles are considered — how a "young boy" becomes a "Man of the Culture" — thus emphasizing Mamet's concern specifically with manhood and its burdens and norms.

This essay, in pointing to the "deviancy" of a man who dabbles in the fine arts, implies that a man who follows this deviant course has first to create a space for himself in the world of man because such a space does not occur naturally (inherently). Secondly, this essay's attempt to validate this space recalls a tradition in American literature by male writers in which they create a space for themselves within the Culture (as Mamet uses the term) that is both useful and manly. This line of argument returns us to David Leverenz's study, referred to in the opening chapter, which discusses the issue of manhood for American writers.

Borrowing from Stephen Greenblatt's "Renaissance Self-Fashioning," Leverenz's *Manhood and the American Renaissance* speaks of the self-fashioning that writers such as Emerson, Thoreau, Whitman, Melville, and Hawthorne underwent in order "to highlight the self-consciousness of being deviant from prevailing norms of manhood," which pervades their works and thoughts (15). Leverenz ascribes the concerns of many of the male writers of the American Renaissance to the same needs that Mamet describes in his essay, arguing that these writers had to forge their careers against the uneasy belief that "conventional American manhood seemed blithely inhospitable to any kind of literary spirit" (13) and that authorship was "a feminized profession" (13). For instance, Leverenz reads James Fenimore Cooper in contrast to more strictly "literary" figures such as Emerson and Thoreau, and shows that Cooper, voicing the traditional view of his day, believed that

to make a social impact ... a man must speak directly, naturally, vigorously, forcefully, without many learned allusions. Real learning — and, implicitly, real manhood — comes through "the jostlings of the world," where a man who may be "existing in a state of dream retrospection, lost in a maze of theories," comes up against antagonists at every turn [14].

The dreamer, the seer, the visionary is not much valued here in Cooper's thoughts, and it is against such concepts that thinkers and dreamers such as Emerson and Thoreau had to forge their sense of literary identity and, as Leverenz implies, their manhood. Like his literary forefathers, Mamet demonstrates in "Some Freaks" a need to express his sense of deviance from a norm, defending his deviance as having a place in the Culture of manhood after all.

Other aspects of the Culture of manhood are explored in the essay "In the Company of Men." Collected about midway through *Some Freaks*, this essay celebrates, albeit in a defensive tone, "The Need of Men to Be Together"—activity "which has been given the unhappy tag 'male bonding'" (*Freaks* 87). This activity is set up in clear contrast to and even in defiance of women and their ideas about men. Mamet locates both the need for brotherhood and the defensive attitude he takes, or feels he is forced to take, in the late twentieth-century confusion about relationships that has been exacerbated by (or perhaps created by?) "the Correct Liberal Political Line of Equal Rights" or feminism (86). He distinguishes this communion of men as something unique to men, something that women do not have together because "women do not, on the whole, get *along* with other women" and when they are together they tend "to indulge in the ... intrafemale activities of invidious comparison, secrecy and stealth" (86). He sums up:

> For the true nature of the world, as between men and women, is sex, and any other relationship between us is either an elaboration, or an avoidance. And the true nature of the world, as between men, is, I think, community of effort directed towards the outside world, directed to subdue, to understand, or to wonder or to withstand together, the truth of the world [90–91].

Interestingly enough, despite the frustration this essay indicates concerning women, one of the implied reasons for getting together with the guys, according to Mamet, is so that "perhaps she [your significant female other] will begin to find you interesting" (91). Even in finding and defending a masculine space, the motives remain connected to ideas of women.

"In the Company of Men" develops the ambivalence about women that Mamet has expressed in interviews and in his plays as well. "Why can't men and women get along?" he wonders in one interview that was prompted by a production of *Sexual Perversity in Chicago* (Wetzeon 103). In "Women," also collected in *Some Freaks*, he asserts that "all exchanges with women [are] negotiations" and describes how

> men will waste their time in pursuit of the utterly useless simply because their peers are all doing it. Women will not. They are legitimately goal-oriented, and their goals, for the most part, are simple: love, security, money, prestige. These are good, direct, meaningful goals, especially as opposed to the more male objectives of glory, acceptance, and being well-liked [22].

This essay sets up women (the good women) in the familiar role as better and more moral beings than men; i.e., "Men *generally* expect more of women than we do of ourselves" (24). At the same time it posits that women (the bad women) can be hard and uncompromising. Overall, this essay is an interesting jumble of sexual desires and attitudes, a response to disillusionment with the Hugh Hefner/James Bond image of woman (and, mainly, of sexual relations), an uncomfortable coming to terms with the women's movement, and an assertion that women are distinctly other than men. These contradictory and ambivalent concepts of women are the ideas against which the concepts of men and of manhood are developed in Mamet's essays, interviews, and plays, and they perhaps help to explain why his male characters are often misogynists. His characters resent female assertiveness of any kind, whether real or imagined, in large part because Mamet's men tend to be insecure about their own identities, which they have based on opposition to women.

In a 1976 article in the *New York Times* entitled, interestingly enough, "Mamet's Plays Shed Masculinity Myth," Mamet is quoted as saying:

> My sex life was ruined by the popular media. It took a lot of getting over. There are a lot of people in my situation. The myths around us, destroying our lives, such a great capacity to destroy our lives [Fraser 7].

Later in the same article he describes "the myths that men 'go through'":

> You have to sleep with every woman that you see, have a new car every two years — sheer utter nonsense. Men never have to deal with it, are never really forced to deal with it, deal with it by getting colitis, anxiety attacks and by killing themselves [7].

Aside from how clearly these two passages mimic the cadences of his characters' speech, the thoughts therein reflect the entrapments of his male characters from *Lakeboat* and *Sexual Perversity in Chicago* to *Glengarry Glen Ross* and *Speed-the-Plow*. In some ways Mamet's characters seem to be an extension of his own confusion, an expression of his own frustration about masculinity myths as voiced in his essays and interviews. Although his plays are not strictly autobiographical, any more than are the writings of any other playwright who draws upon life experiences for fictional material, they reflect Mamet's key themes concerning masculinity and manhood in America.

Curiously, however, his critics have tended towards silence concerning these themes. In his 1985 study of Mamet's work, C. W. E. Bigsby emphasizes the morally bankrupt world that Mamet's characters inhabit, noting as well the loss of values that would offer these characters redemption from the exploitation and betrayal they suffer. Bigsby locates this loss within American society, particularly within its economic systems that turn all relationships into negotiations and "commodity exchange" (132). Although his concluding remarks note briefly that "Mamet's is, to a surprising degree, a male world" often devoid of female characters, he fails to develop further the connections between Mamet's social critique and this male world (131). Dennis Carroll's 1987 book, entitled *David Mamet*, mentions male bonding and male interaction as being part of plays such as *Lakeboat*, *Sexual Perversity*, and *Glengarry Glen Ross*, but he too shies away from issues of masculinity in favor of a reading of Mamet's plays that views their central concern as a more general American decline or dilemma.

Other critics such as Jack Barbera, June Schlueter, Elizabeth Forsyth, and Matthew C. Roudané read Mamet's plays as expressing themes concerning critiques of business and capitalism and the decline of American values. Anne Dean's book on Mamet analyzes in great detail his celebrated use of language, but discusses this language in terms of "dramatic action" rather than its masculine ethos. Guido Almansi is the earliest critic to focus on the maleness of Mamet's language. Although Almansi simply glorifies the language as being masculine, Robert Vorlicky's recent book, *Act Like a Man*, digs deeply into the male discourse within Mamet's *Glengarry Glen Ross* and *American Buffalo* in order to explore how they reflect the semantic and semiotic dynamics among men in male-cast plays. In doing so, he offers some pertinent commentary regarding how Mamet's men are limited by their adherence to traditional myths of masculinity. Previous to Vorlicky, Hersh Zeifman's discussion in *David Mamet: A Casebook* offers an extended examination of the machismo of Mamet's business worlds in *American Buffalo* and *Glengarry Glen Ross*, and David Radavich's article in *American Drama* explores the homosocial in Mamet's theater. Other than Vorlicky, Zeifman, and Radavich, however, Mamet's critics, while sometimes noting his fascination with male characters and worlds, are usually comfortable in overlooking the issues of masculinity he treats in order to view his male world as representative of such things as American society and the world of business. My purpose here is not to argue against the various interpretations of these critics, many of which I find useful and pertinent to an understanding of Mamet's work. However, having focused on the socioeconomic structure of the lives of Mamet's men, many of these critics have failed to consider how the sense of failure and loss experienced by these characters is located also in attitudes toward masculinity that are shaped as much by private as by public life. The discontents that so many critics have identified in Mamet's work may have less to do with "America" and "capitalism" or even "business" per se than with certain assumptions concerning maleness in America, which his characters attempt to locate within systems of business and commodity exchange.

Mamet's emphasis on male issues is made clear within his drama by his favoring of male-cast plays (*Lakeboat, Duck Variations, A Life in the Theater, American Buffalo, Glengarry Glen Ross*) and plays that only nominally include women or women's concerns (*Sexual Perversity in Chicago, Edmond, The Woods, Speed-the-Plow*). His plays are also structured by the search for male identity, for a masculine space, a search that often becomes complicated by competition among men as they seek to establish identities at the expense of other characters. This search for masculine identity is entangled with assumptions concerning women, particularly a fear and hatred of women coupled with an intense physical desire for women or for what they can represent to a man. These conflicts are often communicated through obscene, degraded, and inarticulate language that comes to represent characters' insecurities and confusion. All of these issues are present in varying degrees in the plays to be examined in this chapter: *Edmond* (1982), *Sexual Perversity in Chicago* (1974), *Lakeboat* (1970), *Glengarry Glen Ross* (1983), *American Buffalo* (1976), *Speed-the-Plow* (1988), and *Oleanna* (1993).

The Search for Selfhood: *Edmond*

Edmond, in particular, merits close study in regard to issues of masculine identity, for it presents in the style of a nightmarish fable one man's quest for identity and his failure to find it through traditional means. Edmond, an Everyman figure of sorts,[1] leaves his wife and begins a journey to discover a place for himself in his world. The journey becomes not so much a rite of passage as a search for one. As Edmond encounters increasingly threatening stereotypes of male activities, his position and identity become ever more complicated and unresolved.

Mamet's comments about *Edmond* offered in an interview for the *Profile of a Writer* series for British television set up a clear connection between the world of *Edmond* and the socioeconomic state of the America in which women have begun performing a variety of new roles within society—a change that seems to be bringing about something of an apocalypse, in Mamet's view, for both men and women. In this interview, Mamet bemoans how American society is "falling apart," and he discusses the problems he sees that face women now that the security of marriage is no longer primary for them: "that which would give woman a place in the male mythology, which is as a partner in marriage," is disappearing. His vision of possibilities for women expressed here is, of course, extremely limited, and his concept of marriage has much in common with the usual position (that of subjugation) of women in patriarchal society, but his real concern is not for women in this situation but for men. Mamet explains that marriage for a man now means being "encumbered with a partner who is going to both increase your debts and witness your shame." Although this shame is never explained, Mamet describes how the continuity of relations between men and women has always been upheld "by the possession of woman" so that having women in the marketplace vying for equal positions in a "man's world" seems the reason that the old value system in this country is breaking down.

Edmond is certainly confused about his relationships with women and about his own identity. When we first meet Edmond, he is already experiencing an identity crisis that has led him to seek counsel from a fortune-teller. This woman tells him:

> You are not where you belong. [...] The world seems to be crumbling around us. You look and you wonder if what you perceive is accurate. And you are unsure what your place is. To what extent you are cause and to what effect ... [221].

Edmond believes himself to be in a world that has fallen apart, where traditional roles and interactions do not work for him anymore, if they ever did. He is unsure where he stands now and seeks to redefine himself or, at least, to "find" himself. But this search for identity is complicated by theories of biological determinacy: that, as the man in scene 3 says to Edmond, "we're *bred* to do the things that we do" (226). Edmond is caught between the belief that actions are predetermined (that we are programmed to behave a certain way and that there is a certain position to stand in) and the reality that the environment for which he was "bred" has changed. The implied question throughout Edmond's journey is what his options are when the rules of identity keep changing. What choices or what tools for survival does Edmond have?

The choices are quickly narrowed for Edmond by a conversation in scene 3 with an older man in a bar, a total stranger with whom Edmond discovers a common bond due, as much as anything, to his gender and race. Edmond is soon involved in sympathetic dialogue with this stranger, and each expresses the uncomfortableness that has driven him to this bar in the late afternoon:

> Man: A man's got to get *away* from himself...
> Edmond: ... that's true ...
> Man: ... because the pressure is too much.

When Edmond inquires what this man does to "get away," the man replies:

> What are the things to do? What are the things *anyone* does? ... (Pause) *Pussy* ... I don't know ... *Pussy* ... *Power* ... *Money* ... uh ... *adventure* ... (Pause) I think that's it ... uh, self-*destruction* ... I think that that's it ... don't you? ...
> Edmond: Yes [227].

While aware that there is something uncomfortable about the position that these men take, the two cannot think of any way "out" except, ironically, through the same values that have positioned them in the "pressure[d]" situation they wish to escape. How can they escape what they are bred to do? Disillusioned, they are nonetheless controlled by the construct of self that they continue to enact, the construct of self based upon gender or, more specifically, upon sex. After Edmond confesses, apologetically, that he has just broken up with his wife, the man responds, "Believe me, that's alright. I know that we all *need* it, and we don't know where to *get* it, and I know what it *means*, and I understand" (228). Encouraged by this vague reference to Edmond's many problems, Edmond continues:

> ... I feel...
> Man: I know. Like your balls were cut off.
> Edmond: Yes. A long, long time ago.
> Man: Mm-hm.
> Edmond: And I don't feel like a man.
> Man: Do you know what you need?
> Edmond: No.
> Man: You need to get laid.
> Edmond: I do. I know I do [228].

Having lost his place in regard to his wife, Edmond feels emasculated. Evidently his identity has relied on sex with a woman for its very existence. Although Edmond seems to derive initial comfort from his conversation with this man, he has also been further trapped into limited definitions of manly behavior. He has accepted the traditional version of the "man's" way out — pussy, power, money, adventure — that leads to self-destruction and to destruction of others. Following this limited definition, Edmond accepts that the traffic in women is crucial to his identity as a man. To prove himself as a man, Edmond must possess a woman: he must get laid.

The longest section of the play details Edmond's unsuccessful attempts to buy a woman. However, only after winning a rather desperate street fight with a pimp does Edmond feel powerful enough to attract a woman's attention. Glenna, a waitress in a diner, sleeps with Edmond of her own accord, but when Edmond seeks to exert control over her — to redefine her by his own definitions — she rebels, causing the delicate position that he had set up for himself, based on his image of her, to collapse. Glenna draws a clear distinction between the sex act, with its subtext of female objectification, and their actual subject positions: she tells him, "WHAT DID I DO, PLEDGE MY LIFE TO YOU? I LET YOU FUCK ME. GO AWAY" (271). Her refusal to be controlled or renamed so unsettles Edmond's tentative position for himself that he strikes out against her, calling her "insane" and killing her with the "survival knife" he had bought earlier in a pawn shop.[2]

This murder, unlike the confrontation with the pimp, ends up further confusing Edmond. Even in murdering Glenna, in fixing her position in death, he feels slippage in his control, in his ability to name or define himself and others. This murder has started him on the path to jail, and it is only in jail, where he can no longer run away from his situation and where he thinks he will meet no more challenges to his identity, that he begins to be forced toward some sort of resolution. In jail he resigns himself to his position as being part of his destiny. As he tells his cell mate, "I always knew that I would end up here. Every fear hides a wish. I think I'm going to like it here" (284). At this point, though, Edmond is not aware of the realities of prison life.

In the penal institution, totally run and inhabited by men, where the male is supposedly the absolute master, femininity must be constructed out of masculinity — which is exactly what Edmond's cell mate does with Edmond.[3] By forcing Edmond to perform sex with (on) him, the prisoner erases Edmond's concept of himself and reengenders him. At first horrified by this turn of events, Edmond then becomes motivated to come to terms with his own vulnerability, to reassess his past and his past relationships, and in general to try to communicate with the people around him. The last scene finds Edmond chatting amiably with the prisoner about the reason for their life on earth, and in the closing action Edmond kisses him goodnight.

It is difficult to follow this story of Edmond and not recall the writings of Luce Irigaray who also views patriarchal society as founded upon the commerce of the woman's body, commerce that is actually a displacement of desire. As Irigaray describes the patriarchal system:

> The use of and traffic in women subtend and uphold the reign of masculine hom(m)o-sexuality, even while they maintain that hom(m)o-sexuality in speculations, mirror games, ... which defer its real practice. Reigning everywhere, although prohibited in practice, hom(m)o-sexuality is played out through the bodies of women, matter, or sign, and heterosexuality has been up to now just an alibi for the smooth working of man's relations with himself, of relations among men [172].

These connections between the traffic in women's bodies and the displacement of male "hom(m)o-sexual" desire that Irigaray describes provide possible explanations for the root of Edmond's confusion and for his resolution. As the system breaks down (or "falls apart"), the mirror game and its symbols and signs become increasingly difficult to maintain and control. Identity for Edmond is not a simple process of playing the mirror game, and there is no such thing as "the smooth working of man's relations with himself." Perhaps by the end of the play, Edmond has discovered the inadequacy of using women to define and structure male identity and relationships.

Edmond attempts, in other words, to prove himself a man by seeking sexual domination over women, yet is able to resolve his crisis of self only in sexual relations with another man. If we view the masculine and the feminine, as Edmond seems to, as synonymous with domination and submission, then only through becoming feminized — something that Edmond had feared in previous scenes — can Edmond find peace. Ending up in prison, in an all-male penal institution, he has all power taken away from him and is sexually dominated by his cell mate. But, here, after having all previous concepts of himself erased, he at last is able to struggle toward a new sense of self and of his position in male society (prison being an intensified version of this society), to come to terms with what he accepts as inevitable. It seems to have taken an act as violating of Edmond's preconceived identity as a rape to force him to reevaluate his entire system of defining himself as a man. Oddly enough, after Edmond's initial treatment by his cell mate, the final scene shows Edmond apparently at rest, free from the tensions that had driven him to desperate acts. Yet he also remains trapped, not only physically but psychologically, in the belief that he is being controlled and even punished by some power (aliens? animals?) that he does not understand, thus calling into question the peace he has made with himself and his cell mate.

The last images we have of Edmond highlight the problems with self-image that arise when an individual is defined or defines others solely according to limited notions of gender or sex. What is masculine and what is feminine, what is valued or desired, what is devalued or feared become increasingly hard to pin down as the positions within this play shift. The steps of seeking women, power, money, and adventure all fail to bring Edmond to a sense of his own manhood. Only when all of these are stripped away from him and he is forced to recreate himself without them does he begin truly to examine his past assumptions. His greatest desire is to define and to differentiate masculine from feminine in order to establish a clear identity for the masculine self; his fear is that this differentiation is too difficult to control or maintain, and he attributes this difficulty to the fact that society is "falling apart." Yet it also seems clear that society is "falling apart" precisely because these antagonistic definitions do not work. If, as Edmond says, every fear hides a wish, perhaps the real paranoia and pressure are due to the system's limitations, and the real desire is to escape from or to erase these limitations, a desire that is never allowed to be voiced fully, intentionally, or consciously by any of Mamet's characters.

Apprenticeships to Manhood:
Sexual Perversity in Chicago and *Lakeboat*

While *Edmond* presents the search for masculine identity as a lone journey, a second mode of initiation into manhood explored in Mamet's plays is that of apprenticeship within a mentor-protégé relationship. In this relationship, an older or more experienced man befriends and tutors a younger or less experienced man.[4] Basically the success of this apprenticeship depends on the maturity and knowledge of the mentor. If his ideas of manhood are limited or debilitating, then so will be the protégé's, and in Mamet's worlds, they usually are. In *Sexual Perversity in Chicago*, for example, Danny's failure in his relationship with Debbie is at least partly due to the influence of his mentor, Bernie.

Bernie Litko is the epitome of a man who defines himself by sex and women, yet he resents and even hates women as a result of his dependence on them for his own image. Whenever they are together, Bernie and Dan talk almost exclusively about women or, more specifically, about having sex with women. Talk of sex is what binds these two men together and what helps them to define themselves. When Dan's relationship with Debbie hints at being more than sexual exploitation, Bernie feels threatened. Danny might wish to break away from the sexual attitudes epitomized by Bernie, but, as his scenes with Debbie demonstrate, he does not know how. Because Debbie's experience has trained her to believe that a man's "I love you" means nothing ("It's only words" [41]), she is not receptive to Dan's feeble initial attempts at communication, and so misunderstandings between the sexes prevail.[5] Dan and Deb's relationship soon falls apart in a stereotypical way, and Dan returns to ogling women with Bernie. The protégé returns to his mentor, and nothing changes except perhaps that the hatred between the sexes becomes more pronounced. The closing scene demonstrates Bernie's resentment of women when they cease to be tits and ass and legs and instead become people competing with him for "space." Suddenly feeling surrounded by women, trapped and closed in, Bernie exclaims:

> Coming out here on the beach. Lying all over the beach flaunting their bodies ... I mean who the fuck do they think they are all of a sudden, coming out here and just flaunting their bodies all over? (Pause) I mean, what are you supposed to think? I come to the beach with a friend to get some sun and watch the action and ... I mean a fellow comes to the beach to sit out in the fucking sun, am I wrong? ... I mean we're talking about recreational fucking space, huh? ... huh? [68].

Bernie's desire of women turns to fear and hatred as he feels unable to assert a space apart for himself within the system of sexual identification that he has accepted. His uncomfortableness is expressed in a tirade that stumblingly half-articulates the emotions that prompted it. Following this tirade, however, Bernie refuses to discuss his anxieties. He immediately asserts that he is "okay" in response to Dan's concerned questioning, shutting down any possibility of confronting his sexual fears. With Bernie as his main example of male behavior, how can Dan hope to come to terms with his own confusion and to feel comfortable about his own identity and about sex?

Bernie's expressed desire for a masculine space not defined by women is prevalent in Mamet's plays, yet it is also extremely difficult for his characters to create or maintain because their identities, like Bernie's, rely so heavily on concepts of women. The plays themselves can be seen as attempts to create that masculine space as again and again Mamet writes women off his stage. However, even in his male-cast plays such as *Lakeboat, American Buffalo*, and *Glengarry Glen Ross*, the feminine cannot be fully erased and instead becomes, as in *Sexual Perversity in Chicago*, a powerful, though usually negative, presence within the dialogue of the male characters. In these plays, women tend in general to represent the biggest threats to male identity precisely because, according to the sexual ideology of the male characters, they continue to be what men need in order to define themselves yet are paradoxically what men most fear will deny them that definition.

The 1970 play *Lakeboat*, later revised and restaged in 1980, offers an examination of a masculine space among the blue-collar world of the Great Lakes shipping industry. *Lakeboat*'s world is a world without women, yet its men also demonstrate the obsession with women that Bernie has already experienced. Particularly in the character of Fred, we see sexual exploitation of woman as a defining characteristic of manhood. Yet this play also offers a wider vision of manhood than we saw in *Sexual Perversity*, with the dialogue of its eight-character, all-male cast.

In exploring the lives of these working-class men, Mamet taps into the roots of their fears and desires concerning issues of masculinity. The characters of *Lakeboat* discuss traditionally male interests: poker, sex, horse racing, action-adventure movie heroes, drinking, fellow workers, their jobs, their fears and fantasies. They revel in stereotypes and media myths of masculinity as well as stereotypes of women, and they demonstrate the frictions as well as the camaraderie of men together. Finally, the play presents the emptiness of these men's lives while it also shows their methods of enduring jobs and lives that they know are empty. We are made to see that their jobs are monotonous and all that they have to break the boredom on the boat is talk. Through this talk, various images of maleness emerge, particularly the two versions represented by Fred and Joe.

Dennis Carroll describes *Lakeboat* as the initiation of a young man based on a mentor-protégé relationship: "A young man is accepted by his elders, and he in turn faces the responsibilities of adulthood at the same time as his older associates become aware that their best years have passed them by" (8). The play offers, more fully than *Edmond* and *Sexual Perversity*, multiple examples of male interaction and methods of coping with limitations imposed upon them by the structure of the working class. Dale, a college student, has joined the men who work on the boats of the Great Lakes as his summer job. He is only a temporary part of this world, and provides a fresh audience for its permanent occupants to talk about themselves and their world as they seek to initiate him into their society. Carroll notes that these men perform for Dale, and tell stories of their lives to impress and to teach him; he distinguishes between Fred's reliance on macho lies to build himself up (the Bernard Litko syndrome) and Joe's greater capacity for self-disclosure (86–87).

The opening scene establishes that Dale is already becoming a part of the community of lakeboat men. He is the onstage audience for Pierman's story about a drunken sailor, and he is already keying into the appropriate responses and, especially, language of this world:

> Pierman: And as I understand it, this slut comes on to him, and they leave the bar and he gets rolled.
> Dale: By the whore?
> Pierman: Yeah, I mean he'd had a few ...
> Dale: The bitch.
> ... ...
> Pierman: So, he stumbles back to the gate, drunk and sobbing ...
> Dale: Nothing to be ashamed of....

Pierman: The guards won't let him in! I mean he's bleeding, he's dirty [...] and no
identification. So, of course, they won't let him in.
Dale: Bastards.
Pierman: Yeah, well, they're just doing their job.
Dale: I suppose you're right [130–131].

While Pierman describes the sailor's troubles, Dale responds with lines that are
sometimes accepted, sometimes questioned by Pierman as Pierman, acting as
mentor, indicates the appropriate attitudes and assumptions for a lakeboat man,
thereby teaching Dale how to be one of the "guys."

Dale continues to play this role of listener, reminiscent of the role that Dan
constantly plays for Bernie in *Sexual Perversity*, as the older men on the boat take
advantage of his newness to demonstrate their knowledge and expertise, whether
real or imagined, on everything from sex to salt. His presence offers them a way
to establish authority and identity for themselves as much as, or perhaps more
than, it offers Dale knowledge that will initiate him into manhood. As Pascale
Hubert-Leibler has pointed out in his study of student-teacher relationships in
Mamet,

> Most of Mamet's characters are mediocrities, losers who generally occupy the lower ech-
> elons of American society.... Yet their profound need for dominance is very much alive,
> and because of their disempowerment, can only be expressed through a few particular
> channels.... [One] is the achievement of the position of teacher in a relationship of a ped-
> agogical type [561].

Hubert-Leibler goes on to discuss Joe's positioning of himself as a mentor, which
I will turn to in a moment. Fred, however, also sets himself up in this position,
but his quarrelsome bravado overpowers most of his scenes.

Fred does not make his first lengthy appearance in the play until scene 10 with
Dale. Within seconds of meeting Dale (or of "accost[ing]" him, as the stage directions indicate), Fred takes it upon himself to explain to Dale about the sex lives
of lakeboat men: "Now, the main thing about the boats, other than their primary
importance in the Steel Industry, is that you don't get any pussy.... Except when
we tie up. This is important because it precludes your whole life on the boats"
(159). Fred's eagerness, even urgency, in explaining this point to Dale indicates
the importance that sex must have for Fred. From this abrupt opening, Fred
launches into a sex story which, ostensibly, is intended to teach Dale how to handle women by sharing with him Fred's discovery that "THE WAY TO GET LAID IS
TO TREAT THEM LIKE SHIT" (162), an attitude that Fred shares word for word with
Bernie Litko. The subtext of Fred's story is his desire to assert an image of himself as powerfully masculine, based on his sexual potency, but his influence over
Dale is obviously limited in this scene. Dale's response is an obligatory "yeah" or
"no" or "uh huh" until he can escape back to his work. Having lost Dale as an
audience, Fred nonetheless continues to talk, soliloquizing about muggings, the
mafia, and horse racing. Fred speaking alone, often with great passion, epitomizes
the need for serious, self-disclosing talk that is often denied these men who usually limit their dialogues to stereotypical topics such as sex and liquor. Even with
these topics, the pattern of "dialogue" among the men on the lakeboats is more
often competitive than companionable. Fittingly enough, Fred describes for us

his view of the world as it is epitomized by the race track where competition is continuous and "there are two types of people in the world," winners and losers (168). The competition would seem to be inescapable for these men, even in their main activity — talking.

In contrast to Fred, Joe offers a more complex — and more sympathetic — vision of manhood. He also asserts himself more fully, and seemingly more successfully, as Dale's mentor. It becomes clear in their scenes together that Joe wants to mentor Dale in order to establish a position of authority that he does not otherwise possess.[6] However, perhaps because Joe takes the time to talk *with* Dale rather than *at* him, it becomes clear that Dale is willing to listen to, perhaps also to learn from, but certainly to accept Joe's confessions and confidences. Joe is the only character who asks Dale about himself and his life outside of the boat, expressing concern and interest in Dale's schooling. This scene, significantly titled "The Bridge," prepares the way for further conversation and intimacy between Joe and Dale as Joe sets himself up to teach Dale not to waste his life, offering an empathetic conversation rather than a competition for attention.

The next scene opens with Joe and Dale sharing a beer and confidences while both of them are off watch. Joe opens with a long speech about what he wanted to be when he was growing up. Oddly enough, Joe's dream was to be a ballet dancer, an occupation that does not fit the "norm" of manly pursuits, and is certainly a far cry from the manual labor he performs now. Given the behavior of the other characters on the boat, it is hard to imagine their sympathizing with Joe's dream, indicating that his confession to Dale is the result of an affinity he feels with the young man. Joe explains how he imagined it would feel

> on stage with a purple shirt and white tights catching these girls ... beautiful light girls. Sweating. All my muscles are covered with sweat, you know? But it's clean. And my muscles all feel tight. Every fucking muscle in my body. Hundreds of them. Tight and working. And I'm standing up straight on stage with this kind of expression on my face waiting to catch this girl. I was about fifteen. It takes a hell of a lot of work to be a dancer. But a dancer doesn't even fucking care if he is somebody. He *is* somebody so much so it's not important. You know what I mean? [206].

Joe's rich physical description of this particular dream serves to establish his reason for fantasizing about being a dancer and for sharing the fantasy with Dale. First of all, he emphasizes the physical strength it would take to be a dancer, envisioning "all my muscles covered with sweat." He also stresses that he would enjoy touching and holding the girl dancer, emphasizing his heterosexuality. While Joe's vision of the dancing profession includes the physical labor and lust for women that is part of his life now, he indicates why such a career would be preferable to his current one. Joe, a middle-aged working-class "joe," believes that dancers, like ballplayers and cops (his other childhood fantasy roles) are "somebody," unlike himself. After all, people pay to see a dancer. He is in the spotlight, noticed, important.

After sharing this closely guarded secret, which indicates his sense of failure in his current job, Joe delves even further into the mystique of masculine identity and its pressures as he discusses his attempted suicide. Influenced by media images, Joe's suicide attempt reflects an interesting mixture of childhood fantasies meeting adult realities:

One night in Gary, I had this apartment. I was cleaning my gun and, you know how you do, pretending the cops were after me and doing fast draws in the mirror.... And I said, "What am I doing? A grown man playing bang bang with a gun in some fucking dive in Gary, Indiana at ten o'clock at night?" And I lay down in front of the TV and loaded my gun. Five chambers. You shouldn't load the sixth in case you jiggle on your horse and blow your foot off.... And I put the end in my mouth, and I couldn't swallow and I could feel my pulse start to beat and my balls contract and draw up [207–208].

Joe's fear that he is a nobody, which the first confession indicates, led to an attempted suicide that is itself an attempt to embody a powerful masculine identity, that of the cowboy. This confession is a rare moment in Mamet's plays as a male character purposefully exposes his own vulnerability, a recognition of his tenuous masculinity, and the fear of being a "boy" and not a "man." Certainly all of Mamet's male characters discussed thus far are vulnerable, their identities tenuously formed and tenaciously — though seldom successfully — defended. However, by first establishing a rapport with Dale, by gaining some knowledge of Dale's life and ambitions, Joe seems to believe he has found someone who can listen, understand, and learn from his fears and vulnerability without judging. Certainly Dale does not deride Joe for his confessions. At least between Dale and Joe there seems to exist the ideal male world described in Mamet's essay "In the Company of Men": "an environment where one is understood, where one is not judged, where one is not expected to perform — because there is room in Male Society for the novice and the expert" (*Freaks* 88). At the same time, this accepting environment seems to exist only between Joe and Dale, not among the lakeboat men in general. Joe and Dale have discovered how to communicate beyond the aggressive conversations common among the men of the lakeboat who we hear debating hotly such trivia as which action-adventure movie star is toughest and whose father could drink the most liquor. Though still often caught in limited channels of expression, Joe and Dale are at least able to communicate real fears and desires concerning their lives rather than relying on substitute issues concerning sex, drinking, and gambling that the other characters employ, turning every conversation into rivalry.

Competition for Identity: *Glengarry Glen Ross*

As Mamet's previously quoted comment concerning "masculinity myths" in the popular media coupled with the comments of the lakeboat men makes clear, media images of masculinity, of what it takes to be a man, are both seductive and debilitating. The overriding need of Mamet's male characters is for affirmation of their identity, for comfort, friendship, love, and understanding, yet this need is denied because of the fear that it is weak and unmanly to need anything or not to be secure in one's identity. The only two options, it would seem, are to be brash and cover up the emptiness or to be painfully honest and reveal it, but there is little offered in Mamet's stage world that will convert the emptiness these men feel into meaning. This fear is created by a distrust of the world in which the characters live. Fear of betrayal in sexual relationships, business transactions, and friendships leads to distrust in everyone, and this fear and distrust has its roots in the lack of confidence within the self. In support of this "catch-22" reading of male identity, Stephen Shapiro argues in his study of masculinity that

> male self-mistrust is caused by narcissism and reinforced by male silence, emotional inhi-
> bition, and puerile attitudes and behavior. The division inside men, in the male psyche,
> has the drastic social consequence of weakening trust in all other relationships.... The
> weakening of the bonds of trust in these relationships causes still further decay in male
> self-trust. We have only to regard our social world to see a mirror image of this growing
> mistrust, a tragic reflection of the inner world of men [20].

Reflecting Shapiro's view, Bernie and Edmond, and later characters such as Levene and Fox, are driven by a near hysterical insecurity about their manhood, a sense of powerlessness that they seek to over-compensate for, a need to establish their manhood in the face of real or imagined challenges to it. These challenges are often personal, internal insecurities, and they are regularly projected onto the outside world — often onto women, or else onto fellow businessmen, workers, or friends. More than anything, Mamet's men believe they have something to prove about themselves through competition with others and are therefore locked in a destructive sense of competition that they cannot escape.

Within Mamet's plays, ideals of masculinity are sought through competition and prove to be limiting even when attained. The competition takes place mainly with words — with storytelling — as characters seek to assert some image of themselves and of their actions through their dialogue. Action in Mamet's plays is almost always implied action; it usually occurs offstage and is merely recounted by the characters. Reality, action, the very worlds of these characters are linguistically signified, and since we are sometimes given conflicting information (the stories of the cook in *Lakeboat*) or stories that are too extreme to believe (such as Bernie's sexual exploits), we find it difficult to accept the reality these characters are trying to create for themselves and for their listeners.

Mamet himself recognizes the competition that is at the heart of his plays. In an interview conducted by Matthew Roudané, Mamet explains that "one can only succeed at the cost of, the failure of another, which is what a lot of my plays — *American Buffalo* and *Glengarry Glen Ross*—are about" (74). Although Mamet's comment does not overtly connect this competition with masculine identity, that connection is certainly apparent in his male-cast plays, reflecting what Ray Raphael emphasizes is part of the making of male identity:

> Whether purposely or inadvertently, we create a polarized tension between winning and
> losing in which the success of some is dependent upon the failure of others. Our male rites
> of passage therefore tend to become dysfunctional and counter-productive [Raphael 184].

Glengarry Glen Ross is practically a case study of the conflicts that Raphael describes, particularly because the language throughout the play is gender-coded to set up clearly limited and antagonistic definitions of masculinity. Success of one salesman depends upon the failure of the others — it is the Cadillac, the steak knives, or nothing — and only the top salesman's position is the truly masculine one. While some (one?) of Mamet's salesmen will win and thereby prove their manhood, the others (the losers) are left to wonder, am I really a man? The competition thus ensures failure for the majority, and this failure is not simply a failure to win, but to achieve an identity that is defined as masculine. Ultimately, then, *Glengarry Glen Ross* is less about the need to succeed in business than the need for men to establish and maintain a masculine identity through or within the system of business. In accord with this view, Hersh Zeifman has argued that the portrait of the business world in both *Glengarry* and *American Buffalo* presents "the debased values of an all-male business ethic in which the phallus reigns supreme," a world "in which men *define* themselves as 'men'" (126, 127).

The opening scenes of *Glengarry Glen Ross* establish the dangerous, ego-threatening world that its salesmen inhabit. Levene and Williamson, Moss and Aaronow, and Roma and Lingk play out the humiliating extremes necessary for them to hold onto their jobs. Levene, an older salesman who is not bringing in the revenues he used to, cajoles, bullies, pleads, and finally bribes his boss to give him better leads (names of prospective buyers). Moss, a disgruntled salesman, plans to rob the sales office and steal the leads by manipulating the less aggressive Aaronow into doing the actual break-in. And finally, top salesman Roma dazzles and manipulates the gullible Lingk into purchasing properties in return for Roma's supposed friendship. With these three scenes, act 1 sets up the tensions brewing among the salesmen who have relied on the tentative positions of their jobs for their sense of identity. Act 2 begins to develop more clearly exactly where the lines of identification are drawn and how narrow the space is between them.

Once again, the most often evoked image against which these men seek to define themselves is that of women. Shelley Levene tells Williamson at one point, "a man's his job" (77). The obvious point is that doing a job is what makes a man, what gives a man identity. Levene goes on to say that if "you don't have the balls" to do the job then "you're a secretary" (76–77), a job traditionally held by women. Or, as Roma exclaims to Williamson when the latter messes up a deal:

> Where did you learn your *trade*. You stupid fucking *cunt*. You *idiot*. Whoever told you you could work with *men*? [96].

If being a man relies on performing well at work, then failure to do so defines a worker as not-man, as woman. It is precisely the differentiation of these two narrowly prescriptive positions that offers any sense of identity for these characters. As in previous plays, the feminine is allotted a negative position; it is set up as the failure and lack that a man must overcome in order to establish and maintain his identity as a man. But, this construct of male identity remains extremely tenuous and is constantly threatened by the same competition that is supposed to create it.

The pressure to perform at work in order to maintain an identity is so great that the characters in *Glengarry Glen Ross* continue to submit to that pressure even when they most desire to escape it. While a character such as Edmond journeyed to a greater awareness of himself by embracing his fears and the supposedly negative sides of himself, the characters in *Glengarry Glen Ross* cannot break away from the system that defines them long enough to seek new identity. When Levene is at last revealed as the culprit of the robbery, an act that sought to break down the structure of the business that defines him, he explains his thought at the time of the break-in: "I'm halfway hoping to get caught. To put me out of my…" (101). The desire to be put out of his misery, to escape the pressure, is great enough to drive him to act, yet Levene cannot actually give voice to this desire to escape precisely because this desire is also his greatest fear. If Levene's identity is based upon his job, then escaping the job means negating the self. Levene immediately follows the confession of his desire to escape with a rejection of that desire. He explains:

> But it *taught* me something. What it taught me, that you've got to get *out* there. Big deal. So I wasn't cut out to be a thief. I was cut out to be a salesman [101–102].

This assertion, of course, is belied by Levene's position at the end of the play.

Glengarry Glen Ross has been said to evoke *Death of a Salesman* in its exploration of the failure of the success myth.[7] Interestingly enough, the main concern of Willy Loman was to be "well liked" or accepted in masculine society — given the recognition from other men that Raphael, Shapiro, and even Mamet in his essays describe as being vital to a man's sense of self-worth. But in *Glengarry*, the well-liked motif is rejected for a ruthlessness that Ricki Roma, the top salesman, epitomizes. Roma gains other characters' confidence or liking only so that he can use them for business ends. Although he knows how to act like an interested and sympathetic friend to both customers and fellow salesmen, ultimately he does not care about their opinions of him except as they serve his purpose of getting "on the board." His only desire is to be top salesman, because it is the *position* that gives him power and identity, rather than the admiration of others that Willy Loman desired.

Raphael has argued that "in our culture the practical effect of many of our so-called initiations is to separate the men from the men" (184). *Glengarry Glen Ross* clearly develops this separation and isolation of the male characters. Any comfort they might take from each other, any support or friendship, is constantly undercut by the competition they are locked into. For example, the camaraderie of man-to-man talk developed so vividly in scene 3 between Roma and Lingk is undercut by the realization that all of Roma's shared confidence has been simply a lead-in to a sales pitch aimed at the unsuspecting Lingk. Lingk's desire to believe in Roma's friendship, in their understanding and acceptance of each other as men, continues even as Roma's congame is revealed. Lingk shows up the next day to reclaim his check, but he makes it clear that he has been sent by his wife, that she is what has come between Roma and Lingk. He tells Roma "It's not me, it's my wife" who has driven him to ask for his money back, and this wife has taken away from him "the power to negotiate" (89, 91). Lingk, who evidently feels himself to be powerless, is perhaps drawn to Roma precisely because Roma has power, because his identity as a man is seemingly secure. Even when Lingk discovers that his check has already been cashed, that Roma has evidently been lying to him, he still feels that he, not Roma, has failed in some way. He apologizes to Roma in lines reminiscent of Bobby's at the end of *American Buffalo*: "I know I've let you down. I'm sorry" (95).

Not only is any friendship between customer and salesman made impossible by the exploitative nature of the business, but so is any real respect or friendship between salesmen. In conning Lingk, Levene and Roma fall smoothly into a partnership of lies, but ultimately these men are separated by competition as well. Roma, the more successful, and younger, salesman realizes this while Levene, the failing older salesman, is still trying to operate on an older set of rules, those more along the lines of a Willy Loman. Levene insists that "a man who's your 'partner' *depends* on you ... you have to go *with* him and *for* him ... or you're shit, you're *shit*, you can't exist alone" (98). Roma, the partner to whom Levene refers in this speech, is already setting up to betray Levene. Roma tells Williamson in the closing moments of the play, "I GET HIS [Levene's] ACTION. My stuff is *mine*, whatever *he* gets for himself, I'm taking half. You put me in with him" (107).[8] The "partnership" that Roma is setting up is completely exploitative because Roma realizes that his success is predicated on the failure of other salesmen. Subsequently, Levene has become another mark for Roma, just as Lingk had been, and the men in this play remain separated from each other by a competition that binds them into isolation. No wonder Aaronow, who voices despair throughout the play, has as his closing line, "God, I hate this job." Yet, however much they may hate their jobs, it is clear that these men cannot envision life for themselves beyond the office and its system of identification. As a result, they find themselves clinging to the very system that seeks to destroy them.

Men at Work:
American Buffalo and *Speed-the-Plow*

The salesmen in *Glengarry Glen Ross* are constantly competing for the masculine space of top salesman. They must knock out the competition in order to make room for themselves "on the board." The crisis of identity within business — as that identity is implicated in finding a space for oneself — is developed in two other of Mamet's "men-at-work" plays as well: *American Buffalo* and *Speed-the-Plow*. Separated in creation by a decade that included *Edmond*, *Glengarry Glen Ross*, *The Woods*, and a good deal of work in Hollywood, these two plays nevertheless serve as interesting parallels and at times counterpoints to each other. Ultimately both of these plays explore personal loyalties within business transactions and, further, the search for a space for the self within these transactions. Both also establish a pecking order among their three characters as each struggles to create or maintain an identity within the hierarchy of the play. Each play has two characters competing for the attention and approval of the third. And ultimately, the definitions of masculine identity that the male characters attempt to establish or maintain rely upon antagonistic definitions of women or of the feminine.

American Buffalo is the play that confirmed Mamet's reputation as an important American playwright. Perceived by many early critics as merely a foul-mouthed diatribe, it was soon recognized as an important commentary on American business and ethics. Beyond the larger "American" significance of the three characters in *American Buffalo*, their search seems to focus on an affirmation of self-worth. Each character in this play attempts to assert a place for himself within the lives of the other characters, and each feels threatened by the other characters both on and off the stage.

Mamet has said that *American Buffalo* is really about Donny Dubrow and his decision to betray Bobby (Roudané, "Interview" 76). Don is torn between the role of mentor/protector, which he has set up for himself concerning Bobby, and the role of businessman (his "business" being petty thievery), which he tries to teach Bobby. The opening dialogue establishes this contradiction, as Don tries to teach Bobby that friendship demands loyalty to others and that business demands self-serving interest even when dealing with people that you know. Don explains, "That's what business is... . People taking care of themselves." When Bobby still does not understand, he continues,

> 'Cause there's business and there's friendship, Bobby ... there are many things, and when you walk around you *hear* a lot of things, and what you got to do is keep clear who your friends are, and who treated you like what. Or else the rest is garbage, Bob [...] There's lotsa people on this street, Bob, they want this and they want that. Do anything to get it. You don't have *friends* [in] this life [8].

Using logic such as this passage demonstrates, how can Bobby hope to figure out the lines between business and friendship, or his role in either? Like Lingk of *Glengarry Glen Ross*, Bobby is manipulated by the rhetoric of men who use excessive language in order to deflect their listeners' attention from their lack of logic.

The relationship between Don and Bobby is much like that of Joe and Dale of *Lakeboat* except that Don needs Bobby much less openly than Joe needs Dale. Seemingly, too, in selecting Bobby as his student, Don has chosen someone who can never be fully initiated into masculinity but will remain a "feminized," dependent counterpart to Don's role as provider, protector and teacher. The hierarchy of power can remain intact with Don on top, and it is precisely Don's fear of losing his position within that hierarchy that Teach plays upon throughout the play.[9]

Although playing the mentor figure can help Don appear more knowledgeable and in control — as Hubert-Leibler has indicated — at the same time, appearing too fatherly, too nurturing, would seemingly emasculate Don's image. Anne Dean, in analyzing Don's relationship with Bobby, points out that Don is careful to keep the balance of power in his favor so that he never looks too "soft" in his relationship with the young man. This fear of "softness" with its implications of homosexuality is, after all, exactly what Teach hits upon when he ridicules Don for his relationship with Bobby by telling him, "You're a joke on this street, you and him [Bobby]" (101). To counter this accusation, Don makes sure that he manipulates Bobby into asking for things that Don would otherwise have to offer to him, thereby preventing himself from appearing too solicitous of Bobby's needs.[10] As the early scenes between Don and Bobby indicate, this balance of positions of power is delicately maintained. The dynamics of this play revolve around self-image as each character seeks to assert or regain a masculine image of himself against real or — usually — imagined threats to that image. After all, the robbery that Don plans, talk of which is the central action of the play, is prompted by Don's fear that he has been "buffaloed" by a customer who has duped him by purchasing a buffalo head nickel, the value of which Don had not previously known.

Teach's actions at the start of the play are motivated by a somewhat similar incident of perceived exploitation. He recounts what happened at the Riverside diner that morning:

> So Grace and Ruthie's having breakfast, and they're done. *Plates … crusts* of stuff all over … so we'll shoot the shit. [...] so on. Down I sit. "Hi, hi." I take a piece of toast off Grace's plate [...] and she goes "Help yourself." Help myself. I should help myself to half a piece of toast [...] it's four slices for a quarter. I should have a nickel every time we're over at the game, I pop for coffee … cigarettes … a *sweet roll*, never say a word [10].

Teach's description of this slight from Ruthie demonstrates his concern about his image and the respect, or lack of it, that he commands. Because Ruthie's comment "Help yourself" might just as easily, as Anne Dean points out, have been said teasingly as sarcastically (113), Teach's extreme reaction to it — "The only way to teach these people is to kill them"— is evidence of his own insecurity. Ruthie's comment, like Don's customer, is the event that raises doubts in Teach's mind as to his own position among his "friends and associates." Teach has been made to feel that he has been taken advantage of by these women, just as Don believes that he has been taken advantage of by his customer. Like Don, Teach perceives a need to reassert himself in the face of everything he most fears about his own "softness," gullibility, or inconsequence.

Teach's comments about Ruthie also establish a connection between the fear of emasculation and a fear of the feminine that is developed throughout the play. Each character's relationship with the offstage women indicates how much he feels that his identity is threatened by them. Bobby likes Grace and Ruthie in the same way that he likes Teach and Fletcher and Don. He is basically undiscerning regarding personal character and simply wants to be liked and to please the people he knows. Don, less naive than Bobby and less paranoid than Teach, views Ruthie as a friend and as relatively smart. She did, after all, win money from him in a card game. But Ruthie is not really in the masculine league as epitomized for Don by the mythical Fletcher. Fletcher is, for Don, the ultimate representative of masculine power and know-how:

> He is a fellow stands for something—[...] You take him and you put him down in some strange town with just a nickel in his pocket, and by nightfall he'll have that town by the balls. That is not talk, Bob, this is action. [...] Skill and talent and the balls to arrive at your own conclusion [4].

Don views Fletch as a man's man, a "stand-up guy" who can hold his own and who is, therefore, vastly superior to Ruthie who, even if she is a "dyke," is still a woman. Of course, the irony is that Fletch will not hold his own on the streets but will become the victim of a mugging before the play is over.

Unlike Bob or Don, Teach cannot give credit to any of the offstage characters, male or female, because to do so would, in his mind, encroach upon his own position of power in relation to Don and Bobby. He not only refuses to give them their due but actively seeks to tear them down in the eyes of Don and Bobby. Thus, Ruthie becomes "a Southern bulldyke asshole ingrate of a vicious nowhere cunt" (11). In response to Don's assertion that Ruthie can play cards well, Teach responds: "She is *not* a good card player, Don. She is a mooch and she is a locksmith and she plays like a woman" (14). As absurd as they are in close analysis, both of these statements are meant as insults to Ruthie's status in the same way that both Levene and Roma insult Williamson by calling him derogatory terms for woman. Teach's need to denigrate any image of success or power held by offstage characters extends to Fletcher as well, precisely because he is seen as Teach's rival for the job with Don. Fletcher, too, must be emasculated, like Ruthie, in order for Teach to establish a space for himself in the eyes of the other characters. When Fletcher fails to show up for the robbery and Don refuses to move without him, Teach finally tells him, "The man is a cheat, Don. He *cheats* at cards — Fletcher, the guy that you're waiting for" (80). We, of course, are supposed to connect Fletcher's cheating behavior with the "woman" Ruthie, thus putting Fletch in the feminized position of the other offstage characters.

This image of Fletcher helps Teach to build up a scenario of betrayal by Bobby and Fletcher through which Teach hopes to discredit his two rivals and to place himself squarely in charge as Don's right-hand man — to put himself in a position of power within his small world. Teach's paranoia concerning the double cross, that everyone is a cheat, serves to heighten Don's doubts about the people around him and to lead to the betrayal to which Mamet refers. Not only does Don come to believe that his customer has buffaloed him, but he eventually accepts Teach's story that Fletch and Bobby have double-crossed their deal and pulled off the robbery themselves. Bobby's appearance with a second buffalo head nickel, which he offers Don, helps to confirm Don's suspicion that he is not in control of events but that other characters are taking that control.

Of course, after Teach's terrifying display of violence toward Bobby, we learn that Bobby's offer of the buffalo head nickel had nothing to do with the double cross but stemmed from his desire to give back to Donny what he understands Donny has lost — the nickel that has become for Don the symbol of his dignity. Bobby's simple statement that he bought the nickel "for Donny" indicates that he has learned the lesson of friendship that Don had taught him in the opening scene, but in the world of the junkshop, friendship, like other forms of identification, has to struggle for a space in which to assert itself. Among these three men we have seen what Shapiro has described: male self-doubt that leads to "weakening trust in all other relationships" (20).

Speed-the-Plow works with many of the same issues as *American Buffalo* — loyalty, betrayal, and the fear of emasculation — but it makes the split between masculinity and femininity even more explicit by the actual presence of a female character onstage. The twin poles of business and friendship again pull at the male characters, but their positions are further complicated by the character of Karen, who heightens the competition for establishing and maintaining male bonds. Fox and Gould's buddy system becomes threatened as Karen moves (or is drawn) into their space to claim Gould's loyalty.

The play opens in the office of Bobby Gould, recently promoted movie producer. He and his "friend and associate" Charlie Fox plan yet another buddy-prison film hoping to cash in on an old formula of macho male bonding in order to achieve box-office success. The tentative nature of their own friendship, however, and the emptiness of their work are emphasized by their talk, which is constantly edged with too many protestations of their loyalty to each other. They banter that they are just a couple of "old whores," jauntily establishing that the system of business to which they pay homage is completely exploitative. This definition of their roles also indicates the "feminized" position of men who do not make decisions based upon their own desires but on those of higher-ups who are in turn ruled by the profit motive. Like the salesmen of *Glengarry Glen Ross*, these two men are acutely aware of the tentative nature of their positions in the business, yet they have staked their self-image upon this position.

However, to counteract their positions as manipulated "whores," the two men exert their masculine sexuality over Gould's "temporary" secretary. Fox challenges Gould to seduce Karen, and the bet that the two men place further bonds them through the exploitation of the female body. Karen is set up in the now-familiar role for Mamet's female characters of sexual object, a space upon which men seek to inscribe their identities and exorcise their fears. However, Gould's original intention of establishing his masculine identity through sexual relations with Karen becomes complicated as she asserts an identity of her own.

Karen begins to move from sexual object to acting, thinking subject as she seeks to convince Gould that the book he has asked her to give a "courtesy read" should be made into an important film. By playing on Gould's fears of his own inconsequence, Karen makes a powerful argument for the story of nuclear holocaust, and she makes Gould admit, within himself, his own fears and his own sense of inadequacy. Karen comes to represent for Gould an alternative to the system of mutual exploitation that Fox and Gould participate in and that defines them as manipulated "whores." She offers to Gould the hope of a meaning and purpose beyond money — the chance to choose his own way and to be a "maverick," a "man." This purpose can only be achieved at the cost of the old-boy buddy system of identification already established between Gould and Fox.

The last act becomes a showdown between Fox and Karen as Fox fights to maintain his position within both business and friendship. Gould at first believes he has found a way to overcome the nagging fear of his own inconsequence, which he has heretofore masked by bravado, but he cannot break away from the powerful influence of Fox. Karen, typical of Mamet's women, is given a personality that is overshadowed by the more dynamic — and more driven and paranoid — Fox. Thus Fox convinces Gould that Karen is insincere in her desire to help Gould find purpose and meaning. Fox asks Karen,

> You came to his house with the preconception, you wanted him to greenlight the book.... If he had said "No," would you have gone to bed with him? [77].

When she responds "No," the two men cannot imagine another way of interpreting her reply except that she trades sex only for the chance to get a movie deal. In other words, they believe that she, like them, is nothing but a whore willing to exploit herself for business ends. Convinced that they have discovered her real motives, none of her talk about redemption from their exploited and fearful lives is allowed any further relevance. In their view, Karen has simply moved into their game and is crowding the board and confusing the issues. So, Karen is pushed off the stage as she realizes "I don't belong here" (80), and Fox and Gould's space is resecured. The female character in this play has physically entered the stage space only to be pushed back offstage again precisely because she is too threatening a presence for the play's men to bear. However, even in her absence the system of mutual exploitation will continue, and Fox is prepared to defend the system and his space within it with threats that go beyond the cliché "You'll never work in this town again" to "You ever come on the lot again, I'm going to have you killed" (80).

The desire to differentiate masculinity from femininity is evident in these last three "men-at-work" plays. Yet, oddly enough, it is the men of these plays who enact what Mamet has earlier referred to as the "intrafemale activities of invidious comparison, secrecy, and stealth" (*Freaks* 88). Mamet's ideal of the community among men, briefly established between Joe and Dale of *Lakeboat*, becomes lost completely as his characters seek to define themselves within the competition of business. We have only to look at Roma or at the way Williamson is treated by the other salesmen of *Glengarry Glen Ross* or at Teach of *American Buffalo* or at Fox and Gould in order to see that acceptance and understanding is not common among Mamet's male characters except when it is feigned for a self-serving purpose, as in Roma's supposed concern for Lingk. In the essay "In the Company of Men," Mamet describes leisure activities among men, activities such as card games, sporting events, and hunting, and he differentiates these activities from "the competition of business" (90) wherein the roles a man plays are quite different. However, within the worlds of *American Buffalo*, *Glengarry Glen Ross*, and *Speed-the-Plow*, for example, distinctions between business and personal or leisure activity become blurred. Teach "hangs out" at the junk shop long before he gets involved in a business deal with Don. *Glengarry Glen Ross* begins in a Chinese restaurant where the socializing of the cocktail hour is never far removed from business; it is, in fact, merely an extension of business for the salesmen. Fox and Gould of *Speed-the-Plow* imply that they have a friendship that goes beyond the business of making movies, yet they also know that their friendship is contingent upon the deals they make together, and so they must constantly remind each other of that friendship in order for it to exist.[11]

The men of *Glengarry Glen Ross*, *American Buffalo*, and *Speed-the-Plow*, then, seem to have connections beyond business, yet they cannot ever quit doing business. They are locked into the competition of their jobs in part because the limited construct of identity they try to enact relies on their work as much as it relies on the positioning of women or, more precisely, of the feminine. As each character encounters the crisis of identity so clearly displayed by Edmond, he turns to the system of business in search of a masculine space in which to establish an identity but discovers there only greater challenges to that identity because the separatist system of identification evidently can never exclude fully what it seeks to separate from — women or the feminine.

Fueling the Fires: *Oleanna*

The hysterical fear of women and the feminine that pervades the world of Mamet's plays makes hardly surprising his portrait of Carol in *Oleanna*. Touted by many reviewers, and certainly by advertisers, as a brilliant exposé of sexual harassment, this 1992 play confirms the fear of the feminine that whips Mamet's male characters into such a frenzy.[12] Its timely subject, coming so soon after the Anita Hill/Clarence Thomas confrontation, no doubt contributed to its immense success. Mamet's stated intention was to offer an even-handed look at the issue of sexual harassment that targets both men and women.[13] His tactic relies on the premise that truth is relative to the participant — each participant perceives a different version of their encounter. Although Mamet's intentions are commendatory, the outcome of fair representation does not follow in the text of his play. Mamet's play stacks the deck, perhaps unconsciously on Mamet's part, in favor of his male character, effectively shutting down the possibility of real exposé by its lack of character development in regard to the female character. In doing so, his play reveals the difficulty of speaking fairly from two sides of an argument in which the speaker himself is already immersed. Mamet's choice to deal with the issue of sexual harassment fits comfortably with his concerns about the world of business that he explored in the three "men-at-work" plays, *American Buffalo*, *Glengarry Glen Ross*, and *Speed-the-Plow*. By examining the threatened position that he portrays men encountering in the world of work, we can view *Oleanna* as another facet of this threatened male position, which views the ultimate challenge to men as coming from women, even when women are denigrated, abused, and physically shunned in his worlds of work.

Set in the office of a college professor, this play pits professor John against student Carol. Carol of the first scene is deceptively soft and powerless, seeking help from John because she just does not understand his class, the text, his lectures. Her dialogue further indicates her complete ineptness at even the most basic concepts, although this might be somewhat mitigated by the fact the John is a rather confusing speaker. The first act of this play is a masterpiece of inarticulateness on the part of John, who creates inarticulateness on the part of Carol by never allowing her to finish a sentence. We can see this dynamic quite clearly in the following exchange from early in the play:

> Carol: I'm just: I sit in class I ... (*She holds up her notebook.*) I take notes ...
> John: (*simultaneously with* "notes"): Yes. I understand. What I am trying to *tell* you is that some, some basic ...
> Carol: ... I ...
> John: ... one moment: some basic missed communi ...
> Carol: I'm doing what I'm told. I bought your book, I read your ...
> John: No, I'm sure you ...
> Carol: No, no, no. I'm doing what I'm told. It's *difficult* for me. It's *difficult* ...
> John: ... but...
> Carol: I don't ... lots of the *language* ...
> John: ... please ...
> Carol: The *language*, the "things" that you say ...
> John: I'm sorry. No. I don't think that that's true.
> Carol: It *is* true. I ...
> John: I think ...
> Carol: It *is* true.
> John: ... I ...
> Carol: Why would I ... ?
> John: I'll tell you why: you're an incredibly bright girl.
> Carol: ... I ...

John: You're an incredibly ... you have no problem with the ... Who's kidding who?
Carol: ... I ...
John: No. No. I'll tell you why. I'll tell ... I think you're *angry* [5–7].

At first more concerned with his life outside the classroom — as his constantly ringing phone makes clear — than with helping a wayward student, John quickly comes to pity Carol and offers to let her take the course over in special tutorials with him. By the second scene, we discover that his gestures of goodwill have been interpreted as sexual harassment by this confused student who has filed charges against him, charges that threaten his tenure promotion and his job. The confused and misguided Carol of scene 1 has turned into a vicious harpy out to destroy her professor's livelihood, life, and soul. Her penchant for willfully misunderstanding John's well-intentioned, if highly befuddled, gestures and words provides a convincing argument that sexual harassment charges are bogus and that political correctness is to blame for disrupting an otherwise comfortable, if somewhat paternalistic, system. Ironically, John of scene 1 does manage to be paternalistic, and certainly patronizing, even as he states, out of the blue, "I'm not your father" (9).

More significant perhaps than the truth or falsity of the accusations Carol brings against John is Mamet's method of developing the conflict through character development — or the lack of it. The exposition of this play serves to present Carol as being so distinctly "other" that there is little possibility within the play's logic of rational explanation for her behavior. While we are offered some idea of John's life outside of the classroom — his wife and son, the house he is trying to purchase, his tenure evaluation, and so on — we know nothing of Carol's life except that she has come under the power of some mysterious "group" that seems to equate intolerance with feminism. Alisa Solomon of the *Village Voice* even notes, "Camille Paglia couldn't have invented a more ludicrous spokesperson for feminism" than Carol (104). While we have no personal background on Carol to make her a real person for us, further ways in which she is portrayed serve to distance us from interpreting her as a believable and thereby a sympathetic character. Chief of these is that sometime, mysteriously, between scenes 1 and 2, she learned to speak in a sophisticated vocabulary. While Carol of scene 1 stumbles through

John: I said that our predilection for it ...
Carol: Predilection ...
John: ... you know what that means.
Carol: Does it mean "liking"? (31)

Carol of scene 2 explains her accusations by saying

It is a sexist remark, and to overlook it is to countenance continuation of that method of thought. [...] How can you deny it. You did it to me. Here. You did.... You confess. You love the Power. To deviate. To invent, to transgress ... to transgress whatever norms have been established for us. And you think it's charming to "question" in yourself this taste to mock and destroy. [...] You call education "hazing," and from your so-protected, so-elitist seat you hold our confusion as a joke, and our hopes and efforts with it. Then you sit there and say "what have I done?" And ask me to understand that you have aspirations too ... [51–52]. [And later:] Just don't impinge on me. We'll take our differences and ... [56].

Even later, however, she has to have the word "indictment" explained to her (63), although she is comfortable in her very next speech using legal lingo (64). From not being able to understand John's book, which argues that college education is simply a "hazing" process that "warehouses" the young, by scene 2 Carol is evidently able to understand the complex nuances of the power structure in which John operates, able to explain to him, "You believe not in 'freedom of thought' but in an elitist, in, in a protected hierarchy which rewards you" (67). Whether we are to interpret her comments as a parroting of her "group's" teachings — and John Simon wondered if she were perhaps an "idiot savant whom the Group has coached in some fancy lingo" (102) — or whether her actions are a freely embraced and understood approach to power relations on every level of her life, feminism (i.e., the Group) is given an ugly face in this play — all the more so because its spokesperson is simultaneously facile, dogmatic, and deft.

Given what the audience is allowed to behold in act 1, we are left with the conclusion that John's version of events is the "real" one, while Carol's is the result of her willful misreading of his behavior based on her own sexual fantasies. But the play's non-conflict becomes significant when we consider its message, particularly in regard to the final moments of the play. At the end John, upon discovering that Carol has charged him with rape — or actually battery under the law — physically attacks her. His beating of Carol in the final scene is motivated by tensions and pressures that the audience witnesses occurring onstage as his confrontation with Carol builds. The audience understands why he hits Carol, and so tends to clap or cheer when he does so, as they did the evening that I saw the New York production of the play in the spring of 1992. In contrast, Carol's motivation for her attack on John's character is never made clear. Mamet manipulates us into concluding that Carol is incapable of distinguishing the rational world from her fantasy world, or, to put it another way, has been brainwashed by her group into seeing every gesture of John's as sexist, and as a mark of patriar chal oppression. Through Carol's character, *Oleanna* confirms the fear of the feminine that whips Mamet's male characters into such a frenzy. Carol's leap from idiot to intellectual between scenes 1 and 2 is completely unanticipated. Yet by way of this leap, she comes to embody all that Mamet's men most fear about women's powers. Even the seemingly most helpless and defenseless of women is actually a tigress waiting to pounce.

Certainly it is a modern-day "truth" that truth is subjective, that events are in the eye of the beholder, and such is the supposed premise of this play, as some reviewers and as Mamet himself seem to agree. Mamet, who directed the premiere, chose to have two programs handed out to his audience, one with a woman's figure targeted on the cover, and one with a man's figure targeted. The implication was that both were being targeted equally. The play is supposed to keep from taking sides. However, by allowing us into the details of John's life and obscuring the details of Carol's life, Mamet manipulates our sympathies in favor of John simply because Carol never becomes a real enough character to elicit sympathy. The inability to sympathize with Carol, or more accurately, that the play encourages us to sympathize with John, is reflected in numerous reviews of the original production. Clive Barnes of the *New York Post* wrote that "the professor has no contest in winning our sympathy" (359), while Alisa Solomon, again, of the *Village Voice,* wrote about this "controversial" play: "The pathetic thing is, there's nothing to debate" (104).

Ultimately *Oleanna* is a simplistic reading of gender misunderstandings, fueling the fires of the war between the sexes with its assurances that the gulf between men and women is too wide to be bridged. *Oleanna* affirms the fears of Mamet's male characters and helps to explain why they are so afraid of the feminine, why they are disgusted by women, why they long for their all-male worlds. As cutthroat as the competition is in Mamet's male world, at least his men know the rules there (after all, they made them up). At least there, they can escape the terrifying, inexplicable threat that the female represents to them. No wonder his male characters cling to the fantasy of a male-only world. Compared to the "competition" set forth in *Oleanna,* that of *Glengarry Glen Ross* seems almost palatable. At least in that world, John would have a fighting chance.

Engendering Language

The antagonism between masculinity and femininity, the fear of the feminine, and the attempt to assert masculine identity are present not simply in the actions of Mamet's male characters but most specifically in their language. Guido Almansi's analysis of Mamet helps to spell out the use of language within Mamet's plays to privilege male activity over female activity even, or perhaps especially, as the former faces failure. Almansi describes Mamet as the "chronicler and parodist, of the stag party and of all social occasions and situations precluding women"(191). He also refers to Mamet's "love and need for a degraded language" in which to express "the *cahier de doleances* of the fucked-up male against Mother Nature and her deputies in this world" (193). Mamet's characters may often inhabit worlds without women, but as Almansi points out, through their dialogue they often posit women as the cause or source of their difficulties in their "male" worlds.

If, as Almansi posits, Mamet's characters speak a particularly masculine dialect, what defines their way of speaking as masculine? Certainly the most obvious quality of language in Mamet's plays is the excessive use of expletives. Mamet has said of his language that it is not realist but poetic, designed to create an impression of the way his characters relate to each other (Roudané, "Interview" 76–77). What, then, does the fact that Mamet's dialogue seems to begin and end with sexual expletives indicate about his characters? In addition to the expletives, these characters speak in a rough, streetwise, and extremely argumentative manner, no doubt influenced but not fully explained by the native speech of working class-Chicagoans. Each often seems to be using language to drown out other possible speakers and thus to dominate the stage space that he inhabits. This aggressive use of language has been analyzed by Anne Dean, who describes the forward momentum of speeches by characters, particularly in *Glengarry Glen Ross* and *American Buffalo,* as a way of covering up their vulnerability (25, passim). Mamet's characters also tend to use their speech to override any possible opposition. A clear example of aggressive language is displayed by Fox who, like the ever-performing Roma does with Lingk, hardly lets Karen finish a sentence before he is speaking again, often "for" her. In short, Mamet's male characters usually treat the act of speaking itself as an assertion of power. And the trick they rely on most is the stunning power of expletives.

Probably no other playwright has ever so fully and constantly explored the extent to which the word "fuck" can be employed in dialogue as has Mamet. A violent sexual metaphor, "fuck" implies dominance and submission and seems to stand as the overriding metaphor for all of Mamet's male characters' fears and desires. They want to fuck the competition, fuck women, and fuck their jobs, but they do not want to be the ones who get fucked. In other words, they want to be the ones acting rather than to be the ones acted upon, to be perceived in a masculine rather than a feminine role. By speaking so "viciously" (a favorite word of Mamet's characters), they hope to establish themselves as powerful people. Yet the constant repetition of this expletive, ironically, represents the ultimate powerlessness or sterility, the emasculation, of these characters who usually can do nothing else but speak. "Fucking" is often what these characters want to do but cannot, either metaphorically or literally. Edmond spends most of his time trying to buy someone for this purpose. Fred tells Dale that the men on the lakeboat "say 'fuck' in direct proportion to how bored they are" (52). At the moments of his greatest sense of powerlessness or betrayal, Teach resorts to almost mindless repetition of this word. His first lines reflect the trauma he has just experienced in his encounter with Ruthie: "Fuckin' Ruthie, fuckin' Ruthie, fuckin' Ruthie, fuckin' Ruthie, fuckin' Ruthie" (9). Fox and Gould tell each other "Fuck money … Fuck it. Fuck 'things' too…. Uh huh. But don't fuck 'people'" and then ignore their own advice (21).

Ultimately, all fears and desires for Mamet's men are collapsed into this one word, a word that is burdened with too many signifieds and that itself begins to collapse into non-meaning. The possibilities and options of Mamet's male characters are as reductive as is their language. In part because they can speak only in such limited terms, they remain powerless — even becoming at times ludicrous. They end up asserting their idea of a powerful masculine identity for themselves only within the moment of speech, and that space disappears the moment they are silent.

Mamet's men are men of words rather than actions, a fact that highlights their stagnation. They speak powerfully because they feel powerless. They assert authority because they feel like victims. They attempt to use language to establish a place for themselves that does not exist in the reality of their play worlds. But, if their language is the last masculine space that they can find for themselves, it, too, is ineffective as it breaks down, repeats itself, pauses. Because they have no adequate vocabulary fully to express their fears and desires, Mamet's men end up speaking their confusion in broken syntax and hysterical invectives. They long to displace and divert their identity crises away from the self and onto women or the feminine, yet they remain unable to maintain a stable position for the self as they do so. They seek displacement of the unease they feel rather than seeking to forge new identities that would rely upon a stance less antagonistic not only to the female without but to the feminine within. His men are left with the occasional faint hope that they are at least in the same crisis — that other men, too, feel isolated, confused, inadequate. Yet they are usually unable to use this common ground to forge a pathway out of their problems. In short, Mamet's plays tend to deny the existence of the "male bonding" that his essays seek to assert, of the "masculine space" that his characters so clearly desire. At the end of so many of his plays, Mamet's men are left not to understand or to wonder at but to withstand together any truth in the world, any hope that their system of mutual exploitation can be broken. They remain trapped in this world while seeking to deny their entrapment. *Oleanna* serves to further indicate why his men prefer this entrapment to any alternative. They see alternatives as simply worse than their present state because they believe, along with the Mamet who wrote "In the Company of Men," that the woman's world is filled with an "invidious comparison, secrecy, and stealth" against which their competition pales. Even as they themselves embody this "feminine" behavior that they fear, their paranoid vision of feminine behavior leaves them with little choice but to cling to their machismo as they work under the cliché, "better the hell I know than the one I don't."

Notes

1. Edmond has been read as an Everyman figure by Dennis Carroll, who connects him to Joseph Campbell's hero with a thousand faces (98), and by David Savran, who refers to Edmond as "an American urban, white, middle-class Everyman" (*In Their Own Words* 133).
2. Glenna is the only character besides Edmond who is given a name rather than a noun to define her, indicating that her identity has been personalized — for Edmond as well as for herself — far beyond that of other characters such as "Wife," "Man," and "Prisoner."
3. For an excellent study of gender relations within all male prisons, see John M. Coggeshall's "Those Who Surrender Are Female." Coggeshall shows how "for inmates, the concept of female emerges from the concept of male" and that "the female role models for prison homosexuals are not women but male perceptions of women" (86, 93).
4. Pascale Hubert-Leibler notes that "arguably, age may be the main distinctive feature of Mamet's characters. It is almost always mentioned in the lists of characters, often as the only element which distinguishes them" (560).
5. Dennis Carroll makes a similar point in his discussion of the play (58).
6. For a detailed analysis of this point, see Hubert-Leibler's article.
7. See for example Bigsby 115, Carroll 49–50, and Dean 189.
8. Carroll notes that this line was left out of the American production directed by Greg Mosher (46).
9. Vorlicky reads the relationships among the men in the play as composing a family, thereby placing this play in line with "the American dramatic tradition of realist domestic drama and all its codings" (215). Read in this way, Don becomes a clear father figure, and Teach's concern with gaining Don's approval places him in sibling rivalry with Bobby.
10. See Anne Dean's discussion of the vitamin scene between Don and Bobby (115–116).
11. For further discussion of this blurring of working relationships and friendships, see Roudané, "Private Issues, Public Tensions," passim; and Schlueter and Forsyth, 497, 499.
12. For representative reviews that treat the play as a serious or accurate portrayal of the issues surrounding sexual harassment, see Jack Kroll's "A Tough Lesson in Sexual Harassment," Michael Feingold's "Prisoners of Unsex," and Frank Rich's "Mamet's New Play Detonates the Fury of Sexual Harassment."

13. This intention of even-handedness was set forth in Mamet's choice of program covers for the premiere, which he directed. Each program had either the figure of a woman or the figure of a man with a target drawn over it, implying, as I will discuss further later, that both men and women were being targeted by the play.

Chapter 5

David Rabe: Men Under Fire

You had many fathers, many men, movie men, filmdom's great —
all of them, those grand old men of yesteryear, they were your
father. The Fighting Seventy-sixth, do you remember, oh, I
remember, little Jimmy, what a tough little mite he was, and how
he leaped upon that grenade, did you see, my God what a glory,
what a glorious thing with his little tin hat.— David Rabe from *The
Basic Training of Pavlo Hummel*

Although he originally established himself as a playwright of Vietnam plays, Rabe's central concern does not begin or end with war. His focus is more consistently upon myths of identity. Although he explored some myths concerning women in *In the Boom Boom Room* (1973), his other plays, *The Basic Training of Pavlo Hummel* (1971), *Sticks and Bones* (1971), *Streamers* (1976), *Goose and Tom-tom* (1986), *Hurlyburly* (1984), and even the flawed *The Orphan* (1974), focus on male systems of identification. Rabe's interest in masculinity has become more pronounced with each play he writes. According to an interview with Toby Zinman, he is working on a trilogy of plays concerning the Gilgamesh legend of male friendship as well as a novel about the adventures of the prince in the story of Rapunzel. Rabe even says that he sees Gilgamesh "as potential maleness" (Zinman 6). As his references to Jung in interviews and his own prose indicate, his more recent projects are evidently heavily influenced by Jungian thought and seem to be for Rabe something of the archetype of "maleness," or of the search for what Robert Bly would call the "deep male."[1]

While his works-in-progress reflect a more current influence of Jungian thought on his ideas of masculinity, Rabe's focus on male identity is not new. His earliest Vietnam plays are structured around male protagonists who have as one of their central tasks the sorting out of cultural images of manhood and their own identities in terms of those images. Far from being naive portrayals of the deep male and his power, Rabe's plays uncover the tensions and fracturings of male identity for his characters and the basic immaturity of their thinking about their own identities.

From early reviews of *Basic Training* to recent articles on *Streamers*, the Vietnam plays have been seen as a commentary on men in war and the aftermath that the survivors and their society are forced to confront.[2] Such a reading of Rabe's Vietnam trilogy is pertinent to his purpose in writing the plays, especially considering that the first two were written and performed while America was still involved in Vietnam, but Rabe's focus on the military may have as much to do with that institution's ties to the idea of making men as it has to do with the war in Vietnam, or to war in general. Although the Vietnam plays have war as their backdrop, Rabe is careful to place his soldiers against a societal context that is often seen as separate from war: the home in *Sticks and Bones*, and personal backgrounds and pressures including home life in both *Basic Training* and *Streamers*. By mingling life in the barracks psychically with life "at home," Rabe implies that the violence of one is but an outgrowth of the other. Such a stance encourages a closer examination of the violent images within these plays that are associated so closely with the main characters' struggles to come to terms with the gender influences of their society. Cultural images of manhood as tied to violence and aggression are presented repeatedly, not only in the Vietnam trilogy but in all of Rabe's plays, and his characters seem chiefly to be searching for a self-identity within their culture's myths and fears concerning manhood and manliness.

The Vietnam plays, to be examined in the first half of this chapter, set the groundwork for Rabe's further explorations of how cultural expectations capture and betray men searching for a coherent self-vision: these expectations often lead to violence. The Vietnam plays serve to highlight the instability of the supposedly monolithic image of manhood that the military would like to impose upon American men. This instability has relevance for questions of male friendship that the second half of this chapter explores in Rabe's two plays of the 1980s, *Goose and Tomtom* and *Hurlyburly*. Throughout these five plays, Rabe's characters constantly face loss as they fail to live up to the ideals that the American media presents to its men (for example, the John Wayne of countless westerns and war movies), yet they remain unable to imagine new definitions or positions for themselves that do not recapitulate these ideals. Whether in battle or at home, his male characters are men under fire, pinned down by cultural expectations that confuse rather than clarify who or what they should be. This confusion heightens the level of violence within these male characters, indicating their seeming inability to confront and to move beyond their limited versions of a gendered self.

In the Shadow of War:
The Vietnam Trilogy

Rabe's interest in the Vietnam war springs from his own experiences as a soldier during 1965–1966. Dropping out of college, he was quickly drafted, and he speaks of his experiences in Vietnam as leading him into writing (Rabe, Introduction; Savran, *In Their Own Words* 95–96). As his Vietnam trilogy indicates, Rabe's encounter with the military evidently crystallized for him many issues concerning male identity, issues that Mark Gerzon argues are pertinent to American concepts of the link between war and manhood. In *A Choice of Heroes: The Changing Faces of American Manhood*, Gerzon discusses, in chapters on the soldier and war, that the idea of manhood being created by soldiering and confirmed by war is deeply ingrained in our culture and an intrinsic part of what shaped boys, such as Rabe, who grew up before Vietnam.[3] Gerzon thus sums up the influence that the media had on Vietnam veterans' ideas of the soldier:

> When Vietnam veterans recall what led them to Vietnam, what made them *want* and *need* to go, they do not speak of communism or domino theories or patriotism. They speak of John Wayne [32].

That media images of manhood influence and betray men is also clear throughout Gerzon's study. He recounts personal experiences of several men he interviewed who had to reassess the previously unanalyzed images from films and television of their youth in order to gain control of their lives and their own identities as men. Gerzon's study helps to illuminate the importance of media images that David Rabe also treats in so many of his plays. The television war of Vietnam becomes a fitting metaphor for demonstrating the seductiveness of and yet the confusion created by media images for Rabe's individual men and for the societies they inhabit.

Writing from a feminist perspective, Tania Modleski's examination of media images of war since Vietnam points out that the project of connecting war with manhood has not been noticeably altered by America's experiences with that "bad" war in Vietnam. Modleski argues that war films in general — and recent Vietnam films in particular — share a thematic model that links violence with sexuality for men and portrays a military model of gender relations that is quite antagonistic to women. From *Full Metal Jacket* to *Top Gun*, Modleski notes "that sexual and military conquest are somehow intimately related, and that the relationship has to do with the need to conquer femininity both within and without" (63). The military training portrayed in *The Basic Training of Pavlo Hummel* certainly falls in line with the images that Modleski describes. The rash of films in more recent years that are either set in Vietnam or use that war as a flashpoint for its characters, films such as *Platoon, Full Metal Jacket, Top Gun*, even Rabe's *Casualties of War*, lead Modleski to comment on how many of these films try to recapture the glorious legacy of the military that was tarnished by America's experiences in Vietnam. She writes:

> The desire to rewrite the history of Vietnam to prove that we were not cowardly losers but merely unacknowledged winners — true heroes, in fact — may be seen in many forms of popular culture today; what *Top Gun* makes especially clear is how this rewriting frequently expresses a yearning for a strong paternal figure who will enable young men to go off and "do it right" too, to become heroic soldiers in the new wars to come [71].

Modleski's connection between the need for a positive view of the military and the need for a strong paternal figure is fitting in light of the paternal issues that serve as undercurrents in all three of Rabe's Vietnam plays. His male characters seem uncertain about their manhood in part because of their uncertainty about their fathers.

Gerzon, Modleski, and Dubbert are certainly not alone in noting that the military and its project of war are closely linked with our society's concepts of masculinity and manhood. When *The Basic Training of Pavlo Hummel* was revived starring Al Pacino, Martin Gottfried commented in empathetic response to Pavlo's life that "millions of us who went through military service," and its basic training, "in a real way ... did find manhood there" (59). This idea of "found" manhood — of manhood as an object that can be discovered — ties in with the concept of the military "making" men, "men" being viewed as a monolithic image into which individuals are molded. Both of these concepts of masculinity are demonstrated and critiqued by the events of Rabe's Vietnam trilogy. In both *Basic Training* and *Streamers* we see trainees and recruits seeking to "find" manhood, to mold themselves into the military image of manhood, and we see the disaster that occurs when the image forced upon them does not fit. This need for a set image seems particularly acute for Pavlo and the four recruits of *Streamers* who share a fatherlessness that seems to heighten their insecurities about their own manhood. Yet even the supposed father figure of Ozzie in *Sticks and Bones* is lacking a clear role model for his behavior. Ozzie's struggle is enacted against the backdrop of the war that has led his son to question the family's assumptions about roles and responsibilities. Ozzie's self-questioning is due not simply to his son's return but to Ozzie's own sense of inadequacy, which arises at least in part because — in contrast to his son David — he has never been tested by war.

In all three Vietnam plays, the specter of emasculation haunts the male character, who fears he does not measure up to the norm of manhood, a theme that Rabe will continue into the plays of the eighties. Whether these early characters are literally emasculated by bombs and grenades (Pavlo and Brisbey) or are symbolically threatened with emasculation (as represented by the Jody songs, fear of homosexuality, and fear of losing control or possession of a "home" or its objects), at issue in each of these plays is the desire to embody, while simultaneously failing to understand the cost of, a manliness connected to the violence of soldiering and war. Pavlo, Ozzie, and the four recruits of *Streamers* are trained to accept a limited range of behavior for "real" men, yet this training is precisely what entraps and destroys them.

Media Images of Manhood:
The Basic Training of Pavlo Hummel and *Sticks and Bones*

In his preface to *The Basic Training of Pavlo Hummel*, Rabe comments that Pavlo's "basic training" is "essential" training, "intended to include more ... than the training given by the army" (xiii). This comment encourages us to view Pavlo's training — even Pavlo himself — in metaphorical terms. In this play, Rabe captures the essence of the army's vision of manhood, which is built upon the larger culture's vision as well: aggressiveness, physical strength, and antagonism towards women. In her study of masculinity, Lynne Segal writes that "army training relies upon intensifying the opposition between male and female, with 'women' used as a term of abuse for incompetent performance, thereby cementing the prevalent cultural link between virility, sexuality, and aggressiveness" (18). Sergeant Tower's insulting of the trainees follows this pattern. If the men do not perform strongly enough, they are "pussies" or "slits." This antagonistic positioning of the male and female subject positions is reminiscent of the psychology of Mamet's characters. As in Mamet's plays, here degradation of women is coupled with a glorification of bonds among men. However, *Basic Training* explores, as *Streamers* will also, the conflicts between men that preclude this glorified male camaraderie.

Pavlo's indoctrination into the world of the army highlights the conflicting ideas of male aggressiveness and male camaraderie. Although he embraces the idea of the soldier as the real man who understands army codes (the D and D) and is physically strong and disciplined, Pavlo never understands how to *be* a real soldier and, instead, *plays* at being one. Thus, gender as performance is an underriding issue throughout this play. From his request that Pierce let him perform the Code of Conduct to his desire to perform the role of infantry man, and, most symbolically, as Pavlo is "costumed" in his uniform by Ardell, Pavlo is encouraged to treat masculinity as a performance. In focusing on performing well, Pavlo never fully understands the cost of an identity based on war, except perhaps briefly at the moment of his own death. As the play opens and Pavlo is castrated by an explosion from a grenade, the theme of threatened masculinity is clearly established. Pavlo is then led back by Ardell to relive his life, and we see that even when physically whole, Pavlo has always battled a sense of emasculation, a sense of not being quite up to par in comparison with other men. His training, then, becomes a way of covering up his perceived or actual inadequacies as a man.

Pavlo's search for male identity has led him to the army in the hopes of embodying his desired image of manliness. As the play progresses, we learn that the chief influence in shaping Pavlo's identity prior to the army was the movies that his mother took him to see when he was a child. Pavlo attempts to embody these film versions of manliness, evidently to fill the absence created by his never knowing his own father. Like Shepard's men, Pavlo is hoping to embody a preexisting position of manhood that is traditionally passed down from father to son. Pavlo has substituted the film version of the soldier for that of his unknown father. This substitution was encouraged by Pavlo's mother and her refusal to tell him the identity of his father, giving him instead the following answer:

> You had many fathers, many men, movie men, filmdom's great — all of them, those grand old men of yesteryear, they were your father [75].

Although this response does not give Pavlo the specific answer he wanted to the question of his father's identity, his mother could hardly have spoken more truthfully. Like the men to whom Gerzon refers, Pavlo has formed his myths of gender and has finally chosen to enter the army based on Hollywood images of soldiers, highlighting once again the idea of masculinity as performance. Sergeant Tower (whose name evokes the phallus of manhood that Pavlo wishes to obtain) chastises the trainees for just such delusions: "You think you in the movies? This here real life, Gen'lmen" (46). Once he is in basic training, Pavlo's ideal of the soldier becomes the black Sergeant Tower, ironically an image not prevalent in the white cinema of the fifties and sixties. Pavlo wants to be as good as Tower: "Sergeant, I was wondering how many push-ups you can do. How many you can do, that's how many I want to be able to do before I ever leave" (29). Tower is not sure how to take Pavlo's overeagerness and simply "incredulously" watches him (28).

As his exchanges with Tower indicate, Pavlo has no idea of the dynamics of his relationships with other men or of how he oversteps his boundaries. Throughout his onstage journey, Pavlo fails to analyze the images that he adopts and that constantly fail him or that he fails. Even the faith that he obviously places in his military uniform, believing it to convey an image that commands respect and arouses sexual interest, proves to be ill founded for Pavlo. In his uniform, as Catherine Hughes points out, Pavlo believes that "he is the figure of his fantasies: tough, sure of himself, the potent lover" (80). He is encouraged in this fantasy by the ritual in which he is dressed in his uniform by Ardell and the other recruits. This scene clearly presents the uniform as a costume that supposedly transforms Pavlo so that, as he tells his brother, he is "not an asshole anymore" but a soldier (66). Pavlo's fascination with his uniform mirrors the mystique that military uniforms have had in our culture. Yet Pavlo's experiences indicate what Gerzon and others have noted: after Vietnam, the image of the soldier in uniform became a tarnished image (Gerzon 30–31). After his unsuccessful attempt to pick up girls at a bar in his hometown, however, Pavlo blames his uniform:

> Stupid fuckin' uniform. Miserable hunk of green shit. Don't we go to good bars — why don't you work for me? And there's this really neat girl there sayin' to me how do I like bein' a robot? ... Don't anybody understand about uniforms? [70–71].

Pavlo has relied on his childhood image of movie soldiers to give him a certain social status, yet he cannot fathom the changes that have occurred within those images, or perhaps he simply does not realize his own inability to perform them convincingly. In another sense, Pavlo is confronting the idea expressed in the cliché, "clothes don't make the man," yet he refuses to analyze or confront that fact.

Pavlo's attempt to pick up girls is not the only indication in this play that Pavlo's performance as soldier is linked to an idea of male sexuality. Pavlo's need for the support of props, such as his uniform, to shore up his own sexuality is developed even more explicitly when Pavlo, in bed with the prostitute Yen, responds to the rifle drill that Tower leads. As Pavlo pantomimes the drill, Sergeant Tower tells the men about the rifle:

> You got to have feelin' for it, like it a good woman to you, like it your arm, like it your rib.... You got to love this rifle, Gen'lmen, like it you pecker and you love to make love. You got to care about how it is and what can it do and what can it not do, what do it want and need [83].

The rifle, then, is the prop that compensates for possible emasculation. If the soldier cannot "perform" the sexual act in bed, he can at least perform his drill with his rifle, and in the mise-en-scène of this play, these disparate performances are clearly linked.

The soldier, however, is not the only image of maleness that Pavlo attempts to enact, as Rabe would have us see, yet fails to fully understand. In a note following the published version of *Basic Training*, Rabe writes that Pavlo must be presented as someone who has a "complete inability to grasp the implications of what he does" (110). So, although he plays the rebel ("I bet you never heard of individual initiative" [26]) and attempts to be a streetwise kid by bragging about having stolen cars, both roles get him into trouble with the other trainees. They do not know what to make of his stories and comments and do not accept him as one of them. Parker and Kress in particular voice their anger and confusion at Pavlo, especially after their five-mile run when Pavlo begins doing push-ups. Kress yells at Pavlo: "You're crazy. You really are.... I hate crazy people ... STOP IT OR I'LL KILL YOU" (36). Even as he eagerly performs the actions of a "good" soldier, male camaraderie continually escapes Pavlo.

However, when Pavlo goes back home to talk with his brother, he makes up stories about the respect and friendship that he has supposedly won among his fellow trainees, relying on stories to construct himself in the particular position of military manhood that has evaded him in reality. For instance, he recounts to his brother a completely fictitious event:

> There was this guy Kress in my outfit. We didn't hit it off ... and he called me out ... he was gonna kill me.... We went out back of the barracks. It went on and on, hitting and kicking.... And ... then ... all of a sudden ... this look came into his eye ... and he just stopped ... and reached down to me and hugged me. He just hugged and hugged me. And that look was in all their eyes. All the soldiers. I don't need you anymore, Mickey. I got real brothers now [69].

As Goose and Tomtom will later, Pavlo relies on language to construct for himself what has escaped him in actuality. Pavlo's fictitious account of male friendship created through violence also reflects his indoctrination into the world of film. How often must he have witnessed such scenes of "male bonding" on the silver screen. In fact, David Mamet refers to this type of scene in *Speed-the-Plow* as his two movie producers Fox and Gould summarize the action of the prison-buddy movie they are planning. In this script, Doug Brown, major Hollywood actor, is thrown in prison with a gang of men who are going to rape him. His reaction to this threat demonstrates his lack of fear and his willingness to fight, thus earning the other prisoners' respect so that he is soon their leader rather than their victim. Pavlo has seen the type of movie that the Fox and Goulds of Hollywood produce, and he believes in the codes of behavior that they support. Yet he cannot find the secret to this behavior, to "know it, be it," as he says of the old soldier's knowledge (56). The one moment where he believes that he has finally asserted his position, his claim over the Vietnamese whore, leads to his death. However, even in death, having reviewed his life, Pavlo still cannot make sense of the dynamics that have led to his death and can only sum up his experiences by claiming, "It all shit ... shit ... shit" (107).

If media images of identity are always in the background of Pavlo's life and actions, Rabe's next play foregrounds these same images. *Sticks and Bones* directly develops the connection between television images and confused reality by naming its characters after television's Nelson family: Ozzie, Harriet, David, and

Ricky. War remains in the background of this play against which the Nelson family struggles to maintain their comfortable, middle-class lives. However, David, now blind and recently returned from Vietnam, "sees" more than his family about the nature of their insulated lives. The ghostlike appearances of Zung (David's abandoned Vietnamese lover) together with Ozzie and Harriet's disgusted reaction to the idea of David's having slept with an Asian woman resurrect the theme of racism that, Rabe argues in his introduction to this play, was at the root of the war to begin with.[4] David and Zung disrupt the seemingly smooth surface of the Nelson family's glossy lives, forcing dark undercurrents into the light.[5]

In addition to the anti-war themes, this play explores the latent violence present in the middle-class family's complacency about its self — this institution's willingness to kill whatever threatens that complacency. Most particularly, *Sticks and Bones* connects its violence to the troubled portrait of masculinity played out chiefly by David and Ozzie. This interpretation of the play's focus on masculinity is supported by the fact that the central character in this play is not David, the returning veteran, but Ozzie, the middle-aged father. Rabe himself views Ozzie as the central character of the play, and, read out of the immediate context of returning Vietnam veterans, Ozzie clearly fulfills that role.[6] Although David serves as the catalyst character, the action of the play focuses on his family's adjustment — or lack of adjustment — to his return, and the character clearly thrown into deepest crisis by the play's events is Ozzie.

David's desire to destroy his family home in retribution for his betrayal of Zung and his general involvement in the war — to bring the war home, in other words — highlights his position as that being between worlds, between identities. Ozzie, too, is soon cast into this "between" state by David's return, and, among the other family members, only Ozzie painfully struggles with the questions of self-image that David brings before them all. While David disrupts the lives of Harriet and to some extent of Ricky and Father Donald, none of them is led to question their lives as Ozzie does, to struggle, as Ozzie feels the need to, in order to discover a place for himself within systems of identification that are breaking down due in part to the disruption of David's presence (or, by implication, to the war in Vietnam).[7]

In contrast to Ozzie, Rick, Harriet, and Father Donald barely acknowledge the issues that David has brought into the home. Rick is too busy eating his fudge and going out on dates to concern himself with events in the family. When Rick finally accepts that there is a problem, he immediately moves to get rid of it by making David kill himself, therefore freeing Rick to return to his music and his dates without a second thought about the triviality of his lifestyle. Similarly, Harriet is never led to question her performance as self-sacrificing mother figure to the wayward David but simply moves to reindoctrinate David into his role as a proper son. Harriet eventually turns to Father Donald to help her in David's reindoctrination. Father Donald, who along with Ozzie and the almost mythical Hank has been one of David's "father" figures, becomes simply another image of manhood that fails under the stress of "real" life for David. Aware of his failure with David, Father Donald is still not led to question the efficacy of his religious rituals. He simply retreats from the conflict with the stumbling excuse, "I've other appointments" (192).

Although he is the catalyst that disrupts the family's life, even David remains static within the course of the play. Having witnessed the decay of the gendered images that had sustained him before the war, David has evidently returned home a different person, but he has nothing except hatred and denial with which to replace the images he now accepts as false. As Janet Hertzbach expresses it, "David's sufferings have not increased his capacity for tolerance and compassion; they have only enhanced his capacity to hate" (178). David has returned home with an almost religious zeal for breaking apart his parents' world, but he falls prey to a holier-than-thou attitude that makes any change or growth within himself impossible. Only Ozzie is prompted to seriously rethink his life, the choices he has made. In the character of Ozzie, *Sticks and Bones* holds out a hope for the possibility of creating a self not defined by the limited vision of television's middle-class family sitcom. But this hope is never realized because Ozzie, too, becomes reinscribed in the system of identification beyond which he cannot see.

Ozzie's several speeches about his youth and his present situation indicate that he is suffering from a sense of displacement every bit the equal of David's upon his return home from the war. Like David, Ozzie feels uncomfortable in the family house; the furniture looks strange to him, and he wonders about who he is and how he fits in beyond acting as father and husband. Indeed, he begins to see "father" and "husband" as roles he has been playing or performing, like Pavlo, and he begins to see these roles as an entrapment that he resents. This resentment leads him to wish for an earlier time before he became a part of the family:

I lived in a time beyond anything they can ever know — a time beyond and separate, and I was nobody's goddamn father and nobody's goddamn husband! I was myself! And I could run [150].

Like David, though for different reasons, Ozzie becomes concerned with the masquerade that the family is living, and that concern is most specifically directed toward his own performance of masculinity. David's return initially prompts Ozzie to recall his own limited experience in war as a mechanic. Ozzie regrets that he never really saw any fighting, except when as a kid he used to beat up "Fat Kramer" (126, 143). These initial doubts about his past stir deeper doubts. Ozzie soon comes to feel that he has lost a position for himself that he once possessed but which has left him now with no indication of his past. As he so vividly describes it, "My life has closed behind me like water" (193). Like Shepard's men, he longs for an idealized past, which may in fact exist only in his memory, and to which he can never return.

Ozzie attributes his current position in society, in his home, to his friend Hank Grenweller, who serves in this play much as the illusory Ben served in *Death of a Salesman*. The figure of Hank, often mentioned but never appearing, hangs over Ozzie's life as the guide and mentor that has now forsaken him. Hank comes to represent for the audience — as he does for the characters — an image of manhood that is now in question. We learn that Hank has served as Ozzie's guide and mentor for many years. He and Hank met during the depression, a time of great crisis for Ozzie as it was for many American men, who, unable to find work in order to fulfill their role as provider for the family, experienced personal crises regarding their masculinity (Dubbert 211–225). Before the depression, Ozzie had been a sportsman, specifically a runner — an image of manliness and also of freedom and movement. During the depression, a time when he wandered the country as a bum, Ozzie found Hank, who became his friend, guide, and image of a real man. Hank taught Ozzie to desire women and actually "gave" Harriet to Ozzie, ensuring a heterosexual union and establishing Ozzie in a static position within his current home. In fact, Hank has kept Ozzie in that home even when he wanted to leave it. As Ozzie recalls,

> there was a day ... when I wanted to leave you, all of you, and I wanted desperately to leave, and Hank was there ... with me. We'd been playing cards. "No," he told me. "No," I couldn't, he said. "Think of the children," he said. He meant something by that. He meant something and I understood it. But now ... I don't [204].

If Hank was once by Ozzie's side, his disappearance marks a distinct loss in Ozzie's vision of himself, leaving Ozzie as "fatherless" as Pavlo is, in some sense. He no longer understands what is meant by the home and family that Hank had "given" him. Hank's authority, however, comes into further question because of his illness, which has weakened his power for David and which supposedly explains why he has abandoned the family. David claims that Hank, the image of masculinity not only for Ozzie but for all the Nelsons, is being eaten by a disease that is congenital — inherited from his parents at birth. Significantly, David knows about Hank's disease only because Hank told him before he left for Vietnam, leading, evidently, to David's first major questioning of the influences on his life. Hank's fall from grace in David's eyes prompts him to ask Ozzie, "Why did you make me think him [Hank] perfect?" (141). However, David is not the only one disillusioned by Hank's fall. Ozzie, too, suspects that something is wrong with Hank, and subsequently with the version of masculinity that Hank had "given" Ozzie. Ozzie wants Hank to return and to offer guidance during this troubled time, but he of course never does, remaining instead a vague, uncertain memory for Ozzie. Pamela Cooper notes that "through Grenweller, Rabe signals the rottenness of a powerful, mythologized ideal of American manhood" (619). Ozzie's statement that he used to know what Hank meant but now does not indicates that even within Ozzie that image is decaying, thereby calling into question all previous authority regarding male roles that Rabe's characters have tried to enact.

Lacking Hank's support, and disrupted by David's return, Ozzie feels uncertain about his identity as a man and so lashes out against his family, first at Harriet and then against his children. Searching for a new identity, he decides at one point to take on Rick's by trying to learn guitar. Perhaps Rick reminds him of his own youth when, like Rick, Ozzie was free to come and go without worrying about family entanglements. Shortly after toying with this idea, however, Ozzie decides against it. To take on Rick's identity would erase Ozzie and replace him with another Rick, a realization that is graphically symbolized in a dream that Ozzie recounts to Rick:

> Had a dream of the guitar last night, Rick. It was huge as a building — all flecked with ice. You swung it in the air and I exploded [207].

To prevent being destroyed by this other image, Ozzie decides — much like Willy Loman — that he needs to build something in order to reassert his identity and to protect his self-image, so he plans to build, significantly enough, "a wall" (206). But this plan to build a protective wall also comes to nothing. After these feeble and unsuccessful attempts to assert or protect a new identity for himself, Ozzie finally returns to the self-image that Hank had established for him in the first place — that of breadwinner and provider, husband and father for the family. Ozzie comes to realize that within the system he has accepted, his identity is literally composed of what he has earned and what he has bought with those earnings. Therefore, in order to remind himself of his existence, he inventories his possessions, explaining to the family:

> What I have here is an inventory of everything I own.... And opposite is its price. For instance — here — that davenport — five hundred an' twelve dollars an' ninety-eight cents. [...] Et cetera. Now the idea is that you each carry a number of these at all times. Two or three copies at all times, and you are to pass them out at the slightest provocation. Let people know who I am, what I've done. Someone says to you, "Who are you?" You say, "I'm Ozzie's son." "I'm Ozzie's wife." "Who?" they'll say. "Take a look at that!" you tell 'em [212].

By "buying" into the myth that male worth and identity can be measured by income and property and that a man's wife and children reflect that identity, Ozzie reinscribes himself into the same role he had been playing since Hank first established him in the home with Harriet. The only possibility for progress or change that we have seen in *Sticks and Bones* dies at the moment Ozzie's questioning of role identity ceases. Not long after this moment, Ozzie, Harriet, and Rick, the instigator, help David kill himself in order to rid their house of the person who has disturbed the waters of their lives. David's life, too, is made to "close behind [him] like water," leaving little indication of his previous existence within the family. Ultimately, the family believes it is easier to destroy David, and his war experiences, than to question the roles they have all been enacting, even though Ozzie at least has momentarily confronted the cost of the family's masquerade of complacency.

In the Cadre Room: *Streamers*

Coming five years after *Sticks and Bones*, *Streamers* explores the violence latent in its characters' construction of their own racial and sexual identities. Interestingly enough, it is also much less focused on Vietnam per se than it is on fear and uncertainty among soldiers about to be sent to war. As in *Sticks and Bones*, war in general and the Vietnam war in particular are merely backdrops to the events of the play. Perhaps because it is not so specifically tied to any one war, critics have tended toward universalizing Rabe's themes in this play. Martin Gottfried comments, "How different, really, is the irresponsibility and irrationality of the army from life's own?" ("Streamers" 21). Clive Barnes locates the play's theme as being the nature of violence, and Douglas Watt reads the play as examining "the human condition" (Barnes, "The Stage" 38; Watt, "Streamers" 264). As tempting as it might be to broaden Rabe's themes to a treatment of the "human" condition, doing so does a disservice to the play by fallaciously assuming that manhood or the male dilemma it presents can stand for the human condition. The text of *Streamers* explores quite intricately the tensions, expectations, fears, and myths of American manhood.

The violence in *Streamers* differs, however, from that in both *Basic Training* and *Sticks and Bones* in that there is no evidence of aggression or hardship in the current lives of the four recruits that would seem to prompt it. We see them at leisure, hanging out in their cadre room, going to play basketball, smoking, reading, drinking, preparing to go out on the town. However, the stories told by Cokes and Rooney and the imminent shipment to Vietnam on which Carlyle is particularly fixated set up a feeling of dread — of an impending threat — that contrasts sharply with these leisure moments. Yet even with the threatening images that run through the play, the lives of Richie, Billy, Roger, and Carlyle seem fairly unmilitary. Rather than a battle with external enemies, sexuality and race become the territory over which the characters struggle for control, and this struggle eventually explodes into violence and death. The interior struggle is exteriorized as the recruits argue over the control or ownership of the physical cadre room, representative of "home" (a place where one belongs) for these men. Carlyle becomes the catalyst for this struggle when he intrudes on the space that Richie, Billy, and Roger have evidently been comfortably sharing.

Aggression and camaraderie, hate and brotherly love, competition and collaboration mix in complex ways as each of the men in this play seeks to find and establish his own sense of manhood. The six characters in *Streamers* comprise a microcosm of American manhood. Richie is a white New Yorker, a homosexual, and from a wealthy background, while Billy is a midwesterner from middle-class white America who is trying to hold on to the traditional gender roles in which he was raised. Roger, a black man seeking assimilation into the dominant culture without completely cutting himself off from his background, is set up in contrast to Carlyle, the street-smart black man who is suspicious of assimilation. In addition to these regional and racial differences, these men have profoundly different versions of male identity. Roger and Billy attempt most thoroughly to conform to the military definitions of manhood. They stress discipline, order, physical strength, and conformity, as well as heterosexuality. In contrast, Richie and Carlyle rebel against this model and enact instead a masculinity based upon independence and individuality, using their sexual preference and racial orientation as distinguishing marks that set them outside the dominant structure of the military. Ultimately, in these different versions of masculinity, race and sexual orientation confront or complicate the simplistic stereotyped image of a masculine "norm" (white, middle-class, heterosexual).

Importantly, each character in this play is at a transition point in his development of selfhood, and selfhood within this play becomes intricately connected with gender. Certainly, the army is traditionally one of the places that "makes" men, serving as a rite of passage into manhood, but *Streamers*, like *Basic Training*, makes clear that the army alone does not solve identity crises. It simply offers one more myth of masculine identity, an identity that comes with great sacrifice and that most of its participants have difficulty assuming or enacting. The two sergeants, Cokes and Rooney, introduce this theme as they drunkenly tell of their adventures in the Hundred and First Airborne, clearly establishing lines between the "real" soldiers who have already been to war and are "regular army people" versus the new recruits who are a "buncha shit ... sacks" (45). However, they also establish the fleeting nature of this type of manhood because these "fuckin' hero[es]" are now overweight, drunken slobs who contrast sharply with the idea of the soldier that the clean-cut Roger and Billy present to us. As the play progresses, we see that far from being reliable, male identity is more like the play's metaphor of the streamer — a parachute that fails to open when it is most needed and the failure of which results in death.

Streamers employs homophobia and racism to explore the schisms that exist in any would-be monolithic concept of manliness, such as that which the army seeks to establish. The chief conflict of the play is generated by Billy and Carlyle — the two men who will not compromise their concepts of identity; the two who are, also, the most insecure about their identities and so feel a need to assert them emphatically. In forming their identities, Billy and Carlyle have accepted most fully their disparate cultural upbringings in regard to masculinity. Both men are extremely concerned with power and position and wish to win Richie and Roger over to their separate ideas. Billy cannot stand Richie's "masquerade" of homosexuality, and he is confused as to how much of Richie's behavior is "real" versus "put on," all the while remaining unaware of his own masquerade of a certain version of heterosexual masculinity. As Vorlicky notes, in the presence of Richie, Billy "tries to affect a stalwart male image to deflect attention from his otherwise insecure sense of maleness" (155). Like Billy, Carlyle exhibits a need to assert a certain identity — specifically his blackness — in the presence of the other recruits. Carlyle wants to prevent Roger from assimilating into the white culture and losing his roots because, to Carlyle, Roger's behavior is a denial of Carlyle's world. In the midst of these conflicts, Richie and Carlyle as the "other" men — those not coded by the definitions of "acceptable" masculinity as heterosexual and as white — draw attention to their homosexuality and race, respectively, so that Billy and Roger are forced to acknowledge these elements of their microcosmic society rather than glossing over them. Billy, who denies the importance or existence of either Carlyle's or Richie's differences from himself, is eventually forced to confront not only his own homophobia but also his racism when he is challenged by Carlyle over the control of the cadre room. Carlyle's and Billy's aggressiveness becomes incompatible as the play progresses and each character attempts to exert more control over his space, both within the physical cadre room and within the psychology of the other characters.[8]

Interestingly enough, the violent action of the play follows a moment of shared experience and, seemingly, of mutual trust among the four recruits. Richie, earlier excluded from the heterosexual cathouse adventure by Carlyle, Roger, and Billy, begins to work his way back into their friendship with a story of his father, whom he saw sneaking out of the family home when Richie was very young. Carlyle responds with a story about his father, who stayed in the neighborhood although he never lived with Carlyle and his mother. Their talk of absent fathers begins to bind these men together, as perhaps their search for "father figures" or for some male identity is precisely what has led them to the army in the first place. Certainly these two stories of absent or failed fathers or father figures reflect the concern with father-son relationships that has appeared in so many plays we have already examined, especially in Shepard's plays, as well as in both *Basic Training* and *Sticks and Bones*. Billy participates in their storytelling until it becomes clear that Richie and Carlyle are moving toward a relationship that will entail sharing more than stories. As Richie and Carlyle move towards sexual relations, Roger and Billy become threatened within the space of their shared "home." Seemingly, homosexuality and heterosexuality cannot exist passively together; at least in the limited space of this cadre room, representative as it is of the military's traditional model of competitive masculinity, one must drive the other out. Eventually, by Billy's refusing to give up his space, even as he realizes that he does not "have a goddam thing on the line," Billy's racism surfaces, provoking an edgy Carlyle into violence (88).

Carlyle's murder of both Billy and Rooney indicates how deeply he has felt challenged by the territorial wars the recruits have been waging over issues of race and of sexual preference. Although the scene subtly builds up to the moment of the stabbings, Carlyle's actions still appear shockingly extreme, and precisely in their extremity, the murders affect the surviving characters and the audience. In the matter of a few minutes, congenial relations among men erupt into hatred and violence. Although Carlyle's anger is perhaps no greater than Billy's, Billy recognizes and checks the potential for murder within himself, while Carlyle reacts almost instinctively to what he perceives as a serious threat. Billy, shaped by the relative safety and privilege of middle-class white America, may not "have a goddam thing on the line" in their argument, but for Carlyle, a man of the streets, their confrontation *is* perceived as a life-and-death matter. At the very moment that Billy has perhaps for the first time seriously confronted his own racial and sexual prejudice, he is cut down by Carlyle, who views their confrontation not in the abstract of theory but in the immediacy of physical reality. The murder of Rooney, however, is another matter.

Cokes and Rooney represent another test of manhood that still awaits the young recruits. Having supposedly "attained" the masculine identity of the soldier, these men nonetheless are suffering identity crises precisely because they have basically outgrown their roles, something that will eventually happen to the young recruits as well, if they survive long enough. Old soldiers cannot represent the epitome of manhood. Having already done their duty, they have no place to go within a system that sees them as disposable, and so they are drinking themselves literally into oblivion. The young recruits are the new signifiers of masculinity, but they are obviously still unsure of where they fit in. Cokes and Rooney thus stumble across the battlefield of warring sexuality among the four recruits, and Rooney becomes a victim of his incomprehension concerning this war.

Streamers employs the enclosed environment of the military to percolate and explode the power relations at play within the supposedly monolithic concept of masculinity that the military would seem to offer. Instead of a simple, unified construct, masculinity is set up in a series of contrasts, defined by what it is not — i.e., it is not feminine, not homosexual, and so on — at the same time that those "negatives" are also embodied for us in the men we see onstage as part of their versions of manhood. Thus, the limited definition of the military-made man as initially supported by both Roger and Billy, each in his own way, is deconstructed for us as we realize that each of the four recruits has structured his manhood according to differing definitions. The military may desire to erase differences among its men, but *Streamers* shows that even within this supposedly homogenous group of "soldiers," different definitions of manhood are evident and inevitable. It is precisely the unwillingness to allow room for these multiple definitions that leads to violence and death.

Myths of Male Friendship I: *Goose and Tomtom* Play Dress-Up

Since his Vietnam plays, Rabe's work has become increasingly focused on what Jennifer McMillion has aptly titled "the cult of male identity." As mentioned earlier, his current works-in-progress for the stage are based on the Gilgamesh legend, perhaps the oldest story we have that glorifies and prescribes friendship between men. Discussing the influence of the Gilgamesh legend on ideas of male friendship, Dorothy Hammond and Alta Jablow summarize the legend as the story of Gilgamesh and his friend Enkidu, whom the gods gave to Gilgamesh:

> The friends are heroes: aristocratic, young, brave, and beautiful. In their free and wholehearted response to one another, they openly declare their affection and admiration. They engage in many adventures and battles, sharing danger, loyal to the death ... [valuing] their friendship above all other relationships [247].

That Rabe would have come to treat male friendship in his later plays after writing about the Vietnam war, or war in general, is hardly surprising. Hammond and Jablow note that "warfare is the prime setting for the drama of male friendship" (246). The Gilgamesh legend and its legacy seek to convince us that "men are most manly when they are fighting side by side in a world without women" (Hammond and Jablow 241). Some 3,500 years after the first known record of the Gilgamesh story, Western culture is still attached to this warrior image of manhood even in societies where hand-to-hand combat is practically unknown. If Rabe's or Mamet's plays can be taken as any indication, these stories of male friendships are still clung to even though they may not reflect how such relationships are actually played out among men today. If the previous Vietnam plays explore the blasted possibilities of male identity as they are shaped by male friendship in the traditional realm of war, Rabe's plays of the eighties, *Goose and Tomtom* and *Hurlyburly*, demonstrate the difficulty that male friendship also experiences in other realms of life.

Male bonding holds a privileged place in the psyche of Rabe's male characters (as Pavlo's intense desire for it indicates) even though, as in Mamet's world, male friendship tends not to survive in a contemporary setting. Rather than change their ideals, however, Rabe's men often try to change themselves and the people around them in ultimately futile ways. They are willing to regress in their development, even into a return to a childhood of sorts, in order, paradoxically, to achieve their ideas of manhood. *Goose and Tomtom* plays out these dynamics with cartoon clarity — relying upon bold colors, sharp lines, and exaggerated behavior. So, too, the more realistic *Hurlyburly* presents male characters searching for an identity through some kind of viable relationship with other humans. Both, however, culminate in failure.

The exploration of male stereotypes, fears, and fantasies is given a surrealistic treatment in *Goose and Tomtom* that is markedly different in style than that used in the Vietnam plays. However, Jennifer McMillion argues quite convincingly that far from being the "oddball" of Rabe's work, *Goose and Tomtom* hits at the heart of what Rabe's plays tend to address — male identity in crisis.

Goose and Tomtom takes place in what Rabe refers to in his stage directions as "an apartment in the underworld" (3). The term "underworld" evokes the world of organized crime inhabited by powerful crime moguls, tough-guy detectives, and their entourages. Goose and Tomtom are evidently jewel thieves who seem mainly concerned with proving their toughness and keeping Lorraine, their woman, in diamonds. They have barricaded themselves in an apartment out of paranoia that someone or something (never clearly defined) is trying to get them. During the course of the play, they seem to have kidnapped Lulu, the sister of their associate Bingo. Believing that Bingo has stolen their jewels, they end up killing him. When masked figures enter at the end of the play and carry off Lorraine, the two men turn to Lulu as their replacement for Lorraine, clutching the diamonds that they have left. All of this action takes place in a fractured reality where subject positions are as fluid as language.

The reference points of existence for the male characters in *Goose and Tomtom* are encoded in the gangster/cowboy images of manhood derived from movies and television as well as by the idea of woman as a reflection of male power and prestige. Each has his "cowboy suit," gangster lingo, gun, and mob moll to complete his masquerade of identity, and each clings to these objects as a reflection of self. They "simulate" an identity for themselves based on these objects as signs of their masculinity, and Goose and Tomtom must keep reassuring themselves of their existence through the manipulation of these signs. They constantly remind each other, "I got my gun," "I got my hat," in order to prove that they are present and that they are men. Their plight recalls a culture similar to the one that Jean Baudrillard envisions, in which simulation of reality is the "reality."

In *Simulations*, Baudrillard discusses "successive phases of the image," which move from reflection of a basic reality to masking that reality to masking the *absence* of reality, to bearing no relation to any reality, becoming what Baudrillard calls "its own pure simulacrum."[9] The reality that Goose and Tomtom wish to create concerns their identity as men, and in searching for the images and signs of manhood, they experience these successive phases of the image as it moves farther away from any relation to reality. Although they embrace signs and emblems of masculinity — guns, knives, hats, women, and the more abstract qualities of toughness and tough talk — throughout the play, the power and meaning that these symbols are supposed to reflect concerning American manhood lose any relation to the lives of these characters, who do not have any power or control over their world or over their position in it. Trying to evoke a powerful identity through these signs of masculinity, they actually end up deconstructing those signs by exhibiting how helpless they are in controlling what the signs are supposed to mean about male identity. Both the woman Lorraine and the dark figures that appear at the end of the play to kidnap Lorraine strip Goose and Tomtom of their signs of power and destroy the power positions that they have attempted to establish for themselves. Through the course of the play, the actual disparity between maleness and power is played out through the very symbols that are supposed to represent male power — guns and women-as-objects. Baudrillard's comment concerning power and its signs fittingly sums up the results of the actions of these two characters:

> Power, too, for some time now produces nothing but signs of its resemblance. And at the same time, another figure of power comes into play: that of a collective demand for *signs* of power — a holy union which forms around the disappearance of power [45].

The opening action of the play involves Goose's entrance, which prompts Tomtom to pull his gun for fear that the intruder may be an enemy. After exchanging a hug, which is also a pat-down by these two friends, Goose and Tomtom settle into inane conversation, sprinkled with Pinteresque-style paranoia that seems to be based on their dreams of victimization. Each recounts dreamlike encounters with ghosts and witches in which each was tied up or manipulated. Their lingo is borrowed from Hollywood gangster movies as they try to "get a line on" Bingo, who they suspect is "tryin' to expand his area of influence," and has "iced" somebody (13-14). Through their talk, they establish a chief concern: their identity as men and how they are perceived by others. This identity is based on pop culture images of masculinity, particularly as it is related to the "tough-guy" image so popular among the gangsters, detectives, and cowboys of film.

The desire to be "tough guys" is made clear when Lorraine enters and challenges the two men to prove that they are tough. She tells them how

> Sally and Linda and Darlene and Carla, they was all talkin' about you. What a great coupla guys! And Sally says, "Goose is tougher," and Darlene says, "Tomtom is tougher." They get into this argument over you guys.... So what I figured, we'd have this contest and see who was the toughest by sticking pins in your arms [15].

Goose and Tomtom respond, "That's a good idea, Lorraine" (16). Although later, after the pins have been placed in their arms and Lorraine has left, they both express their pain, leading Tomtom to conclude, "There's somethin' very unfuckin' natural about broads" (19). Nevertheless, throughout the play, he and Goose are much more concerned with performing for Lorraine and keeping her happy than she is concerned with catering to them. As the episode with the pins indicates, both Goose and Tomtom see themselves as being tough, and they value this feature of their personalities. However, their toughness really does not signify anything about their power. Being tough and even being violent does not win these men any advantaged position when it comes to the world outside or to Lorraine. Thus the stereotypical enactments of male power — toughness and violence — become empty performances that expose vulnerability rather than solidify power.

Even the signs of power that they cling to demonstrate the "disappearance of power" that they experience as men. These signs include weapons and clothing that are associated with gangsters and cowboys. Both of these images are clearly modern-day versions of the warrior figure that has been championed by Robert Bly in his articles that culminated in *Iron John*. Goose and Tomtom have their guns (and knives, and Molotov cocktails) and they have their cowboy suits and hats. Whenever either of them is feeling insecure about who he is and what he should be doing, he reminds the other of their "equipment":

> Tomtom: You got your gun?
> Goose: Oh, yeh.
> Tomtom (*pulling out a huge long-barreled pistol from his shoulder holster*): I got my gun.
> Goose: I got my gun. (*He pulls out a glistening pistol from his jacket pocket.*)
> Tomtom: Look at 'em. Look at 'em ... guns.
> Goose: Bang, bang [10].

Tomtom's "long-barreled pistol" recalls Clint Eastwood's Dirty Harry gun, as well as the whole mythos of American westerns and detective films that equates a man's gun with his manhood or his independence. Guns are accepted by these characters as symbols of male power, reflecting their symbolism in popular culture. A fascination with guns as symbols of masculinity appears many times in Rabe's work (exhibited perhaps most vividly by Pavlo's rifle drills), but also makes a significant appearance in Mamet's *Lakeboat*. However, Joe of *Lakeboat* comes to realize the childishness of "a grown man playing bang bang with a gun in some fucking dive in Gary, Indiana at ten o'clock at night" (270), a recognition not shared by Goose and Tomtom. These two characters have ultimate faith in their guns. Early in the play, Goose informs Lorraine that "Tomtom's got a .38 magnum. I got a .38 special" (14). The description of these guns is relevant to how these men imagine themselves. Goose's .38 special is also known as a detective's gun — snub-nosed and easily concealed in a jacket pocket, yet more powerful than a small .22. Tomtom's "magnum" is the type of gun preferred by many male heroes in both film and television from Dirty Harry to Magnum P.I.

In addition to the images evoked by these guns, other significant props and costumes abound in this play to reflect the men's image of themselves. After the two characters have had an exchange of dialogue determining that both are scared and unhappy, Tomtom questions Goose fearfully, "You cryin'?" And when Goose admits that he is, Tomtom offers, "You wanna put on your cowboy suit? We could put on our cowboy suits" (29). And he finally gets Goose to accept "just the hat" in order to make him feel better (29). The cowboy duds, epitomized by the hat, are offered as a mask for the absence of Goose's actual courage and toughness. If the type of guns they have resonate with iconic significance, so do the types of hats. Goose's hat is a Stetson, as Rabe makes explicit in the stage directions (29). While Stetson makes many types of hats, the brand name evokes most prominently the epitome of the cowboy hat — the kind that is supposed to stay on no matter what befalls the cowboy, or, as the commercial for the cologne of that name assures us, "Stetson fits." The hat — being a Stetson after all — miraculously restores Goose's confidence because, as Goose says, "It's a great fuckin' hat" (29).

With this costume, Goose is able to feel more in control of his environment, although visually he could be made to look ridiculous. By putting on the hat, Goose is supposed to represent the hero. In fact, Tomtom wants to put him in that role when he tells Goose: "I wish you was here an' that hat on when them ghosts came by last night" (29–30). Goose with his hat on would have been, in Tomtom's mind, some sort of protection from the threats that haunt him at night. Prompted in part, no doubt, by the change in Goose when he dons his costume, Tomtom soon works on his own costume in order to make him "feel better" too. He begins "breaking out crates of weapons ... putting on additional shoulder holsters, along with knives and pistols strapped to his ankles" (30). Here Tomtom is turning his body into a walking weapon, reminiscent of the macho images portrayed by Sylvester Stallone and Arnold Swarzenegger in such films as *Rambo*, *Commando*, and *The Predator*. Goose and Tomtom's dependence on such props as guns and hats not only highlights their childlike approach to the world as they play "dress-up," but also demonstrates that Goose and Tomtom understand their masculinity as a masquerade, as an act for which they must costume themselves.

Although their dependence upon props and costumes highlights their troubled performance of masculinity, the insecurity of masculinity is reflected in language as well. The instability of language indicates the unstable sign system to which the characters adhere. These men are not only unsure of their masculinity but of their very existence. Each is troubled by the fear that he does not exist outside of his own perceptions, and each needs reassurance that other characters acknowledge his existence. As a result of these fears, the two men must constantly catalog their actions and their surroundings, clutching onto objective reality and ultimately looking to each other for assurance of their existence. "Do you see Goose, Tomtom?" Goose asks anxiously (43). And later, to reinstate his existence in relation to objective reality, Goose declares, "I am Goose and this is a chair!" (43).

In many ways, then, this play is an exercise in speech-act theory. Rabe has commented on his interest in language not as it reflects upon objective reality but as it serves to create it — "that language creates the chair" (Zinman 5). Particularly in reference to *Goose and Tomtom*, Rabe has said that in writing this play he "had the feeling that language can cast a spell on you" (Zinman 5). For the characters in *Goose and Tomtom*, speaking a fear or desire or fantasy makes it real, and other characters immediately act upon that new reality, although neither Goose nor Tomtom is in control of their language or reality. Their tentative hold on reality, and on their masculinity, is reflected in the power they associate with women. When Goose ventures the idea that he was afraid to look into Lorraine's eyes because he thought he might disappear, Tomtom immediately takes up this fear as a reality and exclaims, "You wanna fuckin' disappear? You look into her eyes, you'll fuckin' disappear!" (34). To further emphasize the way that language creates reality in this play, Rabe has Goose suggest that they kidnap Bingo's sister, "tie her up in there [the closet], hang her from the hook, take her out, pump her, man, put her back; she wouldn't know what she was doin', but she'd like it" (19). Not long after this suggestion, Bingo's sister enters from the bedroom, bound and gagged, evidently the victim of Goose's earlier plan. Goose and Tomtom are confused and even frightened by seeing their fantasy come to life yet realize that they must accept Lulu's presence as if they had kidnapped her in order to pretend they have some control over their environment. Even deciding that Bingo is somehow responsible for stealing their jewels becomes a reality when Goose returns from killing Bingo carrying the jewels that were evidently inside Bingo's body. However, neither Goose nor Tomtom understands the power of their words. Far from being in control of their language, they are confused and even frightened whenever an earlier statement is then enacted by other characters.

If saying something makes it so, then the stories that these characters tell of their dreams and pasts are literally "creation" stories that not only report but create their positions within the play. However, the men do not seem to understand how the language game works and so are unable to be in control of the very stories they create. The first stories we get from Goose and Tomtom are retellings of dreams that they have had, although neither is completely sure that these were merely dreams. Both have seen witches and ghosts in their dreams. Goose recounts a meeting he had with a ghost who told him "the secret" that he is actually a frog turned into a person because he "made the ghost a promise," although he is not sure what the promise was (26–27). Throughout the play, Goose is convinced that he was once, and may become again, something subhuman — a frog. This fear heightens his paranoia that encourages him to cling to objects such as his gun and the chair in order to confirm his humanity and his manhood.

Tomtom's story of his encounter with ghosts also has relevance to the end action of the play, although the audience, like Tomtom, remains unsure of how much this story is a prediction of the end and how much it is a cause of that end. Tomtom's "psycho ghosts with evil hearts" under black hoods who came into his bedroom last night looking for "somethin'" eventually return to take away Lorraine in the closing moments of the play (30). The men's stories all recapitulate in one guise or another the male fear of emasculation — of losing control, of becoming object rather than subject.

The last story, told by one of the masked figures at the close of the play, is an amalgamation of the fears that other characters have expressed concerning the power and position of men and women as well as the threat of invasion. The hooded man tells of a simple society that believed "we saw a uniformity in the design of all things in which our place, should we ever come to understand it, would be equally harmonious" (116–117). Sexual difference was established between "those of us who peed standing up and others who peed squatting" and in which the female "mystery" of creating life was recognized and worshipped in "awe" (117). This vision is projected as being harmonious until "barbarians" came and shattered their harmony, indicating a fall from a simple world, one that initiates them into a competitive world where now,

> Though we could not have before conceived of such deeds, we pillage and we are dismayed. We kidnap that which others value ... though we ourselves do not often understand this value, and we are dismayed [117].

These invaders thus explain that their aggressions are fueled by fear that if they do not take what others value, others will take their valuables. Yet, even these figures who display frightening powers of destruction do not see themselves as being fully in control of their own actions. Through the characters' stories, actions are always established as *reactions*.

Reaction rather than original action is prevalent throughout the play and indicates the sense of powerlessness of the titular characters. Neither Goose nor Tomtom sees himself in a secure position, much less a privileged one. The final invasion simply enacts the fearful events against which they have been barricading themselves throughout the play. Even though they can create "realities" through speech, neither is fully aware of this relationship between language and reality. Thus, they simply remain confused as to why events occur as they do. They have barricaded themselves in their apartment, surrounding themselves with weapons, and are intent upon developing elaborate "plans" of what is going to happen next, reviewing their previous activities and wondering how to handle future events. Yet, they remain unaware that the actual instigators of the events in their lives — their own fears and "their" woman Lorraine — remain inside the barricade with them.

Ideas of women in this play provide at least part of Goose and Tomtom's insecurity. The portrait of women is as cartoonish as is the portrait of Goose and Tomtom. Lorraine and Lulu present two extremes of female positioning within a male-ordered world. goddess and whore. However, the positioning of these women as simple objects for the men becomes complicated as the power relationships between them waver. Lulu's stories attempt to rewrite her sexual objectification into a position of power over men, making the bound Lulu seem to be in control of how she came to her current position in the play. Born in some "faraway sky," she is convinced of her "royal and cosmically magnificent origins" that ensure her certain rescue by a hero "with wondrous muscles and grace" (60–61). Although her story seems more like fantasy compared to other stories in the play, which are usually followed by some confirming evidence of their partial reality, the destruction that Lulu speaks of does occur by the end of the play, indicating her story does have relevance to the play's reality.

While Lulu's power is clearly tentative, Lorraine's power is acknowledged by both Goose and Tomtom. Lorraine is both their most prized possession and their greatest threat, raising questions as to how much she is "possessed" by these men and how much they are the ones "possessed" by her. Although she constantly claims that she wants to be beautiful, to bedeck herself with diamonds, only to please Goose and Tomtom, her actual motivations remain an utter mystery to the men. This mystery, this inability to predict what Lorraine wants and what she is going to do next, frightens Goose and Tomtom, encouraging them to act with the uncertainty of children in the face of a demanding parent's discipline and affection. Above all things they fear Lorraine's wrath: "Just don't make her mad, okay?" Tomtom tells Goose (58). Their fear of Lorraine's anger stems from their belief in her supernatural powers. For instance, they believe wholeheartedly that Lorraine has the power to make them disappear, a fear that is connected to woman's role in the sex act as much as it is to woman's supposed role as reflection of man: if she refuses to reflect them, they disappear. Goose and Tomtom also believe that Lorraine can hear everything they say to each other even when she is not present and that she can cast spells and predict the future. Their fear of Lorraine, heightened by their belief in her powers, means that Goose and Tomtom are willing to offer her anything, even their own body parts from penis to liver, in order to appease her.

During the second act, Lorraine parades around the stage clutching a hunk of meat that is supposed to be Goose's liver. While this is perhaps a visual pun on the idea of goose liver pate, her possession of Goose's vital organ, which she acquired after having sex with Goose, again calls into question who "possesses" whom. The sex act earlier played out offstage between Lorraine and Goose further indicates the dominated rather than dominating role of these men in relation to Lorraine. Lorraine initiates the action, and neither Goose nor Tomtom exhibit any real choice in the matter. Evoking the male fear of castration when confronted by the sexual force of women, Goose chronicles his encounter with Lorraine from offstage:

> Tomtom, she's kissin' me. She's kissin me.... She's got my little penis, Tomtom. She's got it. She's doin' stuff to it. Tomtom! ... You there, Tomtom? You there? She's kissing me ... I can't see my little penis. I can't see it.... Is anybody out there? Is anybody out there? [58–59].

Goose's exclamations concerning intercourse reflect how "little" and vulnerable he sees himself in comparison to the engulfing sexuality of Lorraine, which he fears can make him "disappear." During this encounter, Goose loses not only his penis and liver to Lorraine, but also his Stetson — a loss that becomes an objective correlative of his obviously precarious manhood.

Goose's loss of his hat worries Tomtom immensely. In act 2, he asks Goose where it is, and Goose replies, "I left it" (71), evidently meaning that he left it in the bedroom after having sex with Lorraine. A few lines later, Tomtom tells Goose to go get the hat because, he says, "I wanna see you with your hat on.... You could do anything, you was in your hat" (73). Here Tomtom acknowledges that without the hat, Goose is capable of very little because it is the hat that makes the man. Goose's brief search for the hat is futile chiefly because he will not venture back into the bedroom (Lorraine's territory) to look for it. Later, Lorraine enters from the bedroom "flirtatiously putting the cowboy hat on" as Rabe's stage directions tell us (87). She has taken the hat from Goose and possesses it as she possessed him. Slowly she is obtaining Goose's vital organs and vital signs, and in so doing, obtaining the power associated with them.

The fear that the two men exhibit towards Lorraine competes with their desire for her until Lorraine becomes, by the end of the play, another image of witchery, recalling both Tomtom's and Goose's terrifying experiences with witches turning them into animals, which they recount at the beginning of the play. Appearing in the second act in gypsy dress with a crystal ball in hand, Lorraine threatens to cast a spell and then proclaims to Bingo, "You are dead. You stole our jewels and you are dead" (95). Her power to bring death, however, has less to do with the supernatural than it has to do with her control over Goose and Tomtom. Goose is the one who actually takes Bingo away to kill him in order to make valid Lorraine's speech act; yet the men seem unaware of the part they play in Lorraine's power to predict or control events.

Ultimately, the relationship between Lorraine and the two men is detrimental to the male identity in the play, although the men's desire for Lorraine is predicated upon their concept of male identity. Lorraine is the main — perhaps the only — reason why Goose and Tomtom do the things that they do, robbing banks and killing people. They act tough in order to obtain jewels to appease her and so that she will respond by affirming their toughness (maleness) to them. Without her, they have no purpose and no identity, so that as much as they fear her, they fear the loss of her even more. She is supposed to be a part of their trappings of masculinity, a reflection of their power as men, yet she is clearly a sign that they cannot control. In fact, she takes over many of their symbols of masculinity — the cowboy hat, the penis — and basically confiscates their power. By the end of the play, she "owns" their identity because she has obtained many of the most important symbols of their masculinity. Their greatest fear is thus realized at the end of the play when the dark figures take Lorraine away, because in losing Lorraine, Goose and Tomtom also lose many of the trappings by which they have come to identity themselves as men. Lost and upset, they quickly attach themselves to Lulu as the new reference point of their lives, indicating the cyclical nature of their lives — they do not progress to any higher level of understanding concerning their world or their place in it.

In further discussing this play, Jennifer McMillion asserts that Goose and Tomtom value the male bond because it allows them "to submit themselves to a higher order of unified beliefs as a way of evading responsibility for their actions ... and it encourages a reversion to childishness" (179). By depicting so clearly this childishness and the lengths to which these men go in order to avoid responsibilities, Rabe's play indicates the inherent paradox of manhood as it is often still culturally perceived and presented in America. To achieve the fantasy image of the tough guy, hero, "real" man, a man must revert to childish playacting. By depicting so clearly the correlations between sign and identity and the slippery relationship his characters have to the "ownership" of signs and their meanings, Rabe's play indicates the inherent difficulty of maintaining a gender identity that relies on an intricate interplay of symbols for its existence — symbols that form around the actual disappearance of power for the men in this play.

Myths of Male Friendship II: *Hurlyburly*

The incomprehension concerning identity and responsibility played out in *Goose and Tomtom* is treated more realistically in Rabe's next play, *Hurlyburly*. *Hurlyburly* explores the failed dynamics of male friendships in light of changing gender dynamics in America. Rabe writes in his afterword to the first edition of the play that he was interested in exploring "the current disorientation and accompanying anger many [men] feel at having been flung out from the haven of their sexual and marital contexts and preconceptions" (1985, 161). This statement implies that men, through no action of their own, have been banished from a comfortable, secure, simple world. Interestingly, however, these victimized men in *Hurlyburly* are would-be corporate raiders, players, and playboys who would seem to be in powerful positions within the American culture. In the course of the play, however, we witness their confusion and sense of displacement as they try to figure out how to cope with the lives that they, quite obviously to the audience if not to the characters, have created for themselves. Their confusion seems to arise mainly from their inability to see the role they have played in creating their lives, and their pain is intensified by their desire to avoid responsibility for the problems inherent in those lives. "Coping" for these men becomes "escaping" as they turn to drugs and other obsessions, paradoxically, both to escape from and to assert macho attitudes.

As in *Goose and Tomtom*, the men of *Hurlyburly* have only two central images of women: woman as victim (Donna) and woman as desirable sexual object yet also uncontrollable sexual subject (Darlene). The men of this play, again, are lost and confused; they search for an identity out of which to construct themselves yet are unsure in which identities to invest. Separated from meaningful relationships with their wives, they turn to other men for friendship and other women for sexual release. But friendships turn into competitions, and, instead of a means through which they might assert masculinity, sex becomes a method of escaping its responsibilities. The toll that these limitations and demands take on the characters is evident most obviously in Phil's death and Eddie's confusion. The playboy lifestyle is examined in this work as the destructive tendencies of its characters are explored.

Although Philip Kolin, voicing an idea prevalent among other critics, interprets *Hurlyburly* as a reflection of "American society caught in the hurlyburly of dehumanization and despair" ("Staging" 77), it is difficult to imagine Mickey, Eddie, and Phil widely representative of society, or, at least, of its female half. As his working title "Guy's Play" indicates, Rabe's play is about "guys" in contemporary America as they confront tensions unique to their development of masculine identity.[10] Certainly some of their confusion is shared by the women in this play, but the anger and self-doubt of these male characters is made specific to their gendered experience. At the same time that they berate their (ex-)wives, they also wonder about their roles as fathers. They fear for their children yet remain unable or unwilling to be responsible parents, largely because they have not yet learned how to be responsible for themselves. They rely on sex and on drugs to distance themselves from themselves. Much like the characters of Mamet's plays, these men speak aggressively yet end up asserting nothing. Speaking rather than listening, they hope to make up in volume and vigor what they lack in content. Their desire to believe that there is a destiny that shapes their ends is in part a move further to absolve these characters of blame for the directions of their lives.

This desire to displace blame and responsibility exhibited by the male characters of *Hurlyburly* is not an unusual desire for men in American culture. We have already seen such tactics used by the men in Mamet's plays. In addition, we can find similar tactics employed within the more conservative branches of the men's movement. For instance, the ideology exhibited by the characters in *Hurlyburly* is much akin to views expressed by George Gilder, who writes of the dangers of single life for American men. In his 1974 study of unmarried men in America, Gilder comments that "Single men are not in general very good at life.

Often they know little about the most important parts of it. But they are sometimes fiercely ingenious at death" (25). In his argument, Gilder attempts to prove his idea that "Men need women — far more than women need men — for their very survival" because men alone cannot find reason or will to live (28). As proof of this "natural" (inherent) tendency within men, Gilder cites the overwhelmingly high percentages of single men (divorced, separated, widowed, or never married) who abuse drugs, commit violent crimes, are involved in accidents, commit suicide, and suffer from mental disorders. His extremely conservative argument basically absolves men of responsibility for their own lives by making claims to the "inevitability" of the sociobiological destiny of men as destroyers and putting the burden of saving and civilizing men onto women. The men of *Hurlyburly* mirror this attitude toward their own roles and toward those of women, reflecting a perception of male irresponsibility that is often absolved with the well-known phrase, "boys will be boys." Rabe's afterword to this play attributes his male characters' problems to their having been "flung out" of the safe harbor of female nurturance, a description similar to that used by Gilder in his study of single men. This "flinging out" avoids any agency, implying that these men are merely victims of rather than actors in the events of their own lives. Despite Rabe's intention to absolve his characters of responsibility for their actions by presenting them as mere victims of social changes in gender roles, the text also demonstrates, though perhaps unwittingly, that these characters destroy themselves precisely by surrendering responsibility for their own lives.

Aside from blaming women, these men also blame their problems on fate or destiny. To one extent or another, the men in this "Guy's Play" seem incapable of escaping a strong sense of the destiny of their own violent, confused, and tortured lives. They search for connections to life, which they see only in women and children and which they attempt feebly and unsuccessfully to work out in friendships with other men. Ultimately, though, they see their salvation as a return to a world in which women are responsible for healing male wounds and shoring up male ego. That world, however, only exists — if it exists at all — in childhood, and so their search leads to an unproductive, even destructive regression on the part of these men. Having failed or been thrown out of "serious" relationships with wives and girlfriends, the men of *Hurlyburly* turn to brief sexual exploits with "bimbos," "broads," and "bitches," although given the ways they refer to their wives and girlfriends, it is not clear that they actually differentiate among the women they know. Divorced or separated from previous wives, Mickey, Eddie, Phil, and even Artie have not simply retreated into a single's playboy lifestyle but have regressed into an adolescence and childhood that is as destructive as it is unfulfilling.

The key to this interpretation of *Hurlyburly* is in the obviously childish behavior of these men. Even the stage directions in the 1985 Grove Press edition indicate their childish behavior. For instance, at Mickey's first entrance, Eddie and Phil become "like two bad little boys with a babysitter they don't much respect" (25). A few moments later, as Phil waits for Eddie to finish talking with Mickey and come back to him, Phil is "like a kid on a street corner, ... hang[ing] around one of the balcony support beams" (29). The effect of these actions is to make clear that these men are merely "playing" house, and their version of it is the bachelor's pad: "So this is the bachelor life!" Phil exclaims (48). Later when Bonnie returns after Phil has thrown her out of her own car, Eddie has no idea of how to assess the situation and so begins "reacting increasingly as a little boy," mimicking Bonnie's movements and recoiling from her justifiable anger "as a child might" (109). Rabe's revised version of the play published in 1991 does not notably change these types of stage directions, although the revisions of the play are intended to make this childish behavior more understandable to the audience.

In addition to these specific stage directions, the dialogue of these characters clearly indicates juvenile discourse. Mickie, Phil, Eddie, and Artie are constantly playing games of verbal keep-away, and their taunts and teases seem more appropriate to playground pals than to corporate colleagues. Everything about the way they behave, from their dialogue to their body movements, reflects the passions and fury of adolescence (as several critics note, "perpetual adolescence"[11]) in which self-image is not fully formed and so overasserts itself, always in danger of being crushed again. Theirs is the mental age of teenage gangs, secret codes, and insider lingo. The bachelor's pad has become a teen clubhouse, hardly a positioning of these men to be respected or admired or, for that matter, sympathized with, however much Rabe may intend for his audience to do so.

Having abandoned their roles as husbands and fathers, these characters are left only with their friendships, which are anything but secure and reassuring. It becomes clear as the play progresses that these men are able to retain their level of friendship only because their relationships are of the most superficial and self-serving kind, or as Mickey says, they are merely "adequate" (1985, 152). Even Eddie's seeming devotion to Phil is self-interested, as Mickey points out and as critics of the play have agreed. He uses Phil as something of an experiment in order to keep himself relatively in control. Phil gives Eddie perspective, or as Mickey says, "Phil is very safe because no matter how far you manage to fall, Phil will be lower. You end up crawling along the sidewalk, Phil's gonna be on his belly in the gutter looking up in wide-eyed admiration" (1985, 102).

Eddie and Phil's characters were a source of controversy between Rabe and the play's original director, Mike Nichols. Rabe's dissatisfaction with Nichols's direction of the play led to his including a lengthy afterword to the 1985 edition and, eventually, to rewrites and a new staging that Rabe directed before publishing the 1991 revised version. Critics championed the original Broadway run as an important event, if suggesting that the play itself was an interminably long and sometimes flawed piece of work. Perhaps one of the most scathing yet perceptive comments appeared in *Women's Wear Daily*: Howard Kissel noted that "the characters verbalize endlessly, but their capacity to understand anything, especially themselves, obviously cannot be greater than the playwright's" (20). In fact, Rabe's afterword in the Grove Press edition more or less acknowledges his own inability to explain his characters until a chance encounter with some Jungian philosophy helped him along. This afterword, first published in 1985, as well as Rabe's comments on the production he directed in 1988, indicate that Rabe's vision of this play places it close to Gilder's perception of male behavior. By his connecting Eddie's "salvation" with a woman as mother figure, the play unconsciously mirrors even more closely Gilder's ideological stance that only by connecting himself to a woman can a man save himself from certain ruin. It is precisely this closure that Janelle Reinelt argues robs the play of any gender critique and simply reaffirms traditional concepts of gender roles.

In one of the few critical articles devoted to this play, Janelle Reinelt addresses the issue of gender representation in *Hurlyburly* from the point of view of its success or failure in meeting a feminist agenda. Reinelt argues that the women in the play are present only as they reflect, represent, or enforce male subjectivity, and because this is the traditional positioning of women in a patriarchal world, *Hurlyburly* merely reinforces the supremacy of male subjectivity at the expense of women. Certainly the women in this play are positioned by the men, and also by Rabe, to feed male fantasy and to reflect male subjectivity. What Reinelt never acknowledges is the extent to which this tactic fails for the men, and it is because of this failure that *Hurlyburly* ends up offering — most likely unintentionally on Rabe's part — a possible critique of traditional masculinity.

Reinelt notes that the constant repetition of terms such as "bitch," "broad," and "bimbo" objectifies the women in this play and supports the male subject position. However, as in *Basic Training* and *Sticks and Bones*, these terms do not represent the power of male subjectivity so much as the fissures in male identity. Precisely because they cannot construct themselves in any stable identity, they fear and therefore seek to diffuse the power that they envision women holding over them. Use of such terms arises out of fear and doubt, a reactive position that is hardly empowering, although often dangerous. Even Phil's infant baby girl is seen as something to fear by these men in part because she is soon to be a "broad" — something they cannot control. Yet, as much as they fear and fail to understand women, they also believe that they need them. Like Goose and Tomtom, these men believe it necessary to attach themselves to some idea of woman as life force at the same time they fear disappearing into this image. This dilemma is played out in Phil's relationship to his wife, whom we never meet and only hear about through Phil and Eddie. Without her, Phil believes that he has no connection to life and reality, and so he ends up spending his days driving in his car. Despite multiple fights with her, despite clear disparity between her goals and his, he cannot find meaning to his life without her. Phil decides that he must go back to her if he is to survive, even if returning means getting her pregnant, something that Phil fears. Mickey also comments that he is only avoiding reality until he goes back to his wife and family, something he sees as inevitable: "I'm basically on a goof right now. I'm going back to my wife and kids sooner or later" (1985, 53).

Although certainly interested in woman as sex object, as represented by Donna and Bonnie, these men are swayed most by the fertility-goddess image of women, the idea of woman's mystical power to create life, as represented by all their wives who have custody of their children. The men of *Hurlyburly* see themselves as existing in a world completely apart from that of women and children — the life force in their worldview — and instead see themselves in a world of death and destruction so clearly marked off by Gilder's theories. They want to live but fear being consumed by their wives and children. Their concepts limit not only women, however, but also themselves. They want connections to life (Phil and

Eddie, especially) but cannot imagine these for themselves except in a return to childhood and to the mother figure, although mother figures, like all the women in this play (on- and offstage) at one time or another, reject these men.

Even though, as Reinelt points out, they seem to be mostly compliant sexual objects, the three women that appear onstage in *Hurlyburly* still maintain their own space and come and go as they please. Although the men at times hand them around like candy, they do so only as long as the women allow such behavior. Donna, the most clearly exploited of the women, is nevertheless able to assert herself when things have gone too far for her. At the end of act 1, Donna has had enough. As Phil explains to Eddie that he has to return to his wife, that he needs her for his very survival because "I'm lost without her" (1985, 71) — indicating how absolutely dependent on some idea of women these men have become — Donna comes marching down the stairs and proclaims, "You guys have cooked your goose. You can just walk your own dog, and fuck yourselves. These particular tits and ass are taking a hike" (1985, 71). Slamming the door on the sick and defeated Eddie and Phil, Donna's exit establishes that for whatever reasons the audience may not entirely understand, the three women that we see onstage have chosen to be with these men, but they can and do choose to leave them as well. Although at times they undoubtedly serve to complete part of the male subjectivity, this does not fully explain their actions. Darlene's relationships with Eddie and Mickey indicate a will of her own not fully defined by either man. Bonnie also rejects being labelled as an indiscriminate slut who has no right to complain when she is badly treated, emphasizing that her choice to sleep with a lot of men has no reflection on her right to be treated decently. Even Donna's return at the end of the play is precipitated by a need for food and shelter rather than any sense of obligation to or desire for these men.

The fact that these women should and can evoke the audience's sympathy is attested to by Rabe's revision of the play, which he undertook to solidify sympathy for Eddie in response to the original production that Rabe felt did not do Eddie justice. In this revision, Rabe was trying to make Eddie more sympathetic by modelling him along the lines of Jimmy Porter, who was envisioned by his creator as a sympathetic character despite his mistreatment of the women in his life. In recently published comments about the play, Rabe says of Eddie, "I felt that by the end you would be with him completely, and that the play would fall into the tradition of *Look Back in Anger*" (Zinman 223).

This revised version introduces a gun into the action, ostensibly to emphasize how close to the edge these characters really are, but no doubt also unconsciously or consciously drawing upon the idea present in both *Basic Training* and *Goose and Tomtom* that a man needs a phallic "gun" to assert or protect his masculinity. In the closing moments of the 1991 version, Eddie rants and raves with gun in hand, clearly getting ready to shoot himself. Rabe's intention is to show that Eddie is on the brink of suicide and is saved only by Donna's entrance. As Rabe explains it, "if she doesn't come in, he's dead. So she is an accident and she is destiny" (Zinman 225). This ending ties the play even closer to the limiting perceptions of male behavior that Gilder has explored. Donna is Eddie's fantasy of the nurturing, comforting, pleasuring female, and she is, to Eddie, his "savior."

Ready to "fuck" him if necessary, and content just to be off the streets, she is the only version of woman that Eddie and his friends can understand — non-threatening and, so the men hope, endlessly, even mindlessly, giving. But, quite clearly to the audience if not to the male characters, Rabe indicates that even Donna has her own agenda and a subjectivity that the men in search of mothers and playmates cannot recognize. Donna has little real interest in Eddie's state of mind toward her as she wanders around the stage in search of food and drink.

Eddie's behavior in this last scene as rewritten by Rabe is perhaps more of a regression into childishness than the earlier version indicated, especially as Rabe directed it. Rabe tells of directing this scene as a reenactment of the children's book *Are You My Mother*: "As Eddie pursued Donna through that last scene, asking her questions, I told Sean [Penn] who was playing Eddie to play that idea: Are you my mother?" (Zinman 225). Regression into childhood becomes suddenly salvation and resolution, and in this way *Hurlyburly* does follow the tradition of *Look Back in Anger* in which man and woman can find peace only in acting out childish fantasies. However, in *Hurlyburly*, unlike *Look Back in Anger*, it is not clear that the woman participates in these fantasies. The possibility for a less empowered male subjectivity within the play is, then, greater than Reinelt's otherwise strong reading perceives.

Despite Rabe's desire for the audience to sympathize with Eddie, *Hurlyburly* consistently demonstrates the loss and confusion inevitable for men who refuse to take responsibility for their lives and for their own identity. Eddie, Phil, and Mickey turn to women, to drugs, to sex, and to a vague sense of destiny in order to absolve themselves of blame for their current unhappy situations, but they end up increasing rather than lessening their pain and confusion. Even given the textual changes (relatively few) that Rabe made in his revisions of the play, it is not clear that understanding the sources of Eddie's behavior is going to encourage an audience, as Rabe seems to have intended, to sympathize with or to absolve his evasive behavior. Eddie cannot see that his refusal to accept the consequences of his actions is exactly what traps him into a cycle of abuse towards both himself and others. If Donna is the only salvation he can see for himself at the end of the play, it is clear that he is not saved. Rabe's intentions aside, this final image stands as an indictment of the view of male behavior that conservatives such as George Gilder offer us, and that Eddie and his pals have embraced, thus insuring not only their own destruction but the destruction of those who get too close. They keep waiting for someone else to come along and fix their messes, to make everything "ok" again. Their wives have not done this for them, neither have "their" bimbos, and neither have they been able to do this for each other. Rather than take that responsibility upon themselves, their last resort is to believe in destiny — the destiny of death that Phil enacts and that Eddie wants to believe is the message that will put his world to rights. The utter meaninglessness of Phil's suicide note, which Eddie clings to as some great revelation, only further indicates Eddie's inability to understand what is leading these men to destruction. Neither Phil nor Eddie realizes that a blind belief in "destiny" is as much a regression into childhood and an escape from personal responsibility as are drugs and sex and television. By uncompromisingly portraying the failures of his characters' elaborate schemes to shift responsibility for their lives away from themselves, Rabe's *Hurlyburly* demonstrates that such escapism for men is literally a dead end.

With *Hurlyburly*, gender dynamics concerning male evasiveness and female indifference are brought to a head. Both *Hurlyburly* and *Goose and Tomtom* ultimately serve to depict male entrapment as self-created by the unwillingness of their male characters to take responsibility for their own actions, for their own lives. Like the characters in the Vietnam plays who are too influenced by preconceptions of manly behavior to escape the destruction headed their way, so too the men of Rabe's later plays cannot see what is coming. The men remain, like Goose and Tomtom, unaware of the effects their own actions have on their world, unaware of their own ability to change their lives. As in Mamet's plays, no solutions to these male problems are offered, although the problems are made explicit (sometimes unintentionally) in play after play. The task of understanding these dynamics and entrapments, as well as of creating ways out of these destructive dynamics, is simply left to the audience as we watch the characters blindly follow their beliefs into oblivion.

Notes

1. In his interview with Toby Zinman, Rabe discusses the Jungian influences on his current works-in-progress. Also, in his afterword to both versions of *Hurlyburly*, Rabe refers to Jung's *Mysterium Coniunctionis* as a source of inspiration for him in interpreting the layers of meaning in *Hurlyburly*. In the 1985 version, these comments appear on pages 164–166, and in the 1991 version, on pages 202–205.

2. Many of the readings of Rabe's Vietnam plays appear in studies of Vietnam literature or of politics or military institutions. See, for example, Philip Beidler's *American Literature and the Experience of Vietnam*, Catherine Hughes's *Play, Politics, and Polemics*, and Carol Rosen's *Plays of Impasse*.

3. See also Joe Dubbert's *A Man's Place* for further discussion concerning the importance of war for American manhood.

4. See his comments in the foreword to *Basic Training* and *Sticks and Bones*.

5. In his stage directions, Rabe notes that the set of the Nelson's home must "belong to the gloss of an advertisement" (120).

6. Rabe comments in his interview with Philip Kolin that "the real core of the play is Ozzie" (155).

7. Douglas Watt notes in his review of the play that "it is the jumpy father Ozzie, desperately trying to keep the neat pieces of his TV-sitcom family in order, who is [the play's] central figure" ("Sticks and Bones" 364).

8. Carol Rosen (*Impasse* 252) and Janet Hertzbach (*passim*) both mention the turf "war" of this play, waged over control of the cadre room or "home."

9. Jean Baudrillard, *Simulations*, trans. Paul Foss, Paul Patton, and Philip Beitchman (New York): Semiotext(e), (1983) 11. All subsequent references are to this edition and will appear in text.

10. See Rabe's afterword to the 1985 edition, 170.

11. For example, see Beaufort 27 and Kroll 65.

Chapter 6

August Wilson:
Performing Black Masculinity

For many blacks, life is a relentless performance for the mainstream audience and often for each other.... Even when he is offstage, a black male may feel that he is onstage.— Majors and Billson, *Cool Pose: The Dilemmas of Black Manhood in America*

Dutchman is about the difficulty of becoming a man in America. It is very difficult, to be sure, if you are black, but I think it is now much harder to become one if you are white. In fact, you will find very few white American males with the slightest knowledge of what manhood involves. They are too busy running the world or running from it.— Amiri Baraka, "LeRoi Jones Talking"

Attempting to make visible the fracturings and the expectations that surround the performance of normative masculinity, this study has examined many of the powerful images and assumptions that shape characters in plays mainly by white men. The "appropriate" masculinity these characters privilege, however, is not only constructed in contrast to women, to the feminine, and to homosexuality, it also relies on certain assumptions about race and ethnicity. The way that these assumptions about race underlie white male characters' worldviews has appeared, though rarely overtly, in the plays already discussed. Precisely because they are usually not treated as an "issue," these racial assumptions are subconsciously accepted as fact, another "given" to simply accept rather than to change.

Neither Sam Shepard nor his critics have devoted critical attention to the structure of race in his theatrical world. The images against which his white male characters are measured, however, often include that of Native Americans. American Indian mythology, religion, and cultural objects appear in much of his work, usually portraying the Indian as containing a deep spiritual wholeness that the modern white man has lost. Shepard's appropriations are reminiscent of the uses of Native American culture that the Boy Scouts and many of the retreats of the men's movement have employed. Using drums and chants, or taking on "Indian" names, both groups adopt the warrior image, (the Indian as man of the woods, as hunter, as survivalist) and the image of the shaman (the mystic and the healer). Although these images are honored as positive images, taken out of the contexts of their specific cultures, generalized, and mixed with images from variously different tribal cultures, they smack of stereotype. Shepard's unexamined use of Native American images and rituals in plays such as *The Holy Ghostly*, *La Turista*, *Operation Sidewinder*, and *Angel City* attest to how thoroughly that culture has been appropriated and reinscribed by its colonizers, thereby denying that culture validity in its own right.

Shepard has never, evidently, been chastised for these often token appropriations of Native American culture, but his one real commercial and artistic failure occurred with *Operation Sidewinder*, which contains a group of Indians (some designated as Apache and some as Hopi, but all dressed in 1800s outfits of loincloths and moccasins) who kidnap the sidewinder computer because they believe it to be the return of their Snake God. In addition to these Native Americans, the play also contains several black revolutionaries who are reminiscent of the Black Panthers. The original version of the play provoked protests from black students at Yale who blocked the play's production there due to its stereotypical portrait of blacks (Zolotow 38). The play was finally produced two years later in New York, after Shepard rewrote scenes containing the black characters (DeRose 42–43). No similar concern, however, was raised over the stereotypical portrait of Native Americans in the play. Given the response to *Operation Sidewinder*, it would seem that until very recently, race issues dealing with black culture were the only ones "seen" by Americans. Shepard does indicate a somewhat limited awareness of the issues raised when attempting to address race questions. About *Dog*, an unpublished early play that has as one of its two characters an old man identified in the script as "Negro," Shepard told the editors of *Theatre Quarterly* that he has since learned that it was "uncool" for a white man to write a black character (Chubb 194). This interview, coming a few years after the incidents surrounding *Operation Sidewinder*, may exhibit his growing awareness of certain race issues, but at least publicly he has never questioned his uses of Native Americans.

Critics who examine Shepard's entire body of work usually refer to *Operation Sidewinder* as Shepard's one real foray into political issues and (because it is also his one big failure) as evidence that political issues do not really interest him.[1] While Shepard in general avoids political content in his plays, so that his versions of the politics of race tend to remain as unacknowledged undercurrents, David Rabe has stated that he sees race as being one of the main factors in the political event that most influences his theatrical world: the American involvement in Vietnam. American assumptions about Asians as "feminized" and weak, which falls in line with the Orientalism that Edward Said has so vividly defined, certainly led American policy makers during the Vietnam era into political blind spots about Vietnam. Rabe's take on these racial issues is summed up in his comment that it is fear of miscegenation that fueled the war, and his theatrical world in his first two Vietnam plays certainly reflects that. Of *Sticks and Bones*, he comments:

I consider *Sticks and Bones* to be as much about obsession as it is about tribalism — a more inclusive term than "racism" — just as I consider the root of racism to be sex, or more exactly miscegenation [*Stick and Bones*, Introduction xxiii].

The image of Asians in Rabe's plays is female, and it is the male character's involvement with this woman that tears his world apart. Pavlo is destroyed, after all, as a result of a fight over a Vietnamese whore. And David's breakdown occurs over his betrayal of the Asian woman Zung, whom he loved but whom he left in Vietnam because he chose to follow his family's code of acceptable behavior. In the world in which David grew up, a white man does not marry an Asian woman, and the ostracism afforded even the idea of sexual relations between a white man and an Asian woman is made vividly clear by Harriet's reaction to learning that David had slept with Zung. Harriet becomes physically ill, vomiting at the mere thought of a mixing of the races. And while Ozzie tries to understand this involvement as a male thing that has to do only with the sex drive, his references to Zung as a "yellow whore" and "some yellow ass" indicate that he can imagine the relationship in terms of prostitution only, not sincere affection. Although in Rabe's Vietnam trilogy the Asian is stereotyped as a female prostitute, he uses this stereotype to examine American stereotypes of Asians and of the submissive position America envisioned Asian countries should take in response to American political activity. His comment that the root of racism is sex further supports the idea that perceptions of race are closely allied to perceptions of gender.

Sticks and Bones is Rabe's only play that overtly treats Caucasian racism towards Asians, but *Streamers* turns to more familiar racial territory in its examination of conflicts between whites and blacks, and so it has been openly recognized by viewers and critics as dealing with racism, among other issues. Carlyle is the character who "introduces" the issue of race into the cadre room, but it would be more accurate to say that rather than introducing the issue, he simply voices what is already in place. His suspicion of the white man, and his dialogue with Roger warning him not to lose his black identity by conforming to white society, reflect the conflicted positioning blacks face in moving through a world determined by white power. But Billy's worldview is as firmly structured by racial tenets as is Carlyle's. The only difference is that Billy as a white male has the privilege of pretending race issues don't exist until forced to confront them. Billy's ultimate response when threatened by Carlyle is to reveal his own racism, wanting to scream "nigger" and finally to call out "Sambo! Sambo!" The confrontation between Billy and Carlyle points out that although they are thrown together in the same cadre room, the black and white men of *Streamers* finally inhabit different versions of that world because of their different racial positioning in a racist world.

In Mamet's stage world, the characters are almost exclusively white, and are governed by extremely severe and rigid concepts of racial supremacy. Of his plays treated in this study, only *Edmond* contains non-white characters, and those two non-white characters are both black — a black pimp and a black prisoner. These characters are significantly stereotypical versions of black men in American society, offering the portrait of black men as criminals and as sexually aggressive/dangerous. In contrast to the aggressive/dangerous portrait of blacks, the play also

offers the stereotype that blacks are inherently lazy. The white man whom
Edmond meets in a bar immediately connects with Edmond by way of a racist
comment that "niggers" have it easy. He goes on to say, "Northern races *one* thing
and the southern races something else. And what *they* want to do is sit beneath
the tree and watch the elephants" (226). Edmond's easy acceptance of this statement indicates his own racism, which is further exhibited later in the play. When
Edmond gets into a fight with a black pimp, he repeatedly calls the man "nigger,"
"jungle bunny," "coon," and then equates these racial slurs with gender slurs by
also calling the man "cunt" and "cocksucker." Finally, in prison with his black
cellmate, Edmond admits to the man, "I always thought that *white* people should
be in prison. I know it's the black race we keep there. But I thought *we* should be
there [...] to be with black people" (283–284). These last scenes with the black
cellmate bring out a complex image of white male fear, desire, and stereotyping
regarding the black man.

In addition to *Edmond*, *Glengarry Glen Ross* also reveals how the white men
of Mamet's world structure their self-image based on assumptions that they are
superior because of their whiteness. This assumption is so basic that the characters rarely even acknowledge it except in passing comments, such as those made
to and by Edmond. Characters in *Glengarry Glen Ross* employ racial slurs and
stereotypes with full confidence that their colleagues share their assumptions.
Moss, talking to Aaranow about Indians, whom he calls "Patels," comments,

> Fuckin Indians ... You see them in the restaurants. A supercilious race. What is this *look*
> on their face all the time? [...] Their broads all look like they just got fucked with a dead
> *cat*. I don't know [9].

Aaronow simply nods in agreement, just as he nodded in agreement with Moss's
derogatory comments concerning "Polacks." Clearly, Mamet's white men are
right to believe that other white men in their worlds share their racist assumptions.

Although the theatrical worlds of Shepard, Mamet, and Rabe encompass
racial issues, those issues are usually rendered invisible because of being unacknowledged by their male characters. Usually only in the treatment of black-
white conflict do these plays make racial issues apparent, reflecting the fact that
in American culture, racism has often been perceived as limited to black-white
conflict. Asians, Hispanics, Indians, Native Americans, and other ethnic and racial
groups have only recently been acknowledged more widely as facing racial stereotypes and limitations. If blacks have been stereotyped as the representative minority in this country, (largely, no doubt, because of their being the largest minority), then issues of how race intersects with issues of masculinity can readily be
observed in black-white relations.

Confronting August Wilson's theater, it is necessary to consider how ideas of
race intersect with ideas of acceptable masculinity. But to consider that Wilson's
black men confront racism while the white men in the plays of Shepard, Mamet,
and Rabe do not is to ignore the basic tenet of this study: the privileged position
of "normative" masculinity maintains its supremacy by writing over its own constructedness. Thus, the tenets of normative masculinity not only seek to displace

gender and sexual issues onto women and homosexuals, but also seek to displace race problems onto non-whites. Simply put, race issues are a deep part of gender issues because white male power is as dependent on the subjugation of non-whites as it is on women. Viewing issues of masculinity for black men simply makes this fact visible, rather than invisible (as it would seem to be in white male worlds). August Wilson's theater offers excellent texts for reading how race as well as gender factor into male conflicts with and struggles for normative masculinity. Any examination of Wilson's staging of masculinity, however, must take into account multiple contexts for reading his plays: the atmosphere of the time in which they were written (how his plays appear against studies concerning black masculinity); the tradition of staged masculinity in African American theater; and, for this study, the gender issues already raised in the works of Shepard, Mamet, and Rabe.

Black Masculinity

The staging of black masculinity in American culture is one point at which many of our culture's traditional assumptions concerning masculinity and the performance of gender reach their maximum stress. As this chapter's epigraph from the 1992 study by Richard Majors and Janet Mancini Billson indicates, although the performance quality of masculinity can become most evident in the behavior of some black men, that performance of masculinity is typically subject to the harshest judgments and fewest rewards in our masculinist culture. Impulses toward violent behavior that are legitimized by the dominant culture when enacted by white men often become viewed as pathological when "performed" by black men (Majors and Billson 13). This interpretation is supported by the fact that black men are usually penalized more stringently even for the same crimes than are white men.[2] Yet the desire for power, control, and emotional detachment, which are the hallmarks of what Majors and Billson refer to as the "cool pose" among many black men, is basically a version of traditionally violent American masculinity thrown into high relief by the confined spaces of inner cities. Majors and Billson define this "cool pose" as "a ritualized form of masculinity that entails behaviors, scripts, physical posturing, impression management, and carefully crafted performances that deliver a single, critical message: pride, strength, and control" (4). The "cool" refers to America's slang use of the term as indicating a calm, controlled, self-assured attitude. Majors and Billson align their use of the term "pose" with performance, and the term "performance" with Erving Goffman's dramaturgical analyses. They view this cool pose as a "carefully crafted persona based on power and control over what the black male says and does — how he 'plays' his role," noting that this performance changes with shifts in audience and is chiefly an essential tool for survival (28).

Judging by the body of literature currently in print concerning the men's movement, feminism, and civil rights, frustration concerning race, class, and gender seems to be rising. Susan Faludi, in examining the backlash against women in the 1980s, notes that collapsing resources, the rising cost of living, and increasing unemployment brought on by political and economic policies set by a largely white male government have also managed to blame women and minorities for society's economic woes. Economic difficulties have a direct effect on perceptions of manhood because, as Faludi points out, one definition of masculinity has remained constant for American men: a man's role is to be "a good provider for his family" (65). Much of the backlash against women, which Faludi details, grew out of male frustration of being unable to provide for women and children in a manner that affirms an American man's sense of his manhood. This type of backlash is, of course, also aimed at minority groups, as exemplified by the political arguments concerning hiring "quotas" (which many voices in the white culture claim are shutting whites out of jobs in order to give them to "less qualified" blacks and Hispanics) and the "reverse discrimination" allegedly created by affirmative action programs. This talk of quotas and reverse discrimination having such a detrimental effect on employment for white men in competition with black men becomes suspect when confronted with the Bureau of Labor Statistics for 1990 (a year in which the quota debate was especially hot), which reports an unemployment rate of 11.8 percent for black males as compared to 4.8 percent for white males (Majors and Billson 15). If white males, the most privileged members of American society, feel the crunch for jobs in an unstable economic environment, what must the economic environment look like for black males, who are traditionally blocked from the resources and connections allowed the white male? If a black man, like a white man, believes that the chief indicators of his masculinity reside in his ability to earn a living, to provide for and thereby to "head" his family, what happens when the possibility of such behavior is denied a man at the same time it is emphatically insisted upon by his culture?[3]

These issues are central to any study of black masculinity in American culture or American drama. In order to understand something of how concepts of manhood tend to be structured in American society for blacks, we can turn to any of a number of studies provided in the last two decades by African-American scholars. In 1978, James B. Stewart and Joseph W. Scott were the first to treat what they termed the "institutional decimation" of black males in America, examining the economic pressures that drove black men out of schools and legitimate jobs and into crime and the military, pressures that resulted in imprisonment and death for black men in record numbers.[4] 1978 also saw the publication of Michele Wallace's *Black Macho and the Myth of the Superwoman*, which examines how the Civil Rights Movement and especially the Black Power Movement absorbed certain patriarchal assumptions concerning men and women and ended up blaming black women for keeping black men from getting ahead. Wallace, among others, argues that the black man's struggle for liberation led him to abandon the black community and to refocus instead on asserting black masculinity.[5] Robert Staples's *Black Masculinity*, published in 1982, was one of the first book-length studies of the black male's "conflict with the normative definition of masculinity" (2). His discussion examines how this normative definition insists on economic empowerment as the basic evidence of a man's masculinity at the same time that economic disempowerment deprives so many black men of being able to fulfill this definition. In line with this study, the highly influential 1988 publication of

Young, Black and Male in America: An Endangered Species, edited by Jewelle T. Gibbs, marked a culmination of issues concerning conflict within the black community in America that had been treated in articles and books throughout the late 1970s and the 1980s.

The statistics concerning violence among black males are alarming, to such an extent that the terms "institutional decimation" and "endangered species" hardly seem overstated. Gibbs reports in his study that a black male has a 1 in 21 chance of being murdered before age 25, usually by another black male (15). More recently, Jessie Jackson in many of his public addresses has pointed out that more black men are dying today at the hands of other young black men than were killed in the entire history of lynching. Although statistically alarming, what may be even more alarming is that the violent behavior of many black men in America is not in actuality out of line with the country's violent ideological concept of masculinity. Most of the scholars cited above do not interpret most black males' definition of masculinity as greatly different from the definition shared throughout American culture. What they note is the results that occur when black men are offered few legitimate methods of enacting the traditional model of masculinity. In short, the violent and (self-)destructive behavior encouraged by the enactment of traditional masculinity is not qualitatively much different among inner-city black youth than it is within the white culture's traditional ideology of masculinity as represented by, for instance, the cowboys of Sam Peckinpah's westerns or Clint Eastwood's "Dirty Harry" movies — representative mythic images of male America. However, unlike the cowboys and cops of film (or the would-be cowboys of Shepard's plays), urban black men's enactments of this violent masculinity are not culturally condoned. Neither are they usually allowed, like their white counterparts, to subvert the power games into more generally acceptable modes of behavior. Although Mamet's men fight viciously in enclosed spaces over limited resources, at least they can claim the realm of business as the place where they can enact the competitive games that seem vital to their sense of manhood. The high levels of unemployment among black men, and the dominant culture's underlying assumption that black men are generally unhirable, however, removes the space of the business world for many black men in America, leaving them, instead, urban centers such as Harlem and South-Central Los Angeles, where the performances they enact are usually labelled pathological.

In light of the violence enacted by and upon urban black males, August Wilson's drama of blacks migrating to northern urban centers in the first half of this century is a history with particular resonance. Wilson's project of writing a theatrical history of African Americans in this century contains traces and prototypes of the issues of black masculinity that have come to the forefront during the past two decades.[6] In so doing, his plays offer another lens through which to view the stagings of masculinity already treated. Wilson's vibrant portraits of the black community also afford a deeper look into the complexities of what is occurring in America's stagings of masculinity both in and out of the theater, not merely in the way our culture privileges and validates violent "macho" behavior as somehow inherently "American," but — more specifically — in the way that it privileges certain performances of that behavior and condemns others. How the

dominant culture ignores its own failings and shifts responsibility for those failings onto women and "other" men, particularly men of color, becomes more evident when issues of masculinity for white men are placed beside issues of masculinity for black men. Such is my project in this chapter, which examines
Wilson's five major plays produced to date: *Ma Rainey's Black Bottom* (1984),
Fences (1987), *Joe Turner's Come and Gone* (1988), *The Piano Lesson* (1990), and
Two Trains Running (1992).

Masculinity and the Tradition of African American Drama

   Before moving into a discussion of Wilson's plays, it is helpful to contextu-
alize his work within a set of questions about and a tradition of staging of black
masculinity. Wilson's work is affected by and responds to a broad theatrical tradition: it encompasses the white fathers of American drama and the dramatic pre-
decessors who helped to establish a theatrical tradition for African American
dramatists. These two traditions have some similarities to the staging of masculinity that Wilson offers. For instance, Wilson's staging of masculinity reflects
traditional American concepts of masculinity that tend to confuse "male" with
"universal" and to overlook gender issues for men. As noted in regard to both
Miller's *Death of a Salesman* and O'Neill's *The Hairy Ape*, the supposedly universal American dream is structured by both gender and class as being male and
upper class. Within some African American drama, as Baraka's *Dutchman* and
his revolutionary plays reflect, the presentation of masculinity has also been confused with the presentation of the black liberation movement and the fight to
attain for blacks the dignity and humanity all people deserve. Particularly in
regard to the latter issue, not only Baraka but also the highly influential Lorraine
Hansberry offer African American plays now considered canonical presentations
of male conflict as reflecting the culture's conflict. As a result, the black experience has in many regards been equated with the male experience. In sharp contrast to the militant theater of Baraka, Lorraine Hansberry's breakthrough play,
A Raisin in the Sun, stands at the forefront of a realistic style of presenting the
African American family that Wilson's plays evoke.[7]

   A Raisin in the Sun opened a number of doors for future black playwrights
by making it to Broadway and earning a Pulitzer Prize for its young, female
author. Hansberry's play also achieved a seemingly impossible feat in a racist
society: it was simultaneously accepted and lauded by representatives of the dominant class even as it critiqued the ways in which the dominant class maintains
its dominance, and it advocated, albeit subtly, resisting and ultimately over-
throwing such structures.[8] Margaret Wilkerson refers to this play as possessing
"strains of militancy" that were not recognized by early critics, and she comments on the extraordinary position that Hansberry carved for herself:

> That she, a black artist, could tell painful truths to a society unaccustomed to rigorous self-
> criticism and still receive its praise is testimony to her artistry [8].

Hansberry's play examines the Younger family's methods of struggling for their dreams and for a space to call their own in the black, working-class ghetto of Chicago. The family, at the beginning of the play, is matriarchal, as the widowed Mama is in control of her husband's money, in particular a $10,000 life insurance check that arrives during the course of the play. This image of a household headed by "Mama" in the absence of the father, Big Walter, resonates with significance as to the ways the black family structure has been scrutinized and theorized by social investigators. The 1965 Moynihan report on the Negro Family, coming out six years after Hansberry's Broadway debut, is the most influential example of the examination of the supposedly powerful matriarchy within black families that results in the emasculation of black manhood. Although this image of the matriarchy was argued against by many critics, it also sank into the American social perception of the black family.[9] Wallace argues that the perception that black women were part of the problem for black men was present in the culture before Moynihan articulated it, so that Moynihan's report became the confirmation that many black men and women needed to scapegoat the black woman because of her abnormal strength and her "masculine" behavior (30–33).

Given the way the structure of the black family has been debated in this country, the fact that the main conflict in Hansberry's famous play occurs between Mama and her grown son Walter for control of the insurance check further reflects American perceptions of how matriarchal control affects black manhood. Walter's firm belief in his right to the money and his sense of being oppressed by Mama, who initially takes control of the check, reflect the idea of black manhood being limited by the power of the matriarchy. Mama wants to use the money to help her whole family by setting some of it aside for her daughter's education and by using the rest to buy a house for Walter and his wife and children to live in with her. Walter, however, wants the money in order to achieve economic success for himself so that he can provide for his family on his own terms. Chiefly, Walter needs the money in order to feel like a real man in charge of his family rather than like a perpetual adolescent, relying on his mother to take care of him. For the first half of the play, however, he behaves more like an adolescent than an adult, especially in reaction to his wife and in front of his son. Although their money is extremely limited, Walter gives his son Travis a dollar as a way to prove his position as provider for the family in defiance of Ruth, his wife. But, after Travis leaves, Walter must then ask Ruth for carfare since his extravagant gesture has left him penniless. His interactions with his wife before this exchange establish their relationship as more that of a parent to a child than wife and husband. She encourages him to eat his breakfast when he gets distracted by his ideas of how to spend the insurance money, and he complains, sullenly, "There you are. Man say to his woman: I got me a dream. His woman say: Eat your eggs" (21).

Walter's need to fulfill his dream of financial independence finally drives him to despair. Unable to earn the money that he needs to feel like a man in front of his family, he ceases to work and sinks into an alcoholic stupor. To restore his confidence in himself, Mama decides to hand over her dream, by way of the check, into Walter's keeping, designating him the head of the household, the man of the house, because she realizes that by denying him this financial control, she "has been doing to [him] what the rest of the world been doing to [him]" (86). In handing Walter his father's money, Mama also hands him his manhood, which has passed from Big Walter to Walter through Mama. The matriarchy present at the beginning of the play has been a temporary state of affairs that ultimately supports the return of the patriarchy. Walter, however, is clearly not ready to be the patriarch of the family. When he subsequently loses the money to a shady business partner, he is forced to come to terms with his manhood not as economic empowerment but as an assertion of his pride and dignity as a human being. Only in refusing to be bought out by the white member of the housing committee does Walter solidify his family's stance against the racism they are about to confront head on and accept his responsibility to his family as the man of the house. Significantly, however, he learns this responsibility from his mother, who in turn confers on him his manhood by telling Ruth in the closing moments of the play, "He finally come into his manhood today, didn't he? Kind of like a rainbow after the rain..." (130).

The connection made in *Raisin* between the dignity of the black man and that of the black family/community is unmistakable. The family is able to pull itself together once they gain confidence in Walter's leadership. On a certain level, the play's conclusion indicates that the family cannot find its voice and power until it finds a patriarch to replace the deceased Big Walter.[10] Certainly Walter Jr. is not a strong emotional and spiritual advocate of his family until he believes he can control his own destiny as a man, can find his manhood, which is ultimately tied to his role as provider for the family. On the other hand, as Steven Carter argues, Walter learns by the end of the play to speak for his family and to put their needs over his own by learning to find his strength and manhood within his family rather than within the American dream of personal financial success. This interpretation sees Walter's acceptance of his manhood as not antagonistic to but as part of the family (24).

Although Walter learns to stand up for his family's identity, his road to manhood is clearly shaped by his mother in lieu of the absent father, Big Walter. Walter takes on his role most fully when he invokes his father's name for his actions: "We have decided to move into our house because my father ... he earned it" (127–128). Although Walter accepts a patriarchal inheritance much as Shepard's men do, unlike Shepard's men, he receives it through the matriarchal line. Walter's manhood is validated, then, not by other men but by the women in his family — his mother, wife, and sister. This staging of black manhood and its place in relation to the black community — particularly as represented by women and the family — is a recurring theme in Wilson's plays. In particular, *Fences* and *Piano Lesson* treat conflicts similar to those faced by Walter Younger: how does a man trained to view manhood as being marked by financial and emotional independence fit into the family that requires emotional commitment and financial support? This conflict between a man and his family is similar to that discussed in regard to Shepard's theater and its use of the western hero from film. As Laura Mulvey has argued, this western hero is split between self-interest (narcissism) and social responsibility, particularly as represented by women and the family (73). However, unlike Shepard's men, Wilson's male heroes are encouraged to bridge that split in order to achieve their manhood, which is then usually conferred upon them by women.

Wilson has said that his purpose in writing is to give African Americans an image of themselves that might help lead them to a greater self-awareness. He also desires his presentations "to demonstrate that [the black tradition] is able to sustain a man once he's left his father's house" (quoted in Devries, "August Wilson" 29). Like Baraka, who says in his essay "Home" that his chief struggle is "to understand where and who I am, and to move with that understanding" (9), Wilson's project of creating a history for African Americans ultimately posits a male audience as the chief beneficiary of that history. Wilson wants his plays to allow black Americans "in essence ... [to] recognize themselves" (Huang, 73), but the chief responsibility that concerns him is that of black men because "we have been told so many times how irresponsible we are as black males that I try and present positive images of responsibility" (Devries 25). At the same time, his choice to follow traditional theatrical forms of realism and melodrama and to work toward resolution sometimes causes him to write over the conflicts of gender, even as they foreground racial conflicts.[11]

In his portraits of black males, Wilson reflects the stagings of masculinity both within the family as has been set forth by *Raisin* and in contention with white society as portrayed in *Dutchman*. His male characters are affected by the assumption that manhood is often conferred upon or denied a man by women, but they also view their manhood as imperilled by white animosity. These pressures must be negotiated carefully by means of masks and performances such as that of the cool pose or the Uncle Tom pose. Consistently in all five of Wilson's plays, the central protagonist is male and the quest for identity becomes gender-specific for him rather than "universal." In short, the man's performance is what makes or breaks the black culture's image of itself in Wilson's plays.

Blues Men: *Ma Rainey's Black Bottom*

August Wilson's acceptance into the National Playwright's Conference at the Eugene O'Neill Center in 1982 eventually led to the production of his first Broadway play, *Ma Rainey's Black Bottom*, which opened at the Court Theater on Broadway in October 1984 and was directed by Lloyd Richards, the original director of *A Raisin in the Sun*. Wilson's play was initially inspired by the blues women of the '20s and '30s, as the title indicates. In his 1984 interview with Wilson, Feingold notes that "the classic blues singing of the '20s attracted [Wilson] for a variety of reasons: As women making notable careers in a male-dominated world, as artists giving universal expression, and as representatives of a culture with ties to his own black awareness" ("August Wilson" 118). Wilson himself speaks of his own encounter with the blues, particularly Bessie Smith's "Nobody in Town Can Bake a Jelly Roll like Mine," as revelatory: "I felt that someone was talking directly to me. I discovered through her singing an image of myself" (Freedman, "Playwright" 3). This, of course, is Wilson's intention in writing his plays, that they can provide his audience of African Americans with an image of themselves. "The

Blues," then, is fitting territory upon which to stage questions of black cultural awareness and identity. It has been tied so closely with the African American experience as
to prompt Baraka to refer to "the blues people" and the black culture as one and the
same (*Blues, Dutchman* 36). Like Baraka's Clay, who tells Lula that she does not understand Charlie Parker and Bessie Smith and all the "blues people," Wilson's Ma Rainey
says that whites have no clue as to the meaning of the blues for blacks:

> White folks don't understand about the blues. They hear it come out, but they don't know
> how it got there. They don't understand that's life's way of talking. You don't sing to feel
> better. You sing 'cause that's a way of understanding life [82].

The integrity of the blues, however, is challenged in *Ma Rainey* by the changing tastes of the market for which the white producers record Ma's music. As his
play developed during writing, Wilson began to focus on "the economic exploitation of black musicians" (Freedman "Black Writers" 7), and in doing so he shifted
his focus from the blues women as represented by Ma Rainey to the male musicians in her band. As Wilson puts it,

> I came back to the play in 1978 and I began to hear the voices of the band members.... The
> whole time I was writing, I was listening to records in my room. I was listening to the male
> blues singers — Charlie Patton, Son House — because I was writing the men in the band
> [Freedman "Black Writers" 7].

Although he began to write about the blues women as they struggled for success in the face of racism and sexism, *Ma Rainey* became a play about black men —
most specifically, about the troubled and tortured trumpet player, Levee. Levee's
desire to succeed in a white world by abandoning his roots in the black culture
is contrasted to that of Toledo, the older, self-educated man who seeks to learn
about his culture, and to that of Ma, who seeks to maintain the integrity of her
music in the face of exploitation. Assimilation versus separation becomes the
major conflict of the play, and *Ma Rainey* thus becomes a powerful expression of
the choices facing African Americans; however, this conflict is presented as being
faced by the black male, Levee, whose choices are not only racial but also gendered. He must choose between a black tradition represented by a woman and a
new style represented by the white man.

Levee's character offers much to examine regarding issues of black masculinity. In his desire to carve out a space for himself by establishing his own band
rather than playing Ma's music, he equates being in control of his own livelihood
with proof of his manhood. That Levee's chief competition is "Ma" suggests the
supposedly powerful black matriarchy that a black man must overcome in order
to prove his manhood. As in *Raisin*, "Ma" is the repository of the heritage and
holds the only financial power among the blacks in this play. To assert his independence from Ma's control, Levee has written a new version of her signature
song, "Ma Rainey's Black Bottom," which the white producer of the band wants
to use because "times are changing. This is a tricky business now. We've got to
jazz it up ... put in something different" (19). However, Ma resists this new version in favor of the original, and this battle between the original blues and the
new jazz version indicates the conflict between denying and celebrating cultural
roots, and this conflict is presented, in part, along gendered lines.

Understanding one's roots, or one's life, is a necessity echoed in the stories told by the men in the band. They uphold Ma's style of music and her loyalty to their roots, offering stories of their past to support their current position. These stories introduce long monologues into the dialogue, monologues that one critic has called "prose blues" (Smith 179), and through which each man asserts his style or identity within the band. Levee's entrance among the men in the band demonstrates immediately how he differs from them. Beginning with his new shoes, which assert the status he desires, Levee demonstrates his desire to break away from his past — clodhopper, sharecropper — to embrace a flashier, financially more successful future. Levee's purchase of Florsheims for $11 also indicates his willingness to "buy into" the commercialism of the American dream. The three other, older band members reject Levee's goals as being a denial of their backgrounds. Ma, especially, objects to Levee's plans for improving his lot by changing her song. She tells Irvin: "Ma listens to her heart. Ma listens to the voice inside her.... and ... Levee ain't messing up my song with none of his music shit" (63). Both Ma and Toledo point out that in looking out for his own interest, Levee is "messing up" the lives of the other musicians. Philip Smith describes Levee as "a black man alienated from the blues people, [transformed] into a foolish Faustian individualist searching for money, fashion, fame, sexual pleasure" (182). Levee is alienated in this play from the other black men because of the manhood he tries to enact, images that ultimately reinforce white images of black men. As Hansberry's Walter was initially willing to do, Levee will sell his soul to the white producers if it will bring him financial success.

Although not as personally aware of himself as are the other men in the band, Levee does understand, as they do, that navigating the white world is a task necessary for survival. Part of Levee's survival technique is the pose he presents to the white men in the play, a multifaceted pose that changes with his audience. Although to his fellow musicians, Levee plays the "cool" cat, he plays the accommodating Negro to both Irvin and Sturdyvant. Cutler and Slow Drag remark on Levee's "yessuh's" to the "boss" as he is "shuffling them feet" (67). Levee's attitude toward whites is, then, a consciously enacted performance of friendly subservience that differs markedly from the attitude he expresses about whites to the other black men: "I studies the white man. I got him studied good. The first time one fixes me wrong, I'm gonna let him know just how much I studied" (67). Levee's anger towards whites is revealed further in the story he tells of the gang rape of his mother by white men and of his father's revenge. Levee's double-sided pose is similar to that of Clay, whose initially demure demeanor belies his actual rage brought out by Lula. However, Wilson's drama shows that in choosing to play up to the white producer and manager in hopes of smiling his way into his own band, Levee denies the dignity that Ma Rainey demands in her encounters with Irvin and Sturdyvant. Levee envies what he sees as Ma's control over her own life but does not understand what she knows about that life because he does not have her connection with the roots of her culture.

Within moments of Levee's arrival, he and the rest of the band argue over which version of Ma's signature song they are to rehearse, Ma's or Levee's. Levee claims that he and Mr. Irvin have already worked it out to do Levee's version, something that Irvin affirms when Cutler finally asks him. However, Cutler's loyalty is first to Ma, as he tells Levee: "It's what Ma says that counts" (37). In response, Levee argues for Irvin's authority on the matter, claiming "Hell, the man's the one putting out the record! He's gonna put out what he wanna put out!" (37). Toledo, the self-taught intellectualizer, immediately points out the wider implications of the specific argument between Levee and Cutler:

> As long as the colored man look to white folks to put the crown on what he say ... as long as he looks to white folks for approval ... then he ain't never gonna find out who he is and what he's about. He's just gonna be what white folks want him to be about [37].

Toledo's speech echoes much of what Wilson has written about the need to know who one is and where one comes from. In many ways, Toledo functions in this play to remind the other characters of their roots, not only in the American South but also in Africa. This speech also implies that Levee's attempt at "progress" in the white man's world is actually a selling out. Rather than asserting his identity, Levee denies it. In doing so, he is also denying his responsibility to his culture and its people.

Levee's view of himself, however, is quite different from that voiced by the other members of the band. He believes that the other men have given in to the white man by settling for their underpaying jobs as accompaniment musicians. Levee hopes to play his own songs one day rather than someone else's. But his "own" songs themselves pander to the white producer. Unlike Ma, Levee has yet to learn of the exploitation inherent in the white producer-black musician setup, and what it means to hold the line against that exploitation. Although Ma demands to sing her songs her way, and holds out until she gets to, she is also aware of the slim margin of control she has as a musician. Unless she demands everything, she will not get anything, and her ability to make demands relies on the commercial demand for her voice. As she describes her relationship with Irvin and Sturdyvant:

> They gonna treat me like I want to be treated no matter how much it hurt them.... They ain't got what they wanted yet. As soon as they get my voice down on them recording machines, then it's just like if I'd be some whore and they roll over and put their pants on [79].

Ma refuses to pander to these men who control her finances because she is already aware of the game they are both playing. Levee's pandering fails to acknowledge that he needs something to bargain with besides his good manners. When at last confronted with his helplessness in the face of Sturdyvant's control, Levee's reaction further splinters the community of musicians in the play.

Angered at the death of his dreams by the rejection of Sturdyvant, who offers Levee only a few dollars for his songs, Levee vents his anger not on Sturdyvant but on Toledo, whom he stabs in the final scene for stepping on his Florsheims. Levee's actions reflect Majors and Billson's description of the cost of the cool pose:

> When cool behaviors are placed ahead of acknowledging and dealing with true fears or needs, pent-up emotions and frustrations result, which are then released in aggressive behavior toward those who are closest to the black male — other black people [19–20].

Although he had talked earlier about knowing how to handle the wrongs done him by the white man, Levee's murder of Toledo indicates how clearly he is not in control of his own actions, his own performance. The murder of Toledo is a physical acting out of the betrayal that Levee had been flirting with throughout the play. In the violence of his actions, Levee "foreshadows the next generation of blacks" as "a modern urban, alienated man, refusing to recognize that his individualism cripples him" (Smith 184), and, by extension, those whose lives are connected with his.

Family Men: *Fences, Joe Turner's Come and Gone,* and *Piano Lesson*

While *Ma Rainey* established Wilson on Broadway, *Fences* garnered Wilson his first Pulitzer Prize in 1987. This mark of acceptance into mainstream American literature and theater was perhaps influenced by the style and content of this play, which more than one critic has compared to the works of Arthur Miller and Eugene O'Neill.[12] Set in the 1950s, *Fences* explores the responsibilities and limitations of fatherhood and the difficulties of marital commitments for African Americans populating the industrial cities of the North after World War II. Troy Maxson, while more powerful a presence than Miller's Willy Loman, exhibits many of Willy's failings and blind spots. Where Willy was too certain his sons were destined to be successful, Troy is too certain his sons are destined for failure. These two fathers' mutual betrayals of their long-suffering wives are prompted by similar motives. Each turns to another woman to escape the sense of his own failure as a man, and in so doing, betrays the one person who believes in him even when he no longer believes in himself. And as in *Salesman*, *Fences* is ultimately the story of manhood as measured against that illusory American dream of material gain, only this time the struggles of the male protagonist are further heightened by questions of racism.

Fences is the story of Troy Maxson, a 53-year-old former baseball player, who once served time for stealing and now works as a garbage man in Pittsburgh to support his second wife and child. Troy's personality has been shaped by the harshness of his life: first in his contention with his father, a sharecropper in the South who drove Troy out on his own at age 14, and then in his contention with the white world. Although his responsibility to his current family drives Troy to work long hours at an undesirable job, the harshness he has cultivated in order to survive does not leave much room for him to express his love for his family. Troy has developed a pose of emotional detachment to buffer the disappointments in his life and to help him endure the brutal routine that keeps his family fed and clothed. His job means money for food and shelter, which he believes he owes his son and wife and which is a duty he fulfills while denying that it comes out of any sense of love. Troy prefers, instead, to define his actions as his responsibility. As he tells his son Cory:

> It's my job. It's my responsibility! You understand that? A man got to take care of his family.... You my flesh and blood. Not 'cause I like you! Cause it's my duty to take care of you.... Let's get this straight right here... I ain't got to like you [43].

In denying his emotional attachments to his family, Troy defines his achievements by money and sex, both of which are represented in the opening scene of the play. Troy and his buddy Bono enact their Friday night payday ritual of buying a bottle of liquor, which they drink together on Troy's front porch. They talk about their jobs as garbage men and of the women in their lives. Troy's union struggle to become the first black driver of a garbage truck indicates how much his identity is tied into his need to be evaluated fairly at work, however much he also hates the menial nature of his job. He is the breadwinner in his family, supporting not only his wife and teenage son but also his grown son by his first marriage.

Aside from his job, Troy's relationship with his wife Rose helps him to structure his identity along traditional gender lines. Like Willy Loman, Troy brings home his earnings into his wife's keeping, but unlike Willy, Troy asserts his sexual relationship with Rose as a mark of his own virility and as a method of coping with the limitations of his life. When she appears on the porch during his opening conversation with his friend Bono, he tells her, mainly for his own benefit in front of Bono:

> Well, go on back in the house and let me and Bono finish what we was talking about. This is men talk. I got some talk for you later. You know what kind of talk I mean. You go on and powder up [8].

Although Rose teases him in return, it becomes clear that Troy's sexuality is central to his manhood — so much so that he is willing to betray the wife he loves in order to prove to himself that he is still desirable and virile. Yet Troy still manages to evoke sympathy, for Wilson's portrait of him suggests that the hardness in his character results from the harshness of his life.

The way in which Troy represents a whole strata of black masculinity is clearly reflected by the critical reception of the play. Frank Rich writes that James Earl Jones (who originated the role of Troy) "embraces all the contradictions of being black and male in America in his time" ("Family Ties" 3) and that he represents "a generation of black men driven half-crazy by a social status that was half-slave and half-free" ("Wilson's" 17). Brent Staples's review refers to his personal experiences in order to describe how Troy's character resonates familiarly within the black community. Staples refers to Troy Maxson as an accurate portrait of his own father and uncles, describing him as the father figure familiar to a generation of African American men and women growing up in the '40s and '50s:

> Our fathers had by circumstances become nearly impossible to love. They were hard men, tall in green work clothes — just like the ones James Earl Jones wears in the first act of this play. Theirs was the steely love of men who view the world from the angle of one who toils with his muscles [1].

Later in the same article, Staples refers to Troy as

> at once the universal lost father, and in particular that absentee father who fled rural Mississippi or the hellish inner city of the North leaving behind wife and children seeking some place, as Troy puts it "where I can just laugh" [39].

Staples's response to Troy is not simply that he is an accurate portrait of a real life experience, but that in Troy, Wilson has given his black audiences an image of themselves. For men like Staples, he is the father they could not fully understand. And for the women in the audience, Staples reports:

> These women, one might guess, have lived and breathed a Troy Maxson, and they seem to know the specific terrain upon which one deals with a man like him, how he can love, how he can betray, and how he — black and male in the pre-civil rights America of the 1950s — has also been battered and betrayed [39].

Staples's reading of these women implies that they see their own experience reflected not in Rose but in Troy, an image that they have "lived and breathed." This reading also points to the powerful resonance of the character of Troy Maxson as representative of the black experience in America, thereby equating that experience with the male experience.

The gendering of black experience as chiefly a male experience is not mitigated in this play despite the strong voice of Rose, who in act 2 speaks of her disappointments and betrayals. When Troy admits his unfaithfulness after 18 years of marriage *and* brings home a baby from his affair for Rose to raise, she accepts the innocence of the child but refuses to absolve Troy. Like the long-suffering Linda Loman, Rose continues, however, to cook and clean for Troy, and in the last scene of the play, after Troy's death, she defends his failings to Cory in order to bring about a final reconciliation between Cory and his father. Rose's life story is thus made part and parcel of Troy's. So, too, is the life and death of the "other" woman who remains offstage. All that is shown of her is her child, whom Troy brings onstage and who represents the living proof of his sexual power. Paradoxically, however, in proving to himself his own manliness through fathering this child, Troy cuts himself off from his wife and son and breaks apart the life that he and Rose had built together.

Despite his sense of responsibility, Troy manages to alienate not only Rose but also his son Cory. Troy's relationship with his son is reminiscent of the alternately caring and quarrelsome exchanges between Willy Loman and Biff, a relationship that Miller presented as a key part of Willy's vision of himself. Because sons are often considered a reflection of a man's masculinity, Troy, by alienating Cory, can be interpreted as diminishing his own identity as well. By refusing to let Cory compete for a football scholarship to college, perhaps out of jealously rather than out of fatherly concern for Cory's future, Troy pushes his son out of his life. Although Troy thinks he is protecting Cory from the disappointments that he had already experienced as a baseball player in the Negro leagues, Troy has also blinded himself to the changing world around him that is opening up opportunities for black men in professional sports. *Fences'* similarities with the father-son dynamic of *Death of a Salesman* further reflects the male dramatic tradition of father-son conflict that Clive Barnes calls "the classic pattern of the American realistic drama — a family play, with a tragically doomed American father locked in conflict with his son ("Fiery" 317). Troy tries to teach his son the responsibility of manhood but ultimately alienates him. This task of conferring upon Cory his father's teaching is left to Rose after Troy's death. Like Mama of *Raisin*, she supplies the checks on Troy's masculinity as well as the definitions of manhood in his absence, and she teaches the son to take up the mantle of the father. Rose's final duty concerns the maintenance of both her husband's and her son's manhood.

The complex matrix of gender and racial identity is treated again in Wilson's next play, *Joe Turner's Come and Gone. Joe Turner* is the most allegorical of Wilson's plays, as well as his most mystical. Wilson remarks that because the play was set in 1911, much closer to the days of slavery, he took "advantage of some of the African retentions of the characters.... They're Black Americans, they speak English, but their world view is African" (Powers 53). This connection with Africa is most apparent in the African juba that the characters participate in and that drew comment from the majority of New York critics who reviewed the play. Wilson says of this play that he was trying to feature more women because he had "met so many Black actresses who said, 'Why don't you write for us too?'" (B. Staples, "August" 111). And the play does have some nicely drawn parts for women. However, the chief story or quest belongs to a male character — in this case Harold Loomis. Loomis is on a quest to reconstruct himself, to find his humanity, after being enslaved on Joe Turner's chain gang for seven years. Wilson explains that Joe Turner was a real man who "would send out decoys who would lure Blacks into crap games and then he would swoop down and grab them. He had a chain with forty links to it, and he would take Blacks off to his plantation and work them" (Powers 53). Joe Turner became the subject of a song by W. C. Handy that Wilson was listening to when he got the original idea for the play (Kleiman 11).

Harold Loomis's oppression and struggle for identity carry almost iconic significance for the history of African Americans after slavery. However, once again the black man serves, for Wilson, to represent the black experience. The play is set at a boarding house in Pittsburgh run by Seth and Bertha Holly — a center for many types of men and women who have been displaced by the upheavals in the South after abolition. Into this setting comes Loomis with his 11-year-old daughter in tow. Even more clearly than the other wanderers who have come to temporary roost in the boarding house, Loomis is a man haunted by his past and searching for his "song." As in Wilson's previous plays, song represents the souls of the characters in this play. As Bynum tells Loomis:

> Now I can look at you, Mr. Loomis, and see you a man who done forgot his song. Forgot how to sing it. A fellow forget that and he forget who he is. Forget how he's supposed to mark down his life [71].

While all of the roomers at the boarding house are clearly in search of new lives and new identities, the climax of the play is given to Harold Loomis's symbolic rebirth and discovery of his "song." Further, Loomis's ability to "find himself" is tied in his mind, and by the logic of the play, to finding his wife, Martha: she is the object of his quest because he believes that she is his "starting place in the world" (76).

After seven years on the chain gang, Loomis returns to find his wife and child gone. Locating his daughter with his wife's mother, he takes the girl with him on his two-year quest to find his missing wife. Upon finding Martha, he explains, "I just wanted to see your face to know that the world was still there. Make sure everything still in its place so I could reconnect myself together" (89). Without his wife, Loomis finds no continuity in his life. Much as Rose did for Troy, Martha represents Loomis's "center," which both gives him structure and ties him down. After spending all these years looking for Martha, for his center, Loomis immediately declares upon finding her: "I ain't gonna let nobody bind me up!" (91). Taking out a knife, he slashes himself across the chest, rubs the blood on his face and hands in a symbolic baptism, and exclaims, "I'm standing now" as he walks away. This symbolic break from Martha is connected with his break from the control of Joe Turner and the white slavers — yet another equation between women and the forces that "bind up" black men that Michele Wallace has critiqued, and that Baraka employed by using a woman to represent white racism.

The problem of fitting personal identity with family responsibility is not resolved in this play: Loomis frees himself from the ghost of Joe Turner's imprisonment only by freeing himself from his wife and daughter. Like the typical hero of American literature, he departs triumphantly — alone. While this ending positively affirms Loomis's identity after the crushing blows that have been dealt him by Joe Turner's chain gang (read "slavery"), it leaves yet another shattered family in the long tradition of these for African Americans. This conflict between a man and his family also reflects the traditional split of the American hero already discussed in regard to Shepard's male characters. This tradition sets up the female as the presence that the male must exorcise from his life in order to assert his own identity. Just as Huck Finn ran away from Aunt Sally, as Mamet's Edmond and Rabe's Phil left their wives, and as Shepard's western heroes fled the feminine in their lives, Loomis too flees his ties with the feminine and with the entire community of the boarding house. Although on the one hand Loomis's epiphany supports Wilson's intention that Loomis is finally accepting "responsibility for his own presence in the world" (Powers 54), it also leaves us with a familiar, unresolved dilemma: how a man merges the need for self-knowledge and identity with family and community. And we are left to wonder why these two things are usually considered mutually exclusive for men.

This question is brought up again in Wilson's second Pulitzer Prize winning play, *The Piano Lesson*. If *Fences* resonates with echoes of Arthur Miller's stagings of masculinity within the elusive American dream, *Piano Lesson* contains many echoes of Hansberry's staging of masculinity within the black American family. The legacy of a dead father/grandfather is the testing ground for how the main male characters of both *Raisin* and *Piano Lesson* structure their own identity as a man and their role and responsibility within the family. Just as Big Walter's insurance money is the legacy that offers the Younger family a new life, the piano carved by Berneice and Boy Willy's great-grandfather and stolen by their father is the legacy that must be evaluated either for its monetary value or for its symbolic value. And just as the check was held by Mama of *Raisin*, the piano is held by Berneice as the symbol of patriarchal inheritance. Like Walter Younger, "Boy" Willie wants to take possession of his inheritance as a way to claim his manhood, but in order to do so, he must accept a female version of that inheritance. He must move from prolonged adolescence into a recognition and acceptance of a manhood necessitating his taking into account how his life affects his entire family and its history.

The history of the piano is the history of the Charles family's travels from slavery in the old South to working-class struggles and racial inequalities in the urban North. It is also the legacy of violence done to black manhood and the scars this violence leaves for black womanhood. The piano itself, the central issue and emblem of the play, was carved by Willie Boy — the great-grandfather of the current Charles family — during the days of slavery. Willie Boy was ordered by his master to carve the piano with the portraits of his wife and son, who had been traded for the piano. Taking his task seriously, Willie Boy carved the entire family history into the wood of the piano. After abolition, the piano still belonged to the Sutter family, on whose land the Charles family now worked as sharecroppers, until one day Boy Charles (Berneice and Boy Willie's father), along with Doaker and Wining Boy, stole the piano out of the Sutter home. While stealing the piano, Boy Charles was killed, leaving his wife with the piano as her only memory of her husband. Berneice blames Boy Willie's similar "robberies" for the death of her husband, who was killed while helping Boy Willie steal firewood. She refuses to part with the piano because its lesson for her is the cost that the men's struggle to own their own manhood has extracted from the family. She berates Boy Willie:

> You always talking about your daddy but you ain't never stopped to look at what his foolishness cost your mama. Seventeen years' worth of cold nights and empty bed. For what? For a piano? ... All this thieving and killing and thieving and killing. And what it ever lead to? More killing and thieving. I ain't never seen it come to nothing [52].

Yet Boy Willie believes that claiming material objects such as the piano and the land he wants to buy is a move to empower the men in his family in the face of white oppression. He wants to sell the piano and to use the profits to buy Sutter's land — the land his family was once enslaved upon — a gesture every bit as symbolic as his father's theft of the piano. Much like Walter Jr., he hopes to use his father's legacy as a way to become financially independent, like the white man whose property he envies. He tells Berneice that the piano is his legacy left to him by his father and great-grandfather and that he is "supposed to build on what they left me" (51). His approach is extremely pragmatic, looking to the financial future, while Berneice is too tied to the past, refusing to get on with her life. But Boy Willie's plans for the future also run roughshod over his family history, which is nurtured and maintained by the female of the family (Berneice). This question of how to bridge the conflict between male and female versions of family history pervades the play.

When Boy Willie tries to move the piano against Berneice's wishes, Sutter's ghost appears in the house. This ghost is the haunting image of the Charles family's slave past, and in preventing Boy Willie from selling the piano, it teaches Boy Willie the "lesson" that Wilson seems to intend for his audience as well: there must be a balance between abandoning the past, as Boy Willie wants to do, and living too much in it, as Berneice does. The conflict between Boy Willie and Berneice is resolved by the deus ex machina appearance of Sutter's ghost at the end of the play. Boy Willie is at last able to wrestle physically with this ghost of his family's past in a version of the masculine duel/showdown. Berneice, however, is the one who finally exorcises Sutter's ghost by playing the piano again. As in *Joe Turner*, the ghost of the white slaver is finally exorcised for the man by the actions of a woman. After the ghost departs, Boy Willie immediately prepares to leave, admonishing Berneice: "If you and Maretha don't keep playing on that piano ... ain't no telling ... me and Sutter both liable to be back" (108). This decision to give up his plan for selling the piano occurs so rapidly as to leave the portraits of both Berneice and Boy Willie incomplete, a move atypical of Wilson's usually thorough treatment of his main characters and perhaps the result of his inability to resolve fully the different demands for ownership of the family legacy/identity as enacted by his male and female characters.

Men in Groups: *Two Trains Running*

In *Two Trains Running*, Wilson practically avoids the family altogether in order to focus on a group of men who hang out at Memphis Lee's restaurant in Pittsburgh in 1969. Memphis's restaurant once did great business, feeding the men who came to Pittsburgh seeking jobs and new lives but who "d[id]n't have nobody to cook for them" (10). The restaurant's business, however, has fallen off with urban decay, which Memphis chronicles early in the play: "Ain't nothing gonna be left around here. Supermarket gone. Two drugstores. The five and ten. Doctor done moved out. Dentist done moved out" (9). Now, his place is the hangout for only a handful of men still involved in the neighborhood, but a sense of detachment, decay, and dissolution pervades their talk. These men are separated from their families and are left with very little in the way of companionship, especially now that Memphis's restaurant is closing down.

Unlike each of his preceding plays, Wilson's *Two Trains* lacks a central character and that character's central story, something that has prompted one critic to remark that the production is "more an evening of linked monologues than a play" (quoted in Huang 73). Although they are living in the politically volatile years of the 1960s, the men of this play are more interested in their private endeavors than in political issues. Two characters given more attention than the rest, however, are Memphis Lee, who is fighting to get city hall to pay him top price for his restaurant, which the city intends to tear down, and Sterling, who searches for some love interest and excitement after getting released from prison. The central "action" of the play is the talk among Sterling, Memphis, and the other men who frequent the restaurant — Wolf, Holloway, and West. This talk is full of personal experiences and opinions, as well as gossip about the neighborhood and even political discussions concerning the Civil Rights Movement. Throughout all of the talk, a vision of the imperilled position that these men see themselves as inhabiting in relation to the white society becomes clear, as do their methods of coping with this peril.

The talk of the men in this play reflects the sense of loss that fed the growing militancy of the Black Power Movement, as well as foreshadowing the urban centers of violence about which Gibbs, Staples, and Majors and Billson have more recently written. Their talk focuses on four issues related to black male identity, which each of these sociological studies examine as well: guns, employment or unemployment, jail, and women. Each of these issues reflects the characters' understanding that they must navigate a world in which the rules have been made by white men.

Memphis, a resident of Pittsburgh since 1936, derides the "old backward Southern mentality" of certain black men in their deferential behavior to white men: "They walk around here tipping their hat, jumping off the sidewalk, talking about, 'Yessir Captain. How do Major'" (30). Memphis is deriding the Uncle Tom performance that some black men used to navigate the white world. In contrast to this performance, Memphis — prompted by a brief political discussion regarding Malcolm X — later suggests another attitude in dealing with the white man:

> I don't know how these niggers think sometimes. Talking about Black Power with their pockets empty. You can't do nothing without a gun. Not in this day and time. That's the only kind of power the white man understand [42].

Memphis's speech indicates a shift in the performance of black masculinity such as we witnessed in Baraka's portrait of Clay, who began as a placid character, but abandoned that approach for open rage when it became clear that his "Uncle Tomism" was ineffective against the merciless needling of Lula. Significantly, in Wilson's play, this new assertion of masculinity is connected to guns, which are clearly a central prop for asserting the control and power of masculinity for the men in *Two Trains*. Memphis speaks of wanting to return to the South with a 30.06 in order to reclaim the land that was once taken from him (31). When Wilson revised the script of the play — which was first printed in *Theatre* — to move the production from the Yale Repertory Company to Broadway, he cut out several passages that concerned guns, perhaps to dull the militancy that sparkled in the earlier version. In the version published in *Theatre*, Memphis remembers his youth in terms of the gun he used to carry, a .44, explaining, "I used to carry it to keep me from killing somebody. Soon as everybody know you carry a gun they steer a wide circle around you" (64). But this speech is rewritten in the Broadway version where Memphis describes that he had to carry a gun at one point in his life, before he found a better way to make a living by buying his own business, the restaurant:

> Used to carry a pistol and everything. Had a .44. Had me one of them big .44s. Used to scare me to look at it. I give L. D. the fifty-five hundred in cash [for the restaurant]. I didn't find out till after he died that he owed twelve hundred dollars in back taxes ... but I didn't care. I had seen a way for me to take off my pistol [8–9].

This version of Memphis's story does not glorify guns, but indicates they are a substitute for a better way of life. Wilson's textual changes here shift Memphis from advocating violence as a way to assert the power that is associated with manhood to presenting the economic power possible through entrepreneurship as a better way to assert control over one's life.

In contrast to Memphis, who has found his better way of life, the young ex-con Sterling is still looking. Interestingly, most of the references to guns that appear in the Broadway version are made by Sterling. Although Sterling is mainly interested in the waitress, Risa, he feels the need for a gun, in part to protect Risa but mainly to compensate for his lack of control over other areas of his life. When

Risa explains that she does not want to go with Sterling to the Malcolm X celebration because "there might be a riot or something," Sterling voices his understanding of his role as a man:

> If a fight break out you just get behind me. I won't let nobody hurt you. Not when you with me. I don't care if he was King Kong or Mighty Joe Young. He got to come through me first. Mrs. Johnson taught me that. Told me not to let nobody hurt my sister. Say she'd rather see me hurt than her hurt. That made me kinda important. Made me feel strong. Like when I robbed the bank. That made me feel strong too. Like I had everything under control. I did until they caught me [47–48].

This passage is ripe with implications regarding the question as to which gender is privileged. Sterling has been taught that he should sacrifice himself to save a woman, which would indicate that he is more expendable, matters less, than she does. Yet he also says that this duty is what makes him important and powerful.

Sterling's need to feel in control in a society that denies him most legitimate methods of asserting a powerful masculinity has led him to crime (the robbery for which he was jailed) and to a fetish for guns. Halfway through the play, when he has still been unable to find a job, Sterling remarks, "If I can't find no job I might have to find me a gun," and then asks Wolf to find him

> something that shoot straight.... I don't want no .22. A .38 too big and heavy. Everybody can see it's bulging out under your coat. I'll take me a snub-nosed .32 if I can get one. I don't want no silver gun that shine in the dark. I'll take a black one. Other than that I don't care what it is [53].

Sterling also threatens to get a .45 when he learns that the money he won in betting on the numbers has been cut in half by the Alberts, the number-runners. The detail with which not only Sterling but all of these men speak of guns indicates how closely guns are tied to their ideas of protection and of standing up for themselves. Wolf wonders if he ought to get his gun out of hock before breaking the bad news about the money to Sterling (83–84). Although Wolf does not carry a gun with him because "I might kill somebody," his pistol is readily available to him, indicating that threats and fear of death are readily a part of his life as well. At the same time that these men see guns as one alternative for dealing with the problems that arise — even though they do not usually turn to such a solution — they are also aware of how whites stereotype blacks as violent. Holloway comments

> You say the word "gun" in the same sentence with the word "nigger" and you in trouble. The white man panic. [...] He ain't had nothing but guns for the last five hundred years ... got the atomic bomb and everything. But say the word "nigger" and "gun" in the same sentence and they'll try to arrest you. Accuse you of sabotage, disturbing the peace, inciting to riot ... [85–86].

Although these characters voice a willingness to turn to guns in order to protect themselves from threats in their own community as well as from threats from the white man, they also indicate a desire to solve problems in other, less violent ways such as fighting their battles through the court system and working to establish economic power through their own businesses. At the same time, however, guns are undoubtedly understood as visible symbols of virility and power that compensate for the lack of other more legitimate markers of power, such as employment, especially for Sterling.

Sterling's inability to find a job is hotly debated by Memphis and Holloway. Memphis claims Sterling does not want to work, and Holloway claims that he just does not want to work a job requiring hard labor for little money when he can earn about the same by gambling on the numbers and on the occasional crap game. Holloway's argument is similar to those made by sociologists such as Oliver, Stewart and Scott, and Majors and Billson concerning the forces that tear down the black male's incentives to work by setting up so many obstacles to his employment. Despite Memphis's disparagement, Sterling gives every indication of actively seeking work, even to the point of trying to convince the other men to hire him for all sorts of odd jobs. His need to find work is especially pressing because his parole is contingent upon it. Unemployment, however, is what drove him to commit the crime he was jailed for in the first place. Sterling is clearly caught in a vicious cycle of unemployment and imprisonment, which is accepted among the men in the play as simply a part of life for the black male. As Wolf says, "every nigger you see done been in jail one time or another. The white man don't feel right unless he got a record on these niggers" (54). Wolf tells of being thrown in jail because a policeman ran into him while chasing someone else and ended up arresting Wolf "for obstructing justice," but the experience taught him the valuable lesson "to watch where I was going at all times. Cause you always under attack" (54). This "attack" includes the factors responsible for the institutional decimation of black males, which would become even more apparent during the 1970s and 1980s.

Although these men, particularly the younger Sterling, are navigating their way through potentially volatile situations both within their own community and in relation to the white community, the play avoids confrontations in part due to the mitigating presence of women. Without having to fight city hall, Memphis is simply given more than enough money for his restaurant, an outcome that he attributes to his visit with the famed wise woman Aunt Esther, an offstage character. And Sterling, potentially the most volatile of the men, is guided away from violence to calmer behavior by both Risa and Aunt Esther. Risa gives Sterling a sense that he has a reason to get up every morning, or, as he tells West, "Get Risa to be my woman and I'll be alright" (93). His restlessness is further mitigated by Aunt Esther, who counsels him, after his potentially violent encounter with the Alberts, to "make better what you have" and to rely on his "good understanding" (98–99). This advice leads Sterling to turn even more resolutely to Risa as the "angel" who can set his life to rights. His final act of stealing a ham to be buried in Hambone's coffin indicates a shift in him from self-serving scams to a concern with the just treatment of others. Unlike the robbery that landed him in jail, this robbery is committed out of a sense of justice — to at last give Hambone what he had earned in his life. This closing gesture, as Sterling enters "bleeding from his face and his hands" carrying the stolen ham, leaves the audience with an image of sacrifice done in the name of justice, as Sterling has taken for Hambone that which he deserved but had been denied.

Although the content of *Two Trains Running* generally avoids specific references to issues central to the Black Power Movement, many of the views concerning identity that these characters voice are comparable to the views of the leaders of this movement. Although Wilson's play defuses the restlessness and anger among his male characters, the militancy that would define Black Power for many black men after the days of Malcolm X is hinted at in this play and perhaps also foreshadows the well-armored war that can be witnessed on the streets of South Central Los Angeles today. Although he fails to do so in this play, Sterling could have easily become another statistic among the numbers of urban black men killed by violence. Wilson's decision to avoid this ending was no doubt guided by his intention to create positive portraits of male responsibility and to give his audiences hope rather than despair. Interestingly enough, that hope seems to arise from the women in this play, placing male-female relations in a perspective different from the antagonistic stance present in earlier plays.

Black and White Masculinity

The African American community, as part of American culture, is influenced and shaped by the stereotypes and assumptions of the dominant American culture as well as by those within its own subculture. In examining issues of black masculinity in contrast to issues of masculinity for white males in America, it is clear how interconnected and pervasive are the traditional American concepts of masculinity, as well as how these concepts usually fail the men who attempt to enact them. Economic disempowerment of black men and women due to racism, coupled with often conflicted gender role models, creates a complex matrix of issues surrounding the staging of black masculinity in Wilson's plays. The characters of these plays also indicate that their subjugation is a prop for the white man who structures his identity/masculinity upon the black man by exploiting his labor and limiting his gains. This situation is given its clearest articulation in Holloway's long speech describing how the white man has built his world upon slave labor or by what Holloway calls "stacking niggers" (35).

The three contemporary playwrights who precede August Wilson in this study share common socioeconomic, racial, and gender backgrounds that encourage them to blind themselves to the ways that their images of "American" masculinity are structured upon racist and sexist assumptions. However, the black men who populate Wilson's drama stand in a vastly different position regarding their performance of masculinity as a result of their racial subjugation. Having the carrot of power and prestige held out to them as men in a patriarchal society but denied to them as blacks in a white-dominated society, their performance of selfhood is constantly confronted with limitations set by that society. Against such limitations, the coping tactics of their masculine poses become apparent. Race alone is not the only limitation confronting Wilson's men, however. Their economic disempowerment is an equally important issue and one that we have seen affecting the working classes and underclasses in Mamet's and O'Neill's plays as well. The characters of *American Buffalo*, *Lakeboat*, and *The Hairy Ape*, though white, suffer many of the same identity crises as do the economically disempowered men of Wilson's plays. However, mutual poverty does not simply result in brother-hood between white and black America, something of which Wilson's men are keenly aware. Even in similar economic groups, racial inequalities remain. Again, Holloway's discussion of "stacking niggers" refers to the way that white male identity, however impoverished, still receives a cultural legitimization that is usu-ally denied black men. The racial slurs quoted at the opening of this chapter also demonstrate how the white male characters of Mamet, Rabe, and Shepard struc-ture their identities at least in part on racial assumptions that place them in (often unacknowledged) privileged positions.

What a white version of masculinity seeks to make invisible is made highly visible in our culture's perception of masculinity as it is enacted by black men such as Levee or Sterling — precisely that such behavior *is* a performance staged with props (such as clothes and guns) and is often changed according to audi-ence demands. Wilson's portrayal of black masculinity also offers a different ver-sion of the male-female dynamic than witnessed in the preceding playwrights' work by presenting the feminine as that which usually supports and maintains the definitions and limitations of manhood for the black man. At the same time, he indicates the struggles of such characters as Loomis and Boy Willie to claim their patriarchal legacy from the women in their lives.

Wilson's staging of black masculinity responds to and puts in a larger per-spective the issues of masculinity present in works by Shepard, Mamet, and Rabe. However, in the way that manhood becomes the central focus of his history of African Americans, Wilson falls in line with the traditional masculine gendering of American drama, leaving still unanswered a revised version of the question posed in chapter one: If such things as gender, race, and class are ultimately cul-turally staged performances, why can't we perform them differently when the current performances begin to fracture and fray?

Notes

1. For discussion of this play's political content, see book-length studies of Sam Shepard by David DeRose and Ron Mottram.

2. Majors and Billson, as well as Robert Staples, offer statistics supporting this inequity. For a recent example, the acquittal of the four white police officers who brutally beat Rodney King for "resisting arrest" supports the contention that white men have the legitimation of the state for vio-lent behavior, especially toward minority groups. Key to the double standard of "appropriate" white response to "threatening" black behavior is that these officers were acquitted because the prostrate, beaten King was writhing in such a manner that was read as threatening by the white policemen who subsequently continued to beat him.

3. Robert Staples' *Black Masculinity*, Majors and Billson's *Cool Pose*, William Oliver's "Black Males and the Tough Guy Image," and James Stewart and Joseph Scott's "The Institutional Deci-mation of Black American Males" all indicate that a major contributing factor to frustration for black males is their difficulty supporting a family — the defining characteristic for most Americans of a man's role in society.

4. Clyde Franklin's "Surviving the Institutional Decimation of Black Males" connects the insti-tutional decimation that Stewart and Scott discuss not only to black assimilation of certain white models of masculinity such as Robert Staples treats, but also to discrimination by the white com-munity that prevents black men from enacting other aspects of white masculinity, and to the polar-ization of gender roles and expectations for black men and black women.

5. For other studies that treat the increasing dissension between black men and black women in the 1970s and 1980s, see K. Sue Jewell, Delores Aldridge, William Oliver, and Clyde Franklin. Jewell's "Use of Social Welfare Programs and the Disintegration of the Black Nuclear Family" argues that this dissension is exacerbated by the welfare system, while Aldridge's "Toward an Understanding of Black Male/Female Relationships," Oliver (already cited), and Franklin's "Black Male-Black Female Conflict" argue the problem is worsened by the plight and defense mechanisms of black masculinity.

6. Wilson has voiced his intention to write a play that would reflect each decade of the African American experience in the twentieth century in practically every interview he has ever given. For its most recent explication, see Huang 78.

7. Although Wilson claims not to have read *Raisin in the Sun* (Freedman, "A Voice" 36), his figurations of masculinity derive from similar contexts and influences as Hansberry's play. In addition, all five of his plays discussed have been directed by Lloyd Richards, the original director of Hansberry's play. Although a different type of analysis than I am undertaking here would be needed in order to establish Richard's effect on Wilson, it is interesting to speculate how much the style of dramaturgy he brought to *Raisin* resembles what he brings to Wilson's work. In contrast to his lack of knowledge regarding Hansberry, Wilson has said that he not only read but helped to produce plays by Baraka at the Black Horizons theater in the late '60s (Feingold, "August" 117). In fact, in listing his influences among the '60s playwrights, he mentions only male authors such as Baraka and Bullins (*Three Plays*, xii). Taken together, however, Hansberry and Baraka represent diverse traditions of racially and politically motivated theater in both form and content. Both the mainstream style of Hansberry's staging of the African American family and the avant-garde style of Baraka's militant anti-racist plays resonate strains of thought and experience witnessed in Wilson's plays. In addition, both of these plays implicate women as powerful forces standing between men and their manhood, a theme that Wilson treats in his family plays.

8. In contrast to this view, C. W. E. Bigsby and, more recently, Leonard Ashley argue that Hansberry's play succeeded because it was "safe" and unthreatening in its social critique (Bigsby, *Confrontation* 156; Ashley, "Lorraine Hansberry" 1–2). For further readings that argue for the importance of the play in regard to the history of black playwrights on Broadway, see Gerald Weales, "Thoughts on *A Raisin in the Sun*", and Lloyd W. Brown, "Lorraine Hansberry as Ironist."

9. For discussions arguing that the power supposedly held by the black matriarchy is largely mythic rather than actual, see R. Staples and Wallace. Also see Alice Childress's play *Wine in the Wilderness*, which serves to critique this myth as well.

10. Wallace argues that Malcolm X offered this vision of the powerful patriarch who would take care of his people, men, women, and children, but that this vision died with him when he was killed (36–38).

11. For some effective discussions of how the form of realism often serves to normalize patriarchal assumptions of power positions, see Jill Dolan's *The Feminist Spectator as Critic* and the introduction to Robert Vorlicky's *Act Like a Man*.

12. See reviews of *Fences* by Joel Siegel, Jack Curry, and Frank Rich.

Chapter 7

Other Voices, Other Men: Reinventing Masculinity

Performing a different version of the self is a frightening concept for most of the male characters we have encountered in this study. Someone such as Mamet's Shelley Levene, who has based his whole life on a vision of himself as salesman only to have it fail him in the end, admits that he desires to be put out of the misery of that life — yet even so, he cannot imagine himself playing any other role. Much like Willy Loman, Levene cannot reinvent himself even in the face of failure of the image he has embraced. This inability to reinvent the self is perhaps the underlying cause of failure for the majority of men in the plays we have read. O'Neill's Yank, Rabe's Ozzie and Phil, Wilson's Troy and Levee fail in their attempts to create their lives anew. Perhaps their failure lies not simply in these attempts but in the images for which they aim. While Shepard's men at times seem aware of the possibility of multiple images, or performances, in their "'ideas' of men," they still tend to view certain images as inevitable even though those images are often "curses" handed down from their fathers. All too often, the limited possibilities that all of these male characters embrace are unable to withstand the challenges of the various situations the men confront.

Although most of the male characters discussed in this study have put their faith in a set idea of masculinity and manhood, most also suffer confusion and doubt because they feel unable to achieve or maintain that ideal manhood. Mamet's businessmen, Shepard's would-be cowboys, Rabe's soldiers and single men, and Wilson's family men, while sharing some common beliefs about American masculinity, all structure their ideas of manhood by privileging different qualities and structures of that masculinity. In short, although they tend to assume one definition, when set side by side their multiple stories provide multiple perspectives on masculinity. Even within a perspective, such as Shelly Levene's or Levee's, the possibility of other perspectives — of other performances — arises, although these characters try to suppress or discount those options. The predicament of these characters regarding manhood seems to be that in collapsing possibilities in order to solidify their identities, they actually cut off their ability to maintain any identity. Rather than an inherent, unchanging essence, masculinity seems to be, in fact, a construct that needs the mutability these men fear.

Regarding the idea of mutability, it seems pertinent to return to some of the critical concepts raised in the opening chapter, particularly to the ideas posed by James Clifford. Clifford explores both the mutability of human cultures and the impulse to ignore this mutability in favor of accepting culture as monolithic. He argues, however, that the world of the twentieth century has basically made the idea of monolithic culture obsolete: "Twentieth-century identities no longer presuppose continuous cultures or traditions. Everywhere individuals and groups improvise local performances from (re)collected pasts, drawing on foreign media, symbols, and languages" (14). Clifford's analysis of ways for viewing culture, intended to address issues pertinent to anthropologists and ethnographers, offers a useful perspective from which to view the predicament of masculinity in contemporary American drama. Based upon the plays discussed in previous chapters, male characters are all too often lost in a nostalgia for a set version of American manhood that they usually locate in the country's frontier past, but this past is itself merely another construct, a narrative structured a certain way by writing over actual flaws and discrepancies or, as Victor Seidler puts it, by making the differences among actual men "invisible." Joe Dubbert further argues that the idea of a moment in the past in which American manhood was secure is itself a myth that generations of Americans as far back as the 1840s held about a *previous* time. In contrast to this mythologized previous time, the tendency seems to have been to view the *current* moment as one of crisis. This tendency is voiced by both Mamet's and Edmond's belief that the world is "falling apart," and by Austin of Shepard's *True West* when he comments that "nothing is real here." These men, real and imagined, long for a time and place in the tradition of American manhood when the world was whole and "men were men." Although this tradition is largely mythical, to throw out traditions and pasts completely is hardly a solution, as Wilson's Levee and Boy Willie both learn. Instead of embracing or denying *a* history, perhaps the solution is to entertain multiple versions of that history, to accept the "making of masculinities," as Harry Brod entitles his volume of essays on the new men's studies. In short, the solution is to reinvent masculinity. Why does this solution elude the men of these plays, even when confronted in no uncertain terms by the failure of their monolithic concepts? Clifford comments, "It is easier to register the loss of traditional orders of difference than to perceive the emergence of new ones" (15). Perhaps that is the next task in examining the issue of masculinity in contemporary American drama — not to record old versions of masculinity but to recognize and validate new versions.

Although the plays already treated offer characters trapped in intractable images that betray them, what of explorations of new images of manliness, of manhood? Are alternate viewpoints out there? What about male playwrights who acknowledge this question of male identity and its problems, or who indicate awareness of the centrality of this gender bias? The changes in gender attitudes, the questions raised by feminism, men's studies, and gay studies regarding gender, find their place in more recent work for the stage. Some of the best examples are provided by minority playwrights, those stereotypically outside of the mainstream idea of traditional American masculinity — playwrights who typically get "qualified" with adjectives that supposedly limit their universality. The

Chinese-American David Henry Hwang and the gay playwright Tony Kushner offer recent notable examples of powerful drama that explore the problems and entrapments of traditional American concepts of masculinity, and that provocatively critique it. Their plays do not always escape the stereotypes they seek to deconstruct, but their examination is much more consciously disruptive of the traditional portrait of masculinity than are the plays already treated in this study. Although they do not "solve" the gender question for men, they do engage in what Judith Butler calls "gender trouble." By troubling the still waters of the "accepted" version of gender identification, the "accepted" reflection is disrupted, returning a much more distorted image of gender than is usually recognized and leading ultimately to questioning of that image. Instead of writing over the issues that the dominant voice would like to make invisible, these playwrights tend to acknowledge and foreground gender issues for their men.

David Henry Hwang's most well known play, *M. Butterfly* (1988), explores how the Western concept of the masculine West and the feminine East is precisely what entraps the Western man — makes him vulnerable to manipulation because he is unable to see reality for being blinded by his illusions of power/masculinity. At the same time, Hwang explores Eastern complicity in these Western images. Although he takes an East-West scope, Hwang consciously gives his characters a distinctly American dialect that has been noted by some critics. Hwang comments that he chose the American dialect in order to give his "international" story an American voice (DiGaetani 152). Subsequently, the audience should not be tempted to assume that the issues he treats are irrelevant to the supposed melting pot of America.

Hwang's diplomat Gallimard longs to be the dominant, powerful masculine ideal set forth for him in Western ideology. His need to have a woman create this illusion for him leads him to become completely dependent upon Song Liling, a Chinese man masquerading as a woman in order to gain power over this Western diplomat. In defense of the supposed improbability of the play's plot, which is based on fact, Hwang has written in the afterword of the published version:

> From my point of view, the "impossible" story of a Frenchman duped by a Chinese man masquerading as a woman always seemed perfectly explicable; given the degree of misunderstanding between men and women and also between East and West, it seemed inevitable that a mistake of this magnitude would one day take place [98].

In this play, then, Hwang seems to be exploring how preconceptions based on sexual and racial stereotype dictate the way a person interacts with others — regardless, it seems, of the reality being confronted. In fact, in an interview with John DiGaetani, the issue arises as to whether or not it is possible to love without fantasy, since Hwang emphasizes that in *M. Butterfly* "such a fundamental component of the relationship is the fantasy" (146). Such speculations, especially in light of the diverse critical readings of the play, lead us to question the possibility of arriving at any "real" identity that is not filtered through fantasy.

In critical discussions of this play, Gabrielle Cody and James Moy have read Hwang as not questioning but simply reinscribing the gender and racial fantasies he is supposedly critiquing. While both of these critics make a convincing argument up to a certain point, each ends up simplifying the tangled relationships that occur within the play in order to arrive at a final analysis of misogyny and racism, respectively. In contrast to these critiques that tend to collapse the issues treated by Hwang, Janet Haedicke demonstrates how Hwang's play evades these binary critiques (either the play is racist or it is not) by pointing out the multiplicity of readings possible within this play. Haedicke demonstrates that the gaze in Hwang's play is multifaceted, constantly calling into question the viewpoint of each participant in the production, including that of the audience. Ultimately, she asserts,

> Hwang, who finds the East equally "complicit in this dual form of cultural stereotyping" (Interview 141), calls into question a cultural stage on which identity is stabilized only through the creation — by subject and object — of oppositional otherness, which becomes a self-sustained illusion. *M. Butterfly* ... presents for deconstruction the very structure of gendered binaries [37–38].

Haedicke's critique tries to move beyond binary thinking as it is traditionally presented (male/female, East/West, homosexual/heterosexual, subject/object), in much the same way as Hwang's play attempts to do. The multiple layerings of both gender and racial stereotype and the dismantling of them is accomplished through the multiple uses of theatrical representation within *M. Butterfly*— through the layerings of performance.

Although the questions that revolve around Song are the most obvious and perhaps the most enticing at first, the issue that complicates a "simple" reading of the play as reinscribing stereotypes of Asians and of women is in the questions that revolve around Gallimard. While the gender performance of Song Liling is emphasized by the theatricality of having the actor actually remove his costume of "woman" onstage, Gallimard is also participating in a performance of gender. Not to recognize Gallimard's performance is to fall into the misconception that gender is a masquerade only for woman. Gallimard's performance of masculinity leads the audience to questions that cut deeply into issues of how cultural assumptions, stereotypes, and fantasies can become so accepted as to be "unseen," especially by the active participants of these performances. If Song is performing woman so that, as Cody says, "woman" is actually erased, never represented, then what has happened to "man" given that Gallimard is also performing? If the players enact or present the male stereotype of woman, do they not enact the male stereotype of man as well? In short, the "question" of woman is not the only question — and perhaps not even the central question — being examined in this play. Ultimately, it is Gallimard's assumptions about both male and female gender and sexuality that drive the action of this play. Without his assumptions in place, Song would have nothing with which to "play."

Through these dynamics, *M. Butterfly* raises multiple questions about gender. Is Gallimard actually a gay man who simply wants to deny his gayness by pretending to make love to a woman rather than to a man? If so, is he aware at all of his self-deception and simply refusing to end it by not allowing Song to reveal himself to him? Is Song exploiting the image of woman in a masculinist appropriation, or is his performance the only way he can embrace the feminine qualities he desires? In performing woman, does Song end up reinforcing the Western stereotype of the feminized Asian, or does his transformation to manipulative man (in the courtroom scene) negate that previous performance? Such are the questions that are raised for the audience, and, for an audience trained in an either/or mind-set, it becomes difficult to imagine that instead of "an" answer to each question there may be a range of answers.

M. Butterfly ultimately raises more questions about gender positioning and fantasy than it answers. The levels of masquerade become an endless recurso that leaves us wondering if anyone — Song, Gallimard, Hwang, the audience, or critics — can distinguish where fantasy ends and reality begins in the complex matrix of racial, gender, and sexual stereotypes implicit within the relationship between the two main characters. Shrouded in fantasies of race, of gender, and of sexuality, the characters' interactions raise the question not merely of who is playing what role, but who is aware of the roles that are being played. And it seems that it is the latter question that makes the difference between playing and being played upon in the game of representation being enacted by the characters of *M. Butterfly*. Rather than seeking to replace "wrong" thinking about gender and race with "right" thinking, the play's power is the way that it calls into question the whole concept of stereotype, preconception, and fantasy that is not escaped, it seems, by any character in the play. Gallimard, by enacting the suicide of Puccini's Butterfly, remains in the fantasy to the end. Song's final call for his "Butterfly? Butterfly?" indicates that he has not abandoned their mutual fantasies either. Because the audience witnesses the ruin, even the ludicrousness, that results from this fantasy, perhaps we are left with a broader understanding than that afforded the characters regarding what is at stake in their game-playing: self-knowledge. It is in this richness of images, this layering of vision, that Hwang's play finds its strength.

While Hwang's play is enacted on the sweeping canvas of East-West relations, albeit with a distinctly American voice that Hwang insisted upon, Tony Kushner's epic *Angels in America* takes on a wide-angle portrait of America, the first half of which offers us some relevant issues regarding how America's self-image is implicated in issues of gender.

Kushner's part 1 of *Angels in America, Millennium Approaches* (1990), provides a portrait of a decaying American culture. The heart of this decay is located in the tyranny of heterosexuality and competitive masculinity. These two issues are carried chiefly by the stories of Roy Cohn, "a successful New York lawyer and unofficial power broker" (3), and his employee/apprentice Joe Pitt. Like *M. Butterfly*, Kushner's play highlights the gender games being played, and nowhere is the game better mastered than by Roy Cohn. In treating the ideological climate of America at the end of this century, Kushner chooses as his representative of the cutthroat materialism of the 1980s a gay politician who vehemently denies his homosexuality and disparages homosexuals in general for being weak and ineffectual, even as he affirms that he sleeps with men. Roy Cohn's self-image and his value system is rooted upon one principal: power, or what he calls "clout." He associates power with the defining quality of the heterosexual male. Thus his reasoning: because he is powerful, he is not a homosexual but a heterosexual male who happens to sleep with men. Perhaps no other passage in drama, fiction, or poetry so clearly establishes the issues at stake in male fear of homosexuality than does Cohn's rationalization of his orientation. The assumptions and stereo-types regarding male heterosexuality that lead to prejudice and oppression are summed up in Cohn's assertion that the successful American man is supposed to be tough, powerful, dominant, competitive, ruthless, violent, and that these qual-ities are possible only when associated with heterosexual behavior. Cohn is sub-sequently a contradiction in terms in being a powerful, ruthless, and competi-tive man who is also homosexual. He can resolve the contradiction only by denying it because it is impossible for him, in his limited imagination, to com-bine his definitions of self in any way that falls outside of traditional definitions of "acceptable," heterosexual masculinity.

The issue of acceptable masculinity haunts Joe Pitt as well. His confusion regarding his own identity stems from repressed homosexuality, but his sexual-ity is intricately entangled with his ideas of appropriate behavior as taught him by his religion (Mormonism) and by his position (a lawyer) within the world of corporate America. Joe's innocence of the system that Roy rules serves to high-light the corruption of that system. Faced with the corruption of this all-Ameri-can way, Joe finds himself unable to support or to deny such a system. Instead, he offers a rationalization that covers over Roy's belligerent and abusive behav-ior. When asked by Roy to go to Washington to oversee his political dealings there, Joe refuses, saying:

> There's so much that I want, to be ... what you see in me, I want to be a participant in the world, in your world, Roy, I want to be capable of that, I've tried, really I have but ... I can't do this. Not because I do not believe in you, but because I believe in you so much, in what you stand for, at heart, the order, the decency. I would give anything to protect you, but.... There are laws I can't break. It's too ingrained. It's not me [107].

Joe indicates that he sees Roy's ways as being decent, but also that they are ille-gal (indecent). He cannot reconcile this problem, so he decides to quit working for Cohn, even as he indicates his respect and admiration for Cohn.

Roy's response to Joe's desire to equate decency with Roy's methods is to lay out the ultimate incompatibility between decency and the American method of obtaining and maintaining power. He asks Joe, "You want to be Nice, or you want to be Effective? Make the law, or subject to it. Choose" (108). Unlike the hero of the Hollywood western, whom Robert Ray describes as not having to choose between contrasting ideologies, *this* hero is forced to choose between two possi-bilities. Joe is confronted with the fact that good or decent behavior and power-ful or effective behavior are not compatible in Cohn's (America's dominant) ide-ology. Roy stands for America's history of doing wrong for the supposed sake of right, whether that be blacklisting communists, beating and arresting civil rights demonstrators, bombing civilians in Vietnam, selling arms in return for hostages, or ignoring the "homosexual" disease AIDS. And ultimately Roy sees this bel-ligerent, violent, "illegal" behavior as a mark of his masculinity, his manhood. The fact that Roy has AIDS, then, calls into question his power on many levels. By weakening him physically, it prevents him from being "tough." By associat-ing him with the homosexuality he wishes to deny, it connects him with people he perceives to be weaklings.

In contrast to the weakling that Roy assumes every homosexual to be, Kushner offers his audience several gay men whose behavior is as varied as is their situation. Joe, a repressed homosexual, has married a woman whose addiction to valium is exacerbated by knowing that her husband does not really feel for her as a husband should. Joe has wanted to do right, but in following prescribed behavior laid down for him by religious and corporate philosophies, he has brought unhappiness upon himself and his wife. In comparison to the troubled heterosexual marriage of Joe and Harper, Kushner offers the troubled relationship between Louis and Prior, who is dying of AIDS. This relationship offers the audience a portrait in cowardice and courage. Louis's understandable fear of death does not excuse his abandoning his lover, something which Louis is aware of, even as he defends his behavior to their mutual friend Belize. While Louis spends the course of the play trying to escape his responsibilities, both Prior and Joe come to a greater understanding of who they really are and of their own strengths and weaknesses. Prior's hallucinations/visitations particularize his bout with AIDS, moving him away from being a generic "victim." As Prior encounters his ancestry, as he finds out more about his family past, Joe comes to terms with his present family by at last coming out to his mother. Although each of these men's stories is intricately connected to their sexuality in one way or another, their battles are over issues of identity and responsibility that go beyond sex.

Given the range of attitudes and philosophies among these men, it is interesting to note that a recurring critical comment by reviewers of this play is that Kushner's choice of characters to represent America is not appropriately representational because he focuses on gay men. Although some reviewers of this play, such as Clive Barnes and Frank Rich, were comfortable with accepting the themes presented as being "universal," others were uncomfortable with this "gay" portrait of America (Barnes, "Angelically" 210; Rich "Embracing" 15–16). For example, John Simon called this play a "minority report" ("Of Wings" 102). Edwin Wilson commented that *Angels* "presents the closed universe of a homosexual world" (9). In championing the play, John Lahr still commented that it offers a view from the margins, although that view is relevant to understanding the center of the country (137). And Howard Kissel sums up the play as being "about being gay in America" ("Falling" 216). While all of these comments are valid in that the play does treat the lives of gay men and their conflict with the straight culture, the fact that the reviewers assume that homosexuality is a limiting quality to these characters' ability to be representative Americans is quite relevant to the argument at hand. After all, these men are not the established "norm" of heterosexual masculinity, and the critical reluctance to see these non-heterosexual men as the "real" story of America further emphasizes the way that heterosexual masculinity is accepted unquestionably as the universal. Consider, in comparison, that Mamet's heterosexual businessmen in *Glengarry Glen Ross* encountered no such critical reservations for speaking about American business and culture as they encounter some of the same conflicts regarding work and male identity that Kushner's characters face. Of further interest is the fact that although reviewers repeatedly commented on the lack of a heterosexual perspective, none noted that the play offers very little in the way of women's lives and experiences. These critics are not bothered by the masculine bias, but by the issue of homosexuality. The assumption underlying the critique of gay men as representative Americans is that they do not fit into the already accepted representative of American culture whom we have seen in the plays by the previous playwrights. This representative, universal person is male, but he is not gay, Jewish, Mormon, or black as are the main characters in Kushner's play.

Although they treat characters and issues that would seem to be out of the mainstream of appropriate subject matter for drama, these two plays by Hwang and Kushner have been given the stamp of mainstream approval by being awarded two of its most prestigious awards: The New York Drama Critics' Circle Award and the Pulitzer Prize. Both plays met with wide commercial success as well, and have been restaged often in theaters across the country. Do these awards and commercial acceptance indicate a willingness to examine gender issues as now being obviously relevant to America's staging of itself, or do they reflect a desire to make safe these plays by defusing their radicalness? But ultimately, how radical are these two "gender-bending" plays? For all the spectacular staging and plotting, both plays still treat the question of male identity — of what it means to be a real man, although from refreshingly different angles than we have seen in the works of the previous playwrights discussed. In this way, both of these plays fall in line with the critically accepted bias that manhood — its norms and limitations — is the central, universal issue within American drama. These two plays, however, are much less sympathetic to the traditional portrait of the "real" man than are the nostalgic portraits we have witnessed in previous chapters. Indeed, even as they reinforce the idea that to understand American culture is to understand its men (which is, at best, a partial truth), they also critique social assumptions regarding the efficacy of traditional masculinity.

Hwang and Kushner, though, do less for ensconcing the male bias than does the critical reception afforded these two pieces. At the same time that their treatment of male identity calls into question the validity of the traditional concept of manliness, criticism of these two plays tends to overlook the "man question" that they raise in favor of treating the woman question, the race question, or the gay question. Viewers trained to see gender issues as irrelevant to the "norm" of heterosexual man find themselves unable to see any aberrations with that figure. The "aberrations" of woman, of non-white, of homosexual have been made to replace the question raised about white, heterosexual masculinity. Until we can begin to question the norm, how do we hope to address the man question? If Gallimard, Cohn, Troy Maxson, Phil, Teach, and Jake are to be accepted as the "all-American" voice of experience, what kind of gender problems are we writing into our society as normal, acceptable, unquestionable?

Such a question reveals to us a hauntingly pervasive problem within our culture — how "normal" masculinity is often the cause of gender problems that are being displaced upon other genders and upon other issues. In placing such a premium upon a rigidly defined concept of masculinity, and resisting any alterations or evolution of that concept even in the face of its failure to meet contemporary needs, the male characters we have encountered have locked themselves into an image that is fracturing both themselves and their worlds. Audiences and critics alike, in agreeing to "overlook" traditional masculinity and, more importantly, its problems, have helped to ensure the entrapping ideology that locks these men into such (self-)destructive stories. However, perhaps by finally naming the man question, we can at last begin to answer it.

Bibliography

Abbot, Franklin, ed. *New Men, New Minds*. Freedom, CA: Crossing, 1987.

Aldridge, Delores P. "Toward an Understanding of Black Male/Female Relationships." *Western Journal of Black Studies* 8 (1984): 184–191.

Allen, Jennifer. "The Man on the High Horse: On the Trail of Sam Shepard." *Esquire* November 1988: 141–153.

Almansi, Guido. "David Mamet: A Virtuoso of Invective." In *Critical Angles: European Views of Contemporary American Literature*. Ed. Marc Chenetier. Carbondale: Southern Illinois UP, 1986. 191–207.

Ashley, Leonard R. N. "Lorraine Hansberry and the Great Black Way." In *Modern American Drama: The Female Canon*. Ed. June Schlueter. Rutherford: Fairleigh Dickinson UP, 1990. 151–160.

Auerbach, Doris. "Who Was Icarus's Mother? The Powerless Mother Figures in the Plays of Sam Shepard." In *Sam Shepard: A Casebook*. Ed. Kimball King. New York: Garland, 1988. 53–64.

August, Eugene. "*Death of a Salesman*: A Men's Studies Approach." *Western Ohio Journal* 7.1 (1986): 53–71.

_____. "Men's Studies: Introducing a Special Issue." *University of Dayton Review* 18.2 (1986-87): 3–8.

Bank, Rosemarie. "Self as Other: Sam Shepard's *Fool for Love* and *A Lie of the Mind*." In *Feminist Rereadings of Modern American Drama*. Ed. June Schlueter. London and Toronto: Associated UP, 1989. 227–240.

Baraka, Amiri (LeRoi Jones). "American Sexual Reference: Black Male." In *Home: Social Essays*. New York: William Morrow, 1966. 216–233.

_____. *Blues People*. New York: Morrow Quill, 1963.

_____. *Dutchman and The Slave*. New York: Morrow Quill Paperbacks, 1964.

_____. "Home." *Home: Social Essays*. New York: Morrow and Co., 1966. 9–10.

_____. "LeRoi Jones Talking." *Home: Social Essays*. New York: Morrow and Co., 1966. 179–188.

Barbera, Jack V. "Ethical Perversity in America: Some Observations on David Mamet's *American Buffalo*." *Modern Drama* 24 (1981): 270–275.

Barnes, Clive. "Angelically Gay about Our Decay." *New York Post* 5 May 1993. Reprinted in *New York Theatre Critics' Reviews* 53 (1993): 210.

_____. "Fiery *Fences*." *New York Post* 27 March 1987. Reprinted in *New York Theatre Critics' Reviews* 48 (1987): 316–317.

_____. "Mamet with a Thud." *New York Post* 26 October 1992. Reprinted in *New York Theatre Critics' Reviews* 52 (1992): 359.

_____. "The Stage: 'Streamers.'" *New York Times* 22 April 1976: 38.

Bartky, Sandra Lee. *Femininity and Domination: Studies in the Phenomenology of Oppression*. New York: Routledge, 1990.

Baudrillard, Jean. *Simulations*. Trans. Paul Foss, Paul Patton, and Philip Beitchman. New York: Semiotext(e), 1983.

Baumli, Francis, ed. *Men Freeing Men: Exploding the Myth of the Traditional Male.* Jersey City: New Atlantic, 1985.

Baym, Nina. "Melodramas of Beset Manhood: How Theories of American Fiction Exclude Women Authors." In *The New Feminist Criticism: Essays on Women, Literature, and Theory.* Ed. Elaine Showalter. New York: Pantheon Books, 1985. 63–80.

Beaufort, John. "*Hurlyburly* Is Confused Comedy." *Christian Science Monitor* 3 July 1984: 27.

Beidler, Philip. *American Literature and the Experience of Vietnam.* Athens: UP of Georgia, 1982.

Bennett, Susan. "When a Woman Looks: The 'Other' Audience of Shepard's Plays." In *Rereading Shepard: Contemporary Critical Essays on the Plays of Sam Shepard.* Ed. Leonard Wilcox. New York: St. Martin's Press, 1993. 168–179.

Ben-Zvi, Linda. "'Home Sweet Home': Deconstructing the Masculine Myth of the Frontier in Modern American Drama." In *The Frontier Experience in the American Drama: Essays on American Literature.* Eds. David Mogen, Mark Busby, and Paul Bryant. College Station: Texas A & M UP, 1989. 217–225.

Berkman, Leonard. "The Tragic Downfall of Blanche Dubois." *Modern Drama* 10 (1967): 249–257.

Bigsby, C. W. E. *Confrontation and Commitment: A Study of Contemporary American Drama, 1959–1966.* Columbia: U of Missouri P, 1969.

_____. *David Mamet.* New York: Methuen, 1985.

Blau, Herbert. "The American Dream in American Gothic: The Plays of Sam Shepard and Adrienne Kennedy." In *The Eye of Prey: Subversions of the Postmodern.* Bloomington and Indianapolis: Indiana UP, 1987. 42–64.

Blumberg, Paul. "Sociology and Social Literature: Work Alienation in the Plays of Arthur Miller." *American Quarterly* 21 (1969): 291–310.

Bly, Robert. *Iron John: A Book about Men.* Reading: Addison-Wesley, 1990.

Bogard, Travis. *Contour in Time: The Plays of Eugene O'Neill.* Revised edition. New York: Oxford UP, 1988.

Brater, Enoch. "Miller's Realism and *Death of a Salesman.*" In *Arthur Miller: New Perspectives.* Ed. Robert A. Martin. Englewood Cliffs: Prentice Hall, 1982. 115–126.

Brod, Harry, ed. *The Making of Masculinities: The New Men's Studies.* Boston: Allen and Unwin, 1987.

Brown, Lloyd W. "Lorraine Hansberry as an Ironist: A Reappraisal of *A Raisin in the Sun.*" *Journal of Black Studies* 4 (1974): 237–247.

Bruster, Douglas. "David Mamet and Ben Jonson: City Comedy Past and Present." *Modern Drama* 33 (1990): 333–346.

Butler, Judith. *Gender Trouble: Feminism and the Subversion of Identity.* New York: Routledge, 1990.

Carroll, Dennis. *David Mamet.* London: Macmillan, 1987.

Carter, Steven R. *Hansberry's Drama: Commitment Amid Complexity.* Urbana: U of Illinois P, 1991.

Ceynowa, Andrzej. "The Dramatic Structure of *Dutchman.*" *Black American Literature Forum* 17 (1983): 15–18.

Ching, Mei-Ling. "Wrestling Against History." *Theatre* 19.3 (1988): 70–71.

Chubb, Kenneth. "Metaphors, Mad Dogs and Old Time Cowboys: Interview with Sam Shepard." *Theatre Quarterly* 4.15 (1974). Reprinted in *American Dreams: The Imagination of Sam Shepard.* Ed. Bonnie Marranca. New York: PAJ Publications, 1981. 187–209.

Churchill, Caryl. *Cloud Nine.* Revised American Version. New York: Routledge, 1988.

_____. *Owners.* In *Churchill: Plays One.* New York: Routledge, 1985. 1–67.

_____. *Vinegar Tom.* In *Churchill: Plays One.* New York: Routledge, 1985. 126–179.

Clatterbaugh, Kenneth. *Contemporary Perspectives on Masculinity: Men, Women, and Politics in Modern Society.* Boulder: Westview, 1990.

Clifford, James. *The Predicament of Culture: Twentieth-Century Ethnography, Literature, and Art.* Cambridge: Harvard UP, 1988.

Clum, John M. *Acting Gay: A History of Male Homosexuality in Drama.* New York: Columbia Press, 1992.

Cody, Gabrielle. "David Hwang's *M. Butterfly*: Perpetuating the Misogynist Myth." *Theatre* 20.2 (1989): 24–27.

Coe, Robert. "Image Shots Are Blown: The Rock Plays." In *American Dreams: The Imagination of Sam Shepard*. Ed. Bonnie Marranca. New York: PAJ Publications, 1981. 57–66.

Coggeshall, John M. "Those Who Surrender Are Female: Prisoner Gender Identities as Cultural Mirror." In *Transcending Boundaries: Multi-Disciplinary Approaches for the Study of Gender*. Eds. Pamela R. Frese and John M. Coggeshall. New York: Bergin and Garvey, 1991. 81–95.

Cohen, Ed. "Are We (Not) What We Are Becoming? 'Gay Identity,' 'Gay Studies,' and the Disciplining of Knowledge." In *Endengering Men: The Question of Male Feminist Criticism*. Eds. Joseph A. Boone and Michael Cadden. New York: Routledge, 1990. 161–175.

Cohn, Ruby. "Sam Shepard: Today's Passionate Shepard and his Loves." In *Essays on Contemporary American Drama*. Eds. Hedwig Bock and Albert Wentheim. Munich: Hueber, 1981. 161–171.

Cooper, Pamela. "David Rabe's *Sticks and Bones*: The Adventures of Ozzie and Harriet." *Modern Drama* 29 (1986): 613–625.

Corneau, Guy. *Absent Fathers, Lost Sons: The Search for Masculine Identity*. Boston: Shambhala, 1991.

Cott, Jonathan. "The Rolling Stone Interview: Sam Shepard." *Rolling Stone* 18 December 1986: 166–172, 198, 200.

Crum, Jane Ann. "'I Smash the Tools of My Captivity': The Feminine in Sam Shepard's *A Lie of the Mind*." In *Rereading Shepard: Contemporary Critical Essays on the Plays of Sam Shepard*. Ed. Leonard Wilcox. New York: St. Martin's Press, 1993. 196–214.

_____. "Notes on *Buried Child*." In *Sam Shepard: A Casebook*. Ed. Kimball King. New York: Garland, 1988. 73–80.

Curry, Jack. "*Fences* Mends Its Family Conflicts Well." *USA Today* 27 March 1987. Reprinted in *New York Theatre Critics' Reviews* (1987): 322.

Da Ponte, Durant. "Tennessee Williams' Gallery of Feminine Characters." *Tennessee Studies in Literature* 10 (1965): 7–26.

Dean, Anne. *David Mamet: Language as Dramatic Action*. Rutherford: Fairleigh Dickinson; London: Associated UP, 1990.

Demastes, William W. *Beyond Realism: A New Realism in American Theater*. Contributions in Drama and Theatre Studies, Number 27. New York: Greenwood, 1988.

DeRose, David J. *Sam Shepard*. New York: Twayne, 1992.

Devries, Hilary. "August Wilson. A New Voice for Black American Theater." *Christian Science Monitor* 16 October 1984: 29–31.

_____. "A Song in Search of Itself." *American Theatre* 3.10 (1987): 22–25.

DiGaetani, John Louis. "*M. Butterfly*: An Interview with David Henry Hwang." *TDR* 33.3 (March 1989): 141–153.

Di Stefano, Christine. *Configurations of Masculinity: A Feminist Perspective on Modern Political Theory*. Ithaca and London: Cornell UP, 1991.

Dolan, Jill. *The Feminist Spectator as Critic*. Ann Arbor: U of Michigan P, 1988.

Doyle, Robert. *The Rape of the Male*. St. Paul: Poor Richard's Press, 1976.

Drake, Constance. "Blanche Dubois: A Re-evaluation." *Theatre Annual* 24 (1969): 58–69.

Dubbert, Joe. *A Man's Place*. Englewood Cliffs: Prentice Hall, 1979.

Egri, Peter. "'Belonging' Lost: Alienation and Dramatic Form in Eugene O'Neill's *The Hairy Ape*." In *Critical Essays on Eugene O'Neill*. Ed. James J. Martine. Boston: G. K. Hall, 1984. 77–111.

Erben, Rudolf. "Women and Other Men in Sam Shepard's Plays." *Studies in American Drama, 1945–Present* 2 (1987): 29–41.

Falk, Doris V. *Eugene O'Neill and the Tragic Tension: An Interpretative Study of the Plays*. New Brunswick: Rutgers UP, 1958.

Falk, Florence. "Men without Women: The Shepard Landscape." In *American Dreams: The Imagination of Sam Shepard*. Ed. Bonnie Marranca. New York: PAJ Publications, 1981. 90–103.

Faludi, Susan. *Backlash: The Undeclared War Against American Women.* New York: Crown Publishers, 1991.

Feingold, Michael. "August Wilson's Bottomless Blackness." *Village Voice* 27 November 1984: 117–118.

_____. "The Fall of Troy." *Village Voice* 7 April 1987: 85.

_____. "Prisoners of Unsex." *Village Voice* 3 November 1992: 109.

Fiedler, Leslie A. *Love and Death in the American Novel.* New York: Criterion Books, 1960.

Flax, Jane. "Postmodernism and Gender Relations in Feminist Theory." In *Feminism/Postmodernism.* Ed. Linda K. Nicholson. New York: Routledge, 1990. 39–62.

_____. *Thinking Fragments: Psychoanalysis, Feminism, and Postmodernism in the Contemporary West.* Berkeley: U of California P, 1990.

Floyd, Virginia. *The Plays of Eugene O'Neill: A New Assessment.* New York: Ungar, 1985.

Franklin, Clyde W., II. "Black Male–Black Female Conflict: Individually Caused and Culturally Nurtured." *Journal of Black Studies* 15 (1984): 139–154.

_____. "Surviving the Institutional Decimation of Black Males: Causes, Consequences, and Intervention." In *The Making of Masculinities: The New Men's Studies.* Ed. Harry Brod. Boston: Allen and Unwin, 1987. 155–169.

Fraser, C. Gerald. "Mamet's Plays Shed Masculinity Myth." *New York Times* 5 July 1976: sec. 1, 7.

Freedman, Samuel G. "A Playwright Talks About the Blues." *New York Times* 13 April 1984: C3.

_____. "A Voice from the Streets." *New York Times Magazine* 15 May 1987: 36, 40, 49, 70.

_____. "What Black Writers Owe to Music." *New York Times* 14 October 1984: sec. 2: 1, 7.

Gerzon, Mark. *A Choice of Heroes: The Changing Face of American Manhood.* Boston: Houghton Mifflin, 1982.

Gibbs, Jewelle T., ed. *Young, Black, and Male in America: An Endangered Species.* Dover, DE: Auburn House, 1988.

Gilder, George. *Naked Nomads: Unmarried Men in America.* New York: Quadrangle, 1974.

Glover, Margaret E. "The Songs of a Marked Man." *Theatre* 19.3 (1988): 69–70.

Goffman, Erving. *Frame Analysis: An Essay on the Organization of Experience.* Cambridge: Harvard UP, 1974.

_____. *The Presentation of Self in Everyday Life.* Garden City: Doubleday, 1959.

Goldberg, Robert. "Sam Shepard: American Original." *Playboy* March 1984: 90, 112, 192–193.

Gottfried, Martin. "Pacino Revives *The Basic Training of Pavlo Hummel.*" *New York Post* 25 April 1977. Reprinted in *New York Theatre Critics' Reviews* 38 (1977): 225.

_____. "Rabe's *Streamers*—Theater at Its Peak." *New York Post* 22 April 1976: 21.

Haedicke, Janet V. "David Henry Hwang's *M. Butterfly*: The Eye on the Wing." *Journal of Dramatic Theory and Criticism* 7 (Fall 1992): 27–44.

_____. "'A Population [and Theater] at Risk': Battered Women in Henley's *Crimes of the Heart* and Shepard's *A Lie of the Mind.*" *Modern Drama* 36 (1993): 83–95.

Hall, Ann C. "Playing to Win: Sexual Politics in David Mamet's *House of Games* and *Speed-the-Plow.*" In *David Mamet: A Casebook.* Ed. Leslie Kane. New York: Garland Publishing, 1992. 137–160.

_____. "Speaking without Words: The Myth of Masculine Autonomy in Sam Shepard's *Fool for Love.*" In *Rereading Shepard: Contemporary Critical Essays on the Plays of Sam Shepard.* Ed. Leonard Wilcox. New York: St. Martin's Press, 1993. 150–167.

Hamill, Peter. "The New American Hero." *New York* 5 December 1983: 75–102.

Hammond, Dorothy, and Alto Jablow. "Gilgamesh and the Sundance Kid: The Myth of Male Friendship." In *The Making of Masculinities: The New Men's Studies.* Ed. Harry Brod. Boston: Allen and Unwin, 1987. 241–258.

Hansberry, Lorraine. *A Raisin in the Sun and The Sign in Sidney Brustein's Window.* New York: New American Library, 1966.

Harrison, Paul Carter. "August Wilson's Blues Poetics." In *August Wilson: Three Plays.* Pittsburgh: U of Pittsburgh P, 1991. 291–318.

Hart, Lynda. *Sam Shepard's Metaphorical Stages.* New York: Greenwood, 1987.

_____. "Sam Shepard's Pornographic Visions." *Studies in the Literary Imagination* 21.2 (1988): 69–82.

_____. "Sam Shepard's Spectacle of Impossible Heterosexuality: *Fool for Love.*" In *Feminist Rereadings of Modern American Drama*. Ed. June Schlueter. London and Toronto: Associated UP, 1989. 213–226.

Henderson, Heather. "Building *Fences*: An Interview with Mary Alice and James Earl Jones." *Theatre* 16.3 (1985): 67–70.

Hertzbach, Janet S. "The Plays of David Rabe: A World of Streamers." In *Essays on Contemporary American Drama*. Eds. Hedwig Bock and Albert Wertheim. Munich: Hueber, 1981. 173–186.

Huang, Nellie S. "August Wilson Wants His Ham." *M* April 1992: 73.

Hubert-Leibler, Pascale. "Dominance and Anguish: The Teacher-Student Relationship in the Plays of David Mamet." *Modern Drama* 31 (1988): 557–570.

Hughes, Catherine. *Plays, Politics, and Polemics*. New York: Drama Book Specialists, 1973.

Hwang, David Henry. *M. Butterfly*. New York: Plume, 1988.

Irigaray, Luce. *This Sex Which Is Not One*. Trans. Catherine Porter with Carolyne Burke. Ithaca: Cornell UP, 1985.

Jewell, K. Sue. "Use of Social Welfare Programs and the Disintegration of the Black Nuclear Family." *Western Journal of Black Studies* 8 (1984): 192–198.

Kakutani, Michiko. "Myths, Dreams, Realities — Sam Shepard's America." *New York Times* 29 January 1984, sec. 2:1, 26.

Kaufman, Michael, ed. *Beyond Patriarchy*. Toronto: Oxford UP, 1987.

Kimmel, Michael S., ed. *Changing Men: New Directions in Research on Men and Masculinity*. Newbury Park: Sage, 1987.

Kirkpatrick, Melanie. "Theater: Trio of American Plays Rooted in Reality." *Wall Street Journal* 29 October 1992: sec. A, 11.

Kissel, Howard. "Falling Angels: Gay Epic Fails to Take Wing." *New York Daily News* 5 May 1993. Reprinted in *New York Theatre Critics' Reviews* 53 (1993): 216.

_____. "*Hurlyburly*." *Women's Wear Daily* 22 June 1984: 20.

Kleb, William. "Worse than Being Homeless: *True West* and the Divided Self." In *American Dreams: The Imagination of Sam Shepard*. Ed. Bonnie Marranca. New York: PAJ Publications, 1981. 117–125.

Kleiman, Dena. "'Joe Turner,' The Spirit of Synergy." *New York Times* 19 May 1986: C11.

Kolin, Philip C. "An Interview with David Rabe." *Journal of Dramatic Theory and Criticism* 3 (1989): 135–156.

_____. "Staging *Hurlyburly*: David Rabe's Parable for the 1980s." *Theatre Annual* 41 (1986): 63–78.

Kolodny, Annette. *The Lay of the Land: Metaphor as Experience and History in American Life and Letters*. Chapel Hill: U of North Carolina P, 1975.

Kroll, Jack. "Hollywood Wasteland: Off Broadway, an All-Star Cast Makes Theater History." *Newsweek* 2 July 1984: 65, 67.

_____. "A Tough Lesson in Sexual Harassment." *Newsweek* 9 November 1992: 65.

Kroll, Jack, with Constance Guthrie and Janet Huck. "Who's That Tall Dark Stranger?" *Newsweek* 11 November 1985: 68–74.

Kushner, Tony. *Angels in America, Part One: Millennium Approaches*. New York: Theatre Communications Group, 1993.

Lahr, John. "Angels on Broadway." *The New Yorker* 31 May 1993: 137.

Lanier, Gregory W. "Two Opposite Animals: Structural Pairing in Sam Shepard's *A Lie of the Mind*." *Modern Drama* 34 (1991): 410–421.

Lee, John. *The Flying Boy: Healing the Wounded Man*. Deerfield Beach: Health Communications, 1987.

Leverenz, David. *Manhood and the American Renaissance*. Ithaca: Cornell UP, 1989.

Londre, Felicia Hardison. "Sam Shepard Works Out: The Masculinization of America." *Studies in American Drama, 1945–Present* 2 (1987): 19–27.

Majors, Richard, and Janet Mancini Billson. *Cool Pose: The Dilemmas of Black Manhood in America*. New York: Lexington Books, 1992.

Mamet, David. "All Men Are Whores: An Inquiry." In *Goldberg Street: Short Plays and Monologues*. New York: Grove Press, 1985.

_____. *American Buffalo*. New York: Grove, 1976.

_____. *Edmond*. In *The Woods, Lakeboat, Edmond: Three Plays by David Mamet*. New York: Grove, 1987. 213–298.

_____. *Glengarry Glen Ross*. New York: Grove Weidenfeld, 1984.

_____. *Lakeboat*. In *The Woods, Lakeboat, Edmond: Three Plays by David Mamet*. New York: Grove, 1987. 121–212.

_____. *Oleanna*. New York: Pantheon, 1992.

_____. *Sexual Perversity in Chicago and The Duck Variations*. New York: Grove, 1978.

_____. *Some Freaks*. New York: Viking, 1989.

_____. *Speed-the-Plow*. New York: Grove Weidenfeld, 1988.

_____. *Writing in Restaurants*. New York: Viking, 1986.

Marable, Manning. *How Capitalism Underdeveloped Black America: Problems in Race, Political Economy, and Society*. Boston: South End P, 1983.

Marranca, Bonnie. "Alphabetical Shepard: The Play of Words." In *American Dreams: The Imagination of Sam Shepard*. Ed. Bonnie Marranca. New York: PAJ Publication, 1981. 13–33.

_____, ed. *American Dreams: the Imagination of Sam Shepard*. New York: PAJ Publications, 1981.

Martin, Robert A. "Arthur Miller and the Meaning of Tragedy." *Modern Drama* 13 (1970): 34–49.

McDonough, Carla J. "The Politics of Stage Space: Women and Male Identity in Sam Shepard's Family Plays." *Journal of Dramatic Theory and Criticism* 9.2 (1995): 65–83.

McMillion, Jennifer. "The Cult of Male Identity in *Goose and Tomtom*." *David Rabe: A Casebook*. Ed. Toby Silverman Zinman. New York: Garland, 1991. 175–187.

Miller, Arthur. *Death of a Salesman*. New York: Viking, 1952.

_____. "Tragedy and the Common Man." In *Death of a Salesman: Text and Criticism*. Ed. Gerald Weales. New York: Viking, 1967. 143–147.

Modleski, Tania. *Feminism without Women: Culture and Criticism in a "Postfeminist" Age*. New York: Routledge, 1991.

Mottram, Eric. "Arthur Miller: The Development of a Political Dramatist." In *Arthur Miller: A Collection of Critical Essays*. Ed. Robert W. Corrigan. Englewood Cliffs: Prentice Hall, 1969. 23-57.

Mottram, Ron. "Exhaustion of the American Soul: Sam Shepard's *A Lie of the Mind*." In *Sam Shepard: A Casebook*. Ed. Kimball King. New York: Garland, 1988. 95–106.

_____. *Inner Landscapes: The Theater of Sam Shepard*. Columbia: U of Missouri P, 1984.

Moy, James S. "David Henry Hwang's *M. Butterfly* and Philip Kan Gotanda's *Yankee Dawg You Die*: Repositioning Chinese American Marginality on the American Stage." *Theatre Journal* 42 (1990): 48–56.

Moynihan, Daniel P. "The Negro Family: The Case for National Action." Office of Policy Planning and Research, U.S. Department of Labor. U.S. Government Printing Office, March 1965.

Mulvey, Laura. "Afterthoughts on 'Visual Pleasure and Narrative Cinema' Inspired by *Duel in the Sun*." *Framework* (Summer 1981): 12–15.

Nash, Thomas. "Sam Shepard's *Buried Child*: The Ironic Use of Folklore." *Modern Drama* 26 (1983): 486–491.

Oliver, William. "Black Males and the Tough Guy Image: A Dysfunctional Compensatory Adaptation." *Western Journal of Black Studies* 8 (1984): 199–203.

O'Neill, Eugene. *The Hairy Ape. Selected Plays of Eugene O'Neill*. Garden City: Nelson Doubleday, 1979. 94–142.

Orbison, Tucker. "Mythic Levels in Shepard's *True West*." *Modern Drama* 27 (1984): 506–519.

Osherson, Samuel. *Finding Our Fathers: The Unfinished Business of Manhood*. New York: Free Press, 1986.

Oumano, Ellen. *Sam Shepard: The Life and Work of an American Dreamer*. New York: St. Martin, 1986.

Podol, Peter L. "Dimensions of Violence in the Theater of Sam Shepard: *True West* and *Fool for Love.*" *Essays in Theatre* 7 (1989): 149–158.

Powers, Kim. "An Interview with August Wilson." *Theatre* 16.1 (1984): 50–55.

Profile of a Writer: Mamet. Prod. and dir. Alan Benson. London Weekend Television Co., 1985. 55 min.

Rabe, David. Afterword. *Hurlyburly.* New York: Grove, 1985. 161–171.

———. *The Basic Training of Pavlo Hummel and Sticks and Bones; Two Plays.* New York: Viking, 1973.

———. *Goose and Tomtom.* New York: Grove, 1986.

———. *Hurlyburly.* New York: Grove, 1985.

———. *Hurlyburly.* Revised edition. New York: Grove, 1991.

———. Introduction. *The Basic Training of Pavlo Hummel and Sticks and Bones: Two Plays.* New York: Viking, 1973. ix–xxv.

———. *Streamers.* New York: Alfred A. Knopf, 1990.

Rabillard, Sheila. "Sam Shepard: Theatrical Power and American Dreams." *Modern Drama* 30 (1987): 58–71.

Radavich, David. "Man among Men: David Mamet's Homosocial Order." *American Drama* 1.1 (1991): 46–60.

Raphael, Ray. *The Men from the Boys: Male Rites of Passage in America.* Lincoln: U of Nebraska P, 1988.

Ray, Robert. *A Certain Tendency of the Hollywood Cinema, 1930–1980.* Princeton: Princeton UP, 1985.

Reinelt, Janelle. "Gender and History in *Hurlyburly*: A Feminist Response." In *David Rabe: A Casebook.* New York: Garland, 1991. 191–205.

Rich, Frank. "Embracing All Possibilities in Art and Life." *New York Times* 5 May 1993: sec. C, 15–16.

———. "Mamet's New Play Detonates the Fury of Sexual Harassment." *New York Times* 26 October 1992: sec. C, 11–12.

———. "Stage: *A Lie of the Mind* by Sam Shepard." *New York Times* 6 December 1985: sec. 2, 3.

———. "Theater: Family Ties in Wilson's *Fences.*" *New York Times* 27 March 1987: C3.

———. "Theater: Wilson's *Fences.*" *New York Times* 7 May 1985: C17.

Richards, Sandra L. "Negative Forces and Positive Non-Entities: Images of Women in the Dramas of Amiri Baraka." *Theatre Journal* 34 (1982): 233–240.

Riemer, James D. "Integrating the Psyche of the American Male: Conflicting Ideals of Manhood in Sam Shepard's *True West.*" *University of Dayton Review* 18.2 (1986–1987): 41–47.

Robinson, James A. "Buried Children: Fathers and Sons in O'Neill and Shepard." In *Eugene O'Neill and the Emergence of American Drama.* Ed. Marc Maufort. Amsterdam: Rodopi, 1989. 151–157.

Rosen, Carol. "'Emotional Territory': An Interview with Sam Shepard." *Modern Drama* 36.1 (1993): 1–11.

———. "Marooned but Invincible." *Theater Week* 4 (June 10, 1991): 23–27.

———. *Plays of Impasse: Contemporary Drama Set in Confining Institutions.* Princeton: Princeton UP, 1979.

Roudané, Matthew C. "An Interview with David Mamet." *Studies in American Drama, 1945–Present* 1 (1986): 73–81.

———. "Public Issues, Private Tensions: David Mamet's *Glengarry Glen Ross.*" *South Carolina Review* 19.1 (1986): 35–47.

Sarotte, Georges-Michel. *Like a Brother, Like a Lover: Male Homosexuality in the American Novel and Theater from Herman Melville to James Baldwin.* Trans. Richard Miller. Garden City: Anchor/Doubleday, 1978.

Savran, David. *Communists, Cowboys, and Queers: The Politics of Masculinity in the Work of Arthur Miller and Tennessee Williams.* Minneapolis: U of Minnesota P, 1992.

———. *In Their Own Words: Contemporary American Playwrights.* New York: Theatre Communications Group, 1988.

Schickel, Richard. "Failing Words, *Hurlyburly*." *Time* 2 July 1984: 86–87.

Schlueter, June, and Elizabeth Forsyth. "America as Junkshop: The Business Ethic in David Mamet's *American Buffalo*." *Modern Drama* 26 (1983): 492–500.

Schvey, Henry I. "The Master and His Double: Eugene O'Neill and Sam Shepard." *Journal of Dramatic Theory and Criticism* 5.2 (1991): 49–60.

Schweinitz, George D. "*Death of a Salesman*: A Note on Epic and Tragedy." *Western Humanities Review* 14 (1960): 91–96.

Segal, Lynne. *Slow Motion: Changing Masculinities, Changing Men*. New Brunswick, NJ: Rutgers UP, 1990.

Seidler, Victor J. *Rediscovering Masculinity: Reason, Language and Sexuality*. New York and London: Routledge, 1989.

Shapiro, Stephen A. *Manhood: A New Definition*. New York: G. P. Putnam's Sons, 1984.

Sharma, P. P. "Search for Self-Identity in *Death of a Salesman*." *Literary Criterion* 11.2 (1974): 72–79.

Shepard, Sam. *Angel City*. In *Fool for Love and Other Plays*. New York: Bantam Books, 1988. 59–111.

_____. *Buried Child*. In *Sam Shepard: Seven Plays*. New York: Bantam Books, 1986. 61–132.

_____. *Cowboy Mouth*. In *Fool for Love and Other Plays*. New York: Bantam Books, 1988. 145–165.

_____. *Curse of the Starving Class*. In *Sam Shepard: Seven Plays*. New York: Bantam Books, 1986. 133–200.

_____. *Fool for Love and Other Plays*. New York: Bantam Books, 1988.

_____. "Language, Visualization and the Inner Library." In *American Dreams: The Imagination of Sam Shepard*. Ed. Bonnie Marranca. New York: PAJ Publications, 1981. 214–219.

_____. *A Lie of the Mind*. New York: Plume, 1987.

_____. *Motel Chronicles*. San Francisco: City Lights Books, 1982.

_____. *Operation Sidewinder*. In *The Unseen Hand and Other Plays*. New York: Bantam Books, 1986. 197–254.

_____. *States of Shock, Far North, Silent Tongues*. New York: Vintage Books, 1993.

_____. *Tooth of Crime*. In *Sam Shepard: Seven Plays*. New York: Bantam Books, 1986: 201–251.

_____. *True West*. In *Sam Shepard: Seven Plays*. New York: Bantam Books, 1986. 1–59.

Shewey, Don. *Sam Shepard: The Life, the Loves, behind the Legend of a True American Original*. New York: Dell, 1985.

Siegal, Mark. "Holy Ghosts: The Mythic Cowboy in the Plays of Sam Shepard." *Bulletin of the Rocky Mountain Modern Language Association* 36 (1982): 235–246.

Siegel, Joel. Review of *Fences*. WABC-TV. 26 March 1987. Review transcribed in *New York Theatre Critics' Reviews* 48 (1987): 321.

Simard, Rodney. *Postmodern Drama: Contemporary Playwrights in America and Britain*. New York: UP of America, 1984.

Simon, John. "Of Wings and Webs." *New York* 17 May 1993: 102–103.

Smith, Philip E., II. "*Ma Rainey's Black Bottom*: Playing the Blues as Equipment for Living." In *Within the Dramatic Spectrum*, VI. Ed. Karelisa V. Hartigan. New York: UP of America, 1986. 177–186.

Solomon, Alisa. "Mametic Phallacy." *Village Voice* 24 November 1992: 104.

Spector, Susan. "Alternative Visions of Blanche DuBois: Uta Hagan and Jessica Tandy in *A Streetcar Named Desire*." *Modern Drama* 32 (1989): 545–559.

Stanton, Kay. "Women and the American Dream of *Death of a Salesman*." In *Feminist Rereadings of Modern American Drama*. Ed. June Schlueter. London and Toronto: Associated UP, 1989. 67–102.

Staples, Brent. "*Fences*: No Barrier to Emotion." *New York Times* 5 April 1987: sec. 2: 1, 39.

Staples, Robert. *Black Masculinity: The Black Man's Role in American Society*. San Francisco: The Black Scholar Press, 1982.

Steinberg, M. W. "Arthur Miller and the Idea of Modern Tragedy." *Dalhousie Review* 40 (1960): 329–340.

Sterritt, David. "Drama Touches on Political Power." *Christian Science Monitor* 30 October 1992: 12.

Stewart, James B., and Joseph W. Scott. "The Institutional Decimation of Black American Males." *Western Journal of Black Studies* 2 (1978): 82–92.

Timpane, John. "'Weak and Divided People': Tennessee Williams and the Written Woman." In *Feminist Rereadings of Modern American Drama*. Ed. June Schlueter. London and Toronto: Associated UP, 1989. 171–180.

Tolson, Andrew. *The Limits of Masculinity*. New York: Harper and Row, 1977.

Turner, Victor. *The Anthropology of Performance*. New York: PAJ Publications, 1987.

VerMeulen, Michael. "Sam Shepard: Yes, Yes, Yes." *Esquire* February 1980: 79–86.

Vlasopolos, Anca. "Authorizing History: Victimization in *A Streetcar Named Desire*." In *Feminist Rereadings of Modern American Drama*. Ed. June Schlueter. London and Toronto: Associated UP, 1989. 149–170.

Vorlicky, Robert. *Act Like a Man: Challenging Masculinities in American Drama*. Ann Arbor: U of Michigan P, 1995.

Wallace, Michele. *Black Macho and the Myth of the Superwoman*. New York: Dial, 1979.

Wallach, Allan. "Fenced in by a Lifetime of Resentments." *New York Newsday* 27 March 1987. Reprinted in *New York Theater Critics' Review* 48 (1987): 319.

Watt, Douglas. "*Angels in America* Earns Its Wings." *New York Daily News* 14 May 1993. Reprinted in *New York Theatre Critics' Reviews* 53 (1993): 220.

_____. "*Sticks and Bones* Brings Broadway New Power." *New York Daily News* 2 March 1972. Reprinted in *New York Theatre Critics' Reviews* 33 (1972): 364.

_____. "*Streamers* Exerts Its Power Anew." *New York Daily News* 2 March 1976. Reprinted in *New York Theatre Critics' Reviews* 37 (1976): 264–265.

Watt, Stephen. "Simulation, Gender, and Postmodernism: Sam Shepard and *Paris, Texas*." *Perspectives on Contemporary Literature* 13 (1987): 73–82.

Weales, Gerald. "Arthur Miller's Shifting Images of Man." In *Arthur Miller: New Perspectives*. Ed. Robert W. Corrigan. Englewood Cliffs: Prentice Hall, 1969. 131–148.

_____. "Thoughts on *A Raisin in the Sun*." *Commentary* 27 (1959): 527–530.

Wetzeon, Ross. "David Mamet: Remember That Name." *Village Voice* 5 July 1976. 101, 103–104.

Whiting, Charles G. "Images of Women in Shepard's Theatre." *Modern Drama* 33 (1990): 494–506.

Wilcox, Leonard, ed. *Rereading Shepard: Contemporary Critical Essays on the Plays of Sam Shepard*. New York: St. Martin's Press, 1993.

Wilde, Lisa. "Reclaiming the Past: Narrative and Memory in August Wilson's *Two Trains Running*." *Theatre* 22.1 (Winter 1990–1991): 73–74.

Wilkerson, Margaret B. "The Sighted Eyes and Feeling Heart of Lorraine Hansberry." *Black American Literature Forum* 17 (1983): 8–13.

Wilkinson, Rupert. *American Tough: The Tough Guy Tradition and American Character*. Westpoint: Greenwood, 1984.

Williams, Raymond. "The Realism of Arthur Miller." *Critical Quarterly* 1 (1959): 140–149.

Williams, Tennessee. *A Streetcar Named Desire*. Mount Vernon: New Directions Books, 1947.

Wilson, Ann. "Fool of Desire: The Spectator to the Plays of Sam Shepard." *Modern Drama* 30 (1987): 46–57.

Wilson, August. *Fences*. New York: Plume, 1986.

_____. *Joe Turner's Come and Gone*. New York: Plume, 1988.

_____. *Ma Rainey's Black Bottom*. New York: Plume, 1985.

_____. *The Piano Lesson*. New York: Plume, 1990.

_____. Preface. *August Wilson: Three Plays*. Pittsburgh: U of Pittsburgh P, 1991. vii–xiv.

_____. "*Two Trains Running*." *Theatre* 22.1 (1990–1991): 42–72.

_____. *Two Trains Running*. New York: Dutton, 1992.

Wilson, Edwin. "Tony Kushner's Gay Fantasia Arrives on Broadway." *Wall Street Journal* 6 May 1993: sec. A, 9.

Zeifman, Hersh. "Phallus in Wonderland: Machismo and Business in David Mamet's *American Buffalo* and *Glengarry Glen Ross*." In *David Mamet: A Casebook*. Ed. Leslie Kane. New York: Garland Publishing, 1992. 123–136.

Zinman, Toby Silverman. "An Interview with David Rabe." In *David Rabe: A Casebook*. Ed. Toby Silverman Zinman. New York: Garland, 1991. 3–15.
Zolotow, Sam. "Black Students Block Yale Play." *New York Times* 27 December 1968: sec.1, 39.

Index